THE REFORMATION OF WELFARE

The New Faith of the Labour Market

Tom Boland and Ray Griffin

D1612770

BRISTOL UNIVERSITY PRESS

First published in Great Britain in 2023 by

Bristol University Press
University of Bristol
1-9 Old Park Hill
Bristol
BS2 8BB
UK
t: +44 (0)117 374 6645
e: bup-info@bristol.ac.uk

Details of international sales and distribution partners are available at bristoluniversitypress.co.uk

The work of the last author was supported by the HECAT project, funded within the EU
Framework Programme for Research and Innovation Horizon 2020, under grant number
870702.

British Library Cataloguing in Publication Data
A catalogue record for this book is available from the British Library

ISBN 978-1-5292-1132-0 hardcover
ISBN 978-1-5292-1133-7 paperback
ISBN 978-1-5292-1135-1 ePub
ISBN 978-1-5292-1134-4 ePdf

Cover design: blu inc, Bristol
Front cover image: Cadeau (The Gift). Museum: © Man Ray Trust.
Album/Alamy Stock Photo.

Bristol University Press uses environmentally responsible print partners.

Printed in Great Britain by CMP, Poole

In memory of Paddy O'Carroll,
1937–2015

Contents

1

Introduction: Paradoxes
of Welfare

Welfare policy is both in crisis and stagnant, a chronic stasis. Occasionally there are moments of change and transformation – times of reform – yet repeatedly, these yield to the return of familiar tensions and frustrations. This is because there is a contradiction or paradox at the heart of the welfare state; it both 'giveth and taketh away' (Job 1:21) With one hand it supports the unemployed, yet simultaneously it demands certain things of them, mainly that they seek work, but also attend meetings, undergo assessment, write CVs, work on themselves, retrain, and strive continuously to redeem themselves. These demands are usually made with threats of sanctions for non-compliance: reduced payments or being cut off completely. This is known as 'welfare conditionality' or 'activation' in recent academic or policy terms, and obviously the welfare state also provides for others in a different manner, for instance, the retired, but the impulse towards 'reform' has been extended in recent decades, for instance, towards single-parents.

   Intermittently, how the unemployed are treated becomes a contentious public issue, with interest waxing and waning as the dole queue lengthens, and policymakers, scholars and critics incessantly debate the issue and produce research supporting their arguments. Strikingly, key ideas seem to persist over time; for instance, the contemporary idea of 'rights and responsibilities' echoes older ideas of morality or good character. There is a notable confluence of right and left: conservatives argue for more state investment in getting the unemployed back to work, despite their historic antipathy to the 'big state'; socialists argue for policies which ensure that everyone is supported into work.

Even the big 'revolutionary' ideas have advocates across the political divide: the idea of a universal basic income – basically tax-funded support for everyone – is supported by radical leftists like Guy Standing (2015), and right-wing polemicists like Charles Murray (2006). Taking little heed of such radical alternatives, policymakers continue with 'welfare reforms', tinkering with systems of support and activation, to 'get people back to work' at almost any cost. Meanwhile, the looming threats of roboticization or automation and ecological unsustainability are acknowledged but scarcely addressed: what matters is the present, the current rate of unemployment, the effectiveness of existing activation measures. Politicians occasionally announce sweeping new reforms, but under inspection this is 'old wine in new bottles', the repetition or reiteration of strikingly familiar impulses.

Why? In this book we argue that welfare reforms are derived from cultural models within modern society that are decisively influenced by the Judeo-Christian inheritance. Both the impulse to give, to alleviate the suffering of the poor, and the attempt to reform or redeem people have theological or religious roots. These ideas exist in tension, in varying strengths and combinations in modern states, which are the inheritors of the 'pastoral power' of the medieval church. Recognizing and understanding our ideas and impulses towards reform can help us understand social policy in the present.

Herein, we will explore unemployment, work, careers, jobseeking, CVs and more, through strange yet familiar religious ideas – purgatory, vocation, providence, confession, pilgrimage and so forth. This is not an exercise in obscurity – theological or historical expertise is not needed to read this book – but a matter of reflexivity, of recognizing the presence of half-forgotten ideas at the heart of how we think about the world, both at the micro and macro level – individual life and the wider world. Of course, there are many intellectual inheritances, beyond the theological, but these are perhaps the most neglected, due to modern claims to live in a secular world or a post-religious society. Ironically, the claim to have gone beyond superstition is an idea rooted in theology; the rejection of tradition or iconoclasm – literally the breaking of idols – is a constantly retold story in the West. Our work here is neither for nor against religion, nor does it suggest we should believe in anything. Rather, it attempts to recover an awareness of how certain ideas, cultural models and attitudes towards life are derived from religion and shape our lives and institutions, most particularly welfare policy and unemployment.

Our approach

Our approach is best described as archaic anthropology – an attempt to historicize the present, to recognize the presence of the past in the present. These initially incongruous terms, archaic and anthropology, are combined to provoke a rethinking of modern phenomena, to cultivate a sense of the contingency and historicity of everyday society, not of secret origins or underlying structures, but to restore a long-term perspective on state, society, economy and culture, things hidden in plain sight. Archaic, in its original Greek sense of *arche*, refers to central and persistent ideas rather than the contemporary image of lost fragments of the ancient world. Anthropology entails participation and observation; an ethnography of our shared experience. Our work draws on almost a decade of ethnographic engagement in the curious world of unemployment, interviews with the unemployed, explorations of welfare offices, media discourses, policy making, policy submissions, statistics, jobseeking advice and digital platforms; there is no scientific white coat which separates us neatly from our data. These explorations are then illuminated by the genealogical method of Nietzsche, Weber, Foucault and Agamben, who challenge us to recognize the historicity of things and ideas that appear to have no history – key ideas like choice or work or selfhood.

This method does not mean searching for 'origins' but recognizing our deep entanglement in history and that therefore religious ideas have shaped supposedly secular modern phenomena; even economic categories like unemployment, welfare or the labour market. Nietzsche suggested that even though 'God is dead, and we have killed him', religious ideas permeate our contemporary morality and attitudes towards suffering. Weber reveals how religious ethics inform our contemporary economic practices – most famously, the Protestant work ethic provides the 'spirit of capitalism'. Foucault's studies of governmental power illuminate the welfare state as an echo of the pastoral power of the church over its flock. Agamben identified how the economy and the state are interpreted as providential mechanisms within modernity, imprinting a theological model despite secularization. Taken together, these theorists provide an approach to history which allows us to recognize how official policyspeak and academic scholarship create the very things they seek to describe.

Reader beware! This book is not a history of the welfare state or unemployment, or a contribution to policy, or a detailed case study of contemporary experiences of jobseekers. Nor is it an excoriating critique of neoliberal ideology and the contemporary 'dismantling of the welfare state'; it will not suddenly awaken policymakers or politicians to the futility or cruelty of their policies, or inspire resistance or prompt revolution. Nor does it propose any new solution to the intractable problems of welfare. Such books already exist, some of which are reviewed herein. Instead, this book is a call to recognize the presence of history in the present and how religious ideas animate the contemporary world. Such a reflexive and philosophical undertaking is open to any reader, specialist or otherwise, who is open to considering that their ideas may be derived from society or from history, and often in uncomfortable ways – and that even critics may have common ground with their opponents. Recognizing the persistence of history, especially our disavowed religious inheritance, is vital to understanding why perennial problems seem so intractable, and offers a clue as to why utilitarian policy solutions do not fix society. Work and welfare are more foundational, perhaps even primordial, to Western lives than is commonly imagined.

Most critics of welfare insist that the capacity to contest widely accepted definitions of how the world works is an important political tool, and any historical approach asserts that the world was not always thus, and might be remade. Certainly, our approach joins them in rejecting trite generalizations about the inevitability of certain political and social arrangements. An alternative and less comforting implication is that we can only think at all by using historically inherited ideas, and therefore, thinking differently is difficult indeed. Importantly, composing alternative histories or launching critiques or gathering anthropological evidence are practices with a long intellectual history. Rather than changing the world, we emphasize understanding our culture and society, with the acknowledgement that how we think about our world matters. Recognizing neglected historical influences on the present and the tensions and contradictions within them is a crucial precursor to trying to think anew, indeed another meaning of 'radicalism' is returning to roots.

The new trials of Job

Recent times have seen the emergence of the neologism 'jobseeker', basically meaning the unemployed. Words may seem like mere labels for an unchanging economic reality, yet the terms used to describe something shape it. Indeed, the term 'unemployed' is reshaped by the emergence of the statistical category of 'unemployment', which emerged in the late nineteenth century as states began to keep national records of the numbers claiming poor relief (Walters, 2000; Burnett, 2002). This implied that not having work was a temporary economic situation, in contrast to medieval categories of 'pauper' or 'poor' which indicated a permanent state – or terms like 'idler' or 'vagabond' which implied immorality or even criminality (Mollat, 1986).

While the term 'unemployed' evokes the gathering of individuals together into a society-wide category of unemployment, 'jobseeker' envisages a person as a single economic unit. They are imagined as an active participant in the labour market, searching for opportunities, investing in their skills; an entrepreneur selling their labour to employers. Yet, simultaneously, they are unemployed, dependent on the welfare office, enduring months of frustrated jobseeking. The logic of welfare activation and conditionality is that unemployment and welfare jobseeking should be arranged so that an individual is compelled to engage in the labour market. The market competition for work has moral significance.

A revealing parallel to jobseeking is the Old Testament book of Job. Job – Iyov in Hebrew – is a pious and prosperous man who is tested by God at the instigation of the devil in a quixotic story. Catastrophically, his livestock, servants and children die in turn, yet distraught Job still blesses God in his prayers. After further torments, Job's wife beseeches him to curse God. Job's friends suggest that he must have done wrong to receive such a fate, and eventually Job accuses God of being unjust. One of Job's friends chastises Job, saying God is never wrong and that we cannot comprehend all that God does. God appears in a whirlwind, demonstrating his reality and power, and restores Job's good fortune, granting him a long life and children. Suffering here appears not as something to be overcome or circumvented by action or ignored in passivity but as a refiner of faith, a purifier of the soul.

The book of Job presents a poetic parable of suffering and faith – widely read to this day – and addresses the theological conundrum of theodicy – why an all-powerful, all-knowing and benevolent God allows bad things happen to good people. Religions offer justifications, whereas political realism simply says, 'And the weak suffer what they must' (Varoufakis, 2016). The sufferings of Job are also distinctly economic; his fortune depends upon God who then tests his faith by ruining him, yet without harming him personally.

The poetic myth of Job, commonly dated sometime between the 6th and 4th century BC, is a persistent source of food for thought, inspiring reflection on more immediate philosophical and political concerns: Negri (2009) argues that Job reflects labour resisting capitalism; Deleuze (1994) suggests that Job demands recognition and accountability from a capricious deity; Spivack (1958) sees the parable as the development of an inner conscience and personal relationship to God; darker hints of sacrifice are detected by Girard (1987); for Jung ([1952] 2010), the story of Job reveals the devilish dimension of God, despite Christian and Enlightenment banishments of evil – considered simply as the absence of God or reason.

Each theorist attempts to explicate a hidden dimension of the parable, yet really the message is familiar and suffuses Christian, Western and modern culture. Misfortune is a test which tries our fortitude. What doesn't kill us makes us stronger. The sufferings of Job are a trial of faith; those who persist in hope despite everything will eventually succeed. Implicitly, suffering is a way of purifying, purging individuals of their sinful tendencies.

Growth through adversity is not only part of our philosophy of life; it suffuses our policies, and it is institutionalized in how the unemployed are treated. The economy is our primary test, where the invisible hand of the market replicates the hand of God (Cox, 2016). Those who need state support, especially the unemployed, are forced to suffer and put to the test of seeking work. Effectively, the state becomes the incarnation of providence, testing individuals to the limit (Agamben, 2011). Yet, like Job, the jobseeker must not despair but hopefully and interminably seek salvation in the form of employment (Pecchenino, 2015).

Strikingly, Job's good fortune is attributed to him being favoured by God – he is selected or elected by God's predetermined will. Just as swiftly, he is cast out of God's favour, a reversal of fortune faster than economic recession. Yet, he remonstrates with God, demanding justice, a fair test, a second chance (Deleuze, 1994). This enigmatic relationship of fate and faith, tests and trials, purging and redemption animates the modern economy and welfare state to this day.

The problem of unemployment

Politicians, policymakers and the public at large view unemployment as a problem to be solved, principally by jobs, delivered by economic growth, in the pursuit of full employment. Despite occasional recessions, temporary interruptions to continuous and compounded economic growth, almost every year more people work globally to create more goods and services than ever before. Yet since World War II, every decade has seen rates of unemployment edging upwards gradually almost everywhere, somehow, despite repeated economic recovery and growth – there were still people who needed a job. Modern capitalism is a work culture of unlimited growth, but it is also haunted by a nostalgic dream that once upon a time everyone had work and that the economy was stable and functional; states across the Organization for Economic Co-operation and Development (OECD) work tirelessly to reduce unemployment to almost nothing; from their perspective the economic shocks simply temporarily enlarge the problem.

Through boom and bust, states manage unemployment continuously, not just through providing financial supports to alleviate poverty but through active labour market policies (ALMPs). These ALMPs have replaced alms for the poor – supports are no longer charitable, but exist to support work. ALMPs are varied, but basically they are attempts to reform or transform the individual, either by giving them training or education – 'human capital building' – or by putting pressure on them to find work, sometimes known as 'welfare conditionality'. Rather than simply being supported, the unemployed must take part in case-officer meetings, group engagement, psychological and algorithmic profiling and motivational or CV workshops, and must carry out extensive monitored job searches and accept almost any employment or training they are offered. Failure to comply will eventually or immediately lead to sanctions; cuts or suspension of welfare payments, leaving individuals with no support.

Contemporary academic research has explored welfare conditionality extensively in different jurisdictions; for instance, the Danish system is more oriented towards flexible working, the French to rights-based administration, the Irish towards local adaptations and caprice, and the UK system towards increasingly harsher and punitive approaches (Boland and Griffin, 2015; Dwyer, 2019; Hansen, 2019). Across this research, it is clear that welfare sanctions sometimes push people into poverty, debt, homelessness, black-market activity and even suicide, with mental and physical health impacts which are hard to measure. Indeed, even those who are never sanctioned are pressured and stressed by the ever-present threat of sanctions.

Officially, ALMPs, conditionality and sanctions exist to get people back to work, and there is some evidence that they may shorten the average period of unemployment, although such statistical findings have been contested (Card et al, 2015). Critics have suggested that ALMPs simply accelerate a cycle of low-pay/no-pay by pushing individuals to take up precarious work (Shildrick and McDonald, 2012). While the threat of sanction may be a motivation, the actual impact of sanction on an individual may render them less likely to gain employment.

Despite these criticisms, the effort to 'reform' the unemployed intensifies: there is increased psychologized testing and behavioural economics style 'nudges' to 'activate' jobseekers (Friedli and Stearn, 2015; Frayne, 2019). Pressure is applied to more and more groups, for instance, the chronically ill, migrants, people with disabilities, single parents of increasingly young children and those in part-time work (Watts and Fitzpatrick, 2018; Dwyer, 2019). Entitlements become increasingly conditionalized, for instance, the increased use of conditional cash transfers (CCTs) in South America and elsewhere which make support dependent on certain behaviour, re-education or even health or lifestyle choices (Humpage, 2019). Welfare conditionality has gone digital, with jobseekers required to register on certain websites and complete supervised online searches, having their CVs rewritten by motivational coaches.

Beyond examining the largely negative experiences of unemployed people subjected to welfare conditionality, scholars have analyzed the political and media debates around these policies, researched the inner workings of welfare offices and organizations and traced the impact on the experience of work (Demazière, 2020; Dwyer and Wright, 2014; Jensen and Tyler, 2015; Fletcher and Wright, 2018; Jordan, 2018; Whelan, 2020). All this cannot be summarized here, but broadly what emerges is that rather than simply supporting the unemployed, contemporary welfare offices intervene in the lives of individuals; basically, states govern the lives of jobseekers.

Governing the unemployed

The relationship between the welfare office and the unemployed may seem simple, it is even described by policy documents and official forms as a contract; the welfare office provides welfare payments and offers support and guidance in exchange for compliance with requirements for jobseeking by so-called 'clients' (DSP, 2012). Critics point out that this contractualization of welfare entitlements is effectively an offer you can't refuse. Clearly, this is not a free-market arrangement but a power relationship, which we describe herein as disciplinary or governmental power.

This approach is associated with the field of governmentality studies, inspired by the work of Michel Foucault. By joining 'govern' and 'mentality', this approach refers to how states think about society, using academic disciplines, statistics, policy and so forth to conjure up a series of institutions which shape individual lives (Dean, 2010). This is not a simple dystopian nightmare of government control – though historically liberal thinkers have frequently criticized state tyranny – this form of power is taken on by individuals, literally empowering them.

For instance, without the governmentality of education, this book would scarcely be written or read. So, governmentality has multiple effects: its knowledge redefines reality, its disciplinary power pervades society and it shapes individuals' conduct and selfhood.

For Foucault, governmentality implied a certain governing rationality, an orientation towards transforming the lives of individuals and entire societies in pursuit of various ends. Broadly, governmentality assumes that it is always possible to improve and reform, to govern better, and attempts to survey the population and produce interventions and policies which 'optimize' people in specific ways, in an 'eternal optimism' that things can be made better (Miller and Rose, 2013). Yet, this governing rationality is not universal reason or infallible logic but a particular approach, expressing certain values and pursuing particular ends.

Governmental power is most visible at the street level; for instance, the lives of jobseekers are shaped by requirements to attend meetings, account for themselves, prove job-search efforts, undergo assessment, retrain and so forth (Brodkin and Marsden, 2013). Such power is clearly disciplining– shaping people's conduct by exercising intermittent surveillance and demanding compliance. Beyond this, academic disciplines shape how unemployment is interpreted as a problem (Bacchi, 2015). A combination of ideas from economics and sociology – explored in Chapter 4 – suggests that the unemployed will fall into a poverty trap and draw the dole rather than work unless incentivized by welfare conditionality, that they will lose their skills and 'work-readiness' if they are not compelled into jobseeking, and incrementally enter a downward spiral of 'subjective deterioration' because work provides various social and individual goods. Consequently, jobseekers tend to blame themselves for failure to secure employment, rather than the lack of suitable openings or the number of candidates (Sharone, 2013).

Strikingly, two meanings of 'discipline' meet in the welfare office: first, policy is created by academic disciplines – forms of knowledge which define social phenomena in key ways – posing the problem of unemployment in specific ways (Bacchi, 2015). Second, the unemployed are subject to 'discipline'; interventions into their personal conduct, as though joblessness were a sickness or moral failing. Of course, the problem of widespread job shortages is acknowledged, yet ALMPs never create jobs, only reshape individual conduct. While in 1909 Beveridge published *Unemployment: A Problem of Industry,* the underlying assumption since then and long before is that unemployment is a problem of government.

Cruel to be kind?

Why must the unemployed be made to suffer? ALMPs primarily seek to free the unemployed from their situation – even to the point of being considered emancipation (Hansen, 2019). Welfare conditionality clearly has negative impacts, yet officially it is only 'cruel to be kind', a form of tough love, a sort of testing or challenging of the unemployed to motivate them to find jobs, despite being ineffective (Fletcher and Flint, 2018). How can we explain this government rationality? Why is suffering essential to the system? Previously we have described this impulse metaphorically as chemotherapy (Boland and Griffin, 2016), highlighting the medical model imposed upon unemployment, as though it were a pathology to be cured by tough but purifying measures. Yet, there is more at play: ALMPs are not just invasive treatments, and work coaches demand not just better conduct but also that the unemployed examine themselves. Furthermore, the test of the transformation of the unemployed individual is the labour market.

Unsurprisingly, many critics diagnose capitalism as the root problem; for instance, Grover (2012) suggests that these emergent forms of harsh conditionality serve the purpose of 'commodifying labour' – that is, turning individual lives into labour, a useful resource for employers, capitalists who exploit the productivity of real work to accumulate wealth. Furthermore, Grover (2019) argues that the state is complicit in these processes, as it exerts power over citizens, imposing precarity, austerity and inequality through the machinery of the welfare state – the very institution which was supposed to alleviate these difficulties.

Supposedly capitalism is 'liberal' in the sense of cultivating market freedoms, yet welfare conditionality is authoritarian: a paradoxical hybrid of 'liberal authoritarianism'. In *Punishing the Poor* (2009), Wacquant describes the emergence of a hybrid 'centaur state', which deregulates and allows liberties to business and especially financial capitalism, but simultaneously imposes a starkly authoritarian rule upon the poor. This is most noticeable where states are 'tough on crime', through the growth of prisons and militarization of policing, but largely stems from welfare reform – dismantling and conditionalizing the welfare system which drives poverty and racial ghettoization, considered as problems of 'law and order' rather than economics and social policy. While there is something to this punitive-turn thesis, it scarcely accounts for the extensive governmental attempts to transform or reform jobseekers.

For decades researchers have examined the shaming and stigmatization of welfare claimants, and particularly the use of moralizing concepts of the deserving and undeserving poor (Whelan, 2020). Such ideas are expressed in the media, increasingly as a form of popular entertainment (Jensen and Tyler, 2015), in politicized policymaking (Gaffney and Millar, 2019) and are even expressed in the very processes and architecture of welfare activation (Wright, 2016). Strikingly, those who are unemployed often tend to reproduce stigmatizing discourses about other, 'real' unemployed people – the 'skivers/shirkers/spongers' who have supposedly 'never worked a day in their lives' (Shildrick and MacDonald, 2013).

Indeed, stigmatization can be considered as a form of social control: Imogen Tyler's *Stigma* (2020) argues that, beyond temporarily spoiling the identity of individuals through social shaming, concerted political and institutional efforts to stigmatize welfare claimants work precisely to reshape behaviour and leave psychic and even physical marks on the unemployed. Moving beyond the well-established ideas of Goffman about social-role stigmatization and the individual negotiation of shame, Tyler argues that stigmatization is a distinctly political and governmental project which produces docile – and damaged – jobseekers, and can only be resisted through collective solidarity.

Yet beyond the logic of the 'stigma machine', clearly welfare reform has a broader project than simply punishing the poor. Specifically, activation aims to retrain, reform and improve the unemployed, making them better jobseekers and eventually workers. From policymakers to street-level bureaucrats, the ambition is to reform the unemployed, and while moralizing judgements and harsh decisions are part of welfare conditionality, the system is not simply capriciously cruel. To understand this rationality of purifying people through suffering we must turn to theology.

Theology resurrected

For centuries the West has proclaimed its secular nature, yet there is something ironically religious in proclaiming a new age. Many social sciences are experiencing a 'theological turn' (Juergensmeyer, 2013; Schwarzkopf, 2020) which examines the religious roots of meaning, belief and the sacred in modernity (Habermas, 2008). The contemporary reformation of welfare is the result of states incrementally institutionalizing theological ideas through welfare policies, and thereby transforming the lives of individuals – something churches did more directly for centuries.

Most scholars of the welfare state consign the influence of religion to the past: the standard story of the influence of religion on the welfare state is largely confined to the idea of charity. Before there were workhouses and poorhouses, medieval Europe gave alms to the poor and supported the destitute within the parish out of Christian obligation. Early theologians such as Pelagius and Dominus variously debated the morality of riches and obligations to the poor; for instance, St. Francis insisted on the idea of personal poverty, and many apocalyptic preachers demanded the radical redistribution of wealth. Yet, for millennia, Augustinian ideas of charity held sway: all humankind, rich and the poor, are fallen sinners, continuously straying from God's commandments and therefore always in need of redemption, and thus, charity should be a regular yet voluntary obligation (Holland, 2019). Welfare effectively occurred via the religious practice of expiating sins by giving alms to the poor. Eventually, the state took over the care of the poor from the church and parish authorities, along with the moral ideas of Christianity – the condemnation of idleness and the idealization of work.

Crucially, reforming welfare policy is not simply a matter of fine-tuning rules, processes and institutions within the state but follows cultural models. While political discussions often focus on the costs of welfare payments and their impact on the economy, these numbers describe deeper concerns; the lives, the behaviour, the very being of those who claim welfare payments. Ideas like 'incentives', 'culture of dependency' or 'human capital' may initially seem like academic abstractions, but they reflect inherited ideas. Policies which are simply described as 'labour market reforms' or 'activation' are attempts to transform individuals: whether through sticks and carrots of incentives or education and training, the aim is to reshape the attitudes, behaviour and decisions of individuals. This is an attempt at 'reform' – to purify and save the individual.

Architects of welfare conditionality are not coy about this goal; they tend to carefully avoid moralizing and religious language, but they explicitly aim to transform the unemployed into active jobseekers. Obviously, there are different approaches: some focus on incentives – which implies the unemployed are lazy, feckless and greedy, or too proud to take humble work and therefore need reformation; others formulate arguments around the 'culture of poverty' or 'welfare dependency' which imply the unemployed need to be re-educated in the 'work-ethic'. Recognizing that these concepts are shaped at least partially by religious inheritances may help us to better understand these ideas and the hold they exert on the imaginations of policymakers and populations.

Yet, this book is not simply a critique which identifies others as 'ideological' but a reflexive interrogation of how our Judeo-Christian culture shapes our thoughts and lives today. Theological ideas are adapted and adopted by economics, but also sociology, anthropology, psychology and so forth. Specifically, the crucial idea here is that humans can be transformed by their experiences, yet they make their own choices and actions. This is the idea of socialization, but also of salvation. These ideas suffuse Western society beyond the ivory tower – which was hardly their origin in any case – and influence how states govern their subjects.

Crucially, states assume that individuals are transformable and that suffering and challenges will make them stronger. Therefore the state *reforms institutions to reform individuals*, historically by containing them within actual spaces – poorhouses, asylums and even work camps (Fletcher, 2015). Yet now, these are diffused throughout society, and the individual pressured, enticed and empowered to reform themselves in line with the priorities of governance. Perhaps these governmental projects are often ineffectual or may also be partially resisted by those subject to reformation, but what matters is how they permeate our contemporary thinking, almost to the eclipse of any other ideas, as the only way forward.

What is at stake in this book?

This book is intended to be thought provoking, exploring new avenues for understanding the contemporary transformations of welfare. Yet, it is relatively accessible, not requiring the reader to have an expert understanding of the sociology of unemployment, welfare policy, labour-market economics or esoteric theological knowledge. Rather than exposing secret hidden histories, this book restores connections, allowing us to recognize how the relatively well-known ideas of the Judeo-Christian world animate the modern world. These are usually discounted as fairy tales, yet the argument is not that policymakers believe in metaphysics or superstitions, but that our underlying ideas – models of human choice, versions of self-transformation, idealizations of work – inform and animate the welfare state. As such, this book is inevitably centred on the distinctly Western Judeo-Christian inheritance which matters mostly in Europe and in the Americas; the ideas presented here will be less resonant or even irrelevant for other places.

The phrase 'reformation' inescapably evokes Protestantism, which marks the rejection of alms and charity alongside the growth of reformatory institutions. Yet, new modes of 'policing the poor', anticipating the welfare state, predate Luther and Calvin (Michielse and Van Krieken, 1990). Indeed, Catholicism had its own reformation which equally set out ways of reforming individuals; for instance, inventing purgatory and penitential pilgrimages or regular confessions. Thus, this book is about the tensions between different principles which exist within Christianity rather than being for or against its various versions. Any religion or culture has competing demands and ideals within it, rather than a simple coherent ideology, and to an extent this book is an attempt to redress the current imbalance whereby we have drifted towards a punitive rather than forgiving ethic.

Thus, the book is clearly neither for nor against religion – indeed, the whole idea of assessing religion as if from outside is absurd. Claims to be post-religious, atheistic, secular and so forth rely, ironically, on Judaic or Christian models of iconoclasm, anti-idolatry and theological models of separate church and state. Rejecting religious ideas ironically reiterates the gesture of Moses and subsequent prophets who denounced idol worship as vain superstition – our aim is to recognize how these ideas shape us. Our archaic anthropology suggests the importance of recognizing that contemporary culture exists in the aftermath of millennia of organized belief, which not only contributes to how we organize the state and economy but constitutes the deep background of our philosophical ideas which are not mere abstractions, but shape how we experience the world and interpret our lives.

This book attempts to expand the horizons of existing scholarship; there is extensive and excellent research on welfare and unemployment, on individual experiences, social organization, cultural ideas and policy, yet the actual impact of this research is somewhat disappointing – certainly we were disappointed by the impact of our own research which was highly critical of welfare activation in Ireland. Whether in academic papers, the popular press or even in parliament, criticism does not have the desired effect of reversing the turn towards activation and instituting more humane treatment of the unemployed. Perhaps the ideological proponents of welfare activation are more convincing, or governments may be adherents of neoliberal ideology. Or perhaps, things might be even worse were it not for these critiques, which restrain other impulses in a plural public sphere. Perhaps we need more resonant cultural ideas.

We suggest that contemporary critique does not do enough to understand the deeper political and cultural impetus towards welfare activation. Critics often 'reveal' neoliberal ideology in politics or policy which unfairly suggests that others are delusional or evil. Such an approach not only tends to provoke policymakers into defensive positions but also frames the debate in terms of truth and illusion, so that rival think tanks and academics can return the criticism – decrying 'left-wing propaganda' or 'bleeding hearts groupthink'. The capacity of words to reveal the truth and change minds is often overestimated; indeed, criticism suffers from the law of diminishing returns – the more there is, the less effective it is – or the perverse logics of an arms race – the more one side critiques, the more they are critiqued in turn during an endless culture war. This book is not a revelation of other people's illusions, but ruminates upon our shared culture.

Outline

Rather than starting at the next chapter, readers should note that many of the chapters of this book work as stand-alone analyses, particularly from Chapter 4 to 7, and readers are welcome to sample these first. These focus on particular elements of economic life – work, welfare, jobseeking and CVs – and how deeper theological and religious ideas considerably shape our modern practices. These are not obscure ideas but remarkably familiar for Western 'post-Christian' readers, and largely still circulate in popular culture today; ideas of redemptive labour, purgatorial purification, pilgrimages of self-transformation and penitential conversions. Each of these appear initially as arcane superstitions, yet we will argue that they are part and parcel of contemporary thought – how we model human nature and society today.

So, in Chapter 4 we revisit Weber's famous Protestant ethic thesis, to examine the centrality of work in modern culture. Beyond the idea of frugal living and relentless reinvestment of profits, we suggest that work is also considered as a mode of self-transformation. While Weber turned to Benjamin Franklin as his exemplar of capitalism, we analyze Maslow's idea of self-actualization, whereby to work is to test yourself and grow. From there, we examine how the absence of work in unemployment is considered in the popular imagination and sociology. Curiously, the absence of a job is figured as the opposite of monastic life, not just lacking discipline but implicitly damned rather than saved.

Extending an earlier article, 'The Purgatorial Ethic and the Spirit of Welfare', our fifth chapter outlines how contemporary welfare activation derives inspiration from purgatory, imposing purifying and redemptive suffering on individuals. Dismissed as mere superstition in modernity, purgatory returns in the numerous institutions of modernity which manage transformation, from penitentiaries to poorhouses. These buildings are now replaced with individualized treatment, so that jobseekers carry a sense of perpetual obligation to redeem themselves; purgatory pervades their lives.

Initially more hopeful, our sixth chapter focuses on pilgrimage, the ritual of penance through travelling to a shrine, as informing the process of jobseeking – for the unemployed and job-changers or the perpetually precarious. Pilgrims seek out signs of favour and face personal challenges along their road, and thus, economic outcomes are converted into a moral drama of faith in the face of adversity, a balance of hope and despair. Such metaphors persist in modernity, where almost anything can be characterized as a 'journey', yet the idea that it would reform one's character or reveal the truth is a distinctly religious idea. Interestingly, pilgrimage is markedly individualistic, even in supposedly communal medieval culture, so salvation is a personal matter, despite the collective problems of economics.

In Chapter 7 we focus extensively on the CV or résumé, the key document of the labour market, desired by employers and required by welfare officers. Such a practical document nonetheless has a religious history in the obligation to confess, to reflect upon oneself, to tell the truth about oneself, to transform oneself in order to profess oneself to the world. Each tailored CV is a statement of faith in oneself and the labour market, yet in a world of proliferating jobseeking and compulsory applications for the unemployed, these supplications are made over and over again.

Our theoretical position and methodological approach are outlined in Chapter 2, a combination of the sociological and the historical which we term archaic anthropology, an exploration of the presence of the past in the present. Drawing inspiration from key figures, particularly Nietzsche, Weber, Foucault and Agamben, we outline an approach which allows us to recognize how older, ancient, even archaic ideas echo, persist, animate and give meaning to the present. While our concern is welfare in particular, the broader roots of modern states in the pastoral power of the medieval church and the providential interpretation of the economy as the 'hand of God' are introduced to contextualize the impulse towards reform.

Informed by this method, our relatively self-contained chapters combine together into a larger argument centred on the idea of reform, which is explored in depth in our third chapter in regard to both policy reform and the reformation of individual unemployed people through welfare activation. Key ideas which are developed throughout the book are introduced here, particularly the idea of the transformative effect of suffering, imposed by governmentality in an effort to reform, and the idea of the economy as a test or even of life itself as a trial which reveals the truth. While punitive and stigmatizing impulses are part of the process, the governance of welfare is oriented towards reform, demanding work discipline and personal transformation, but also incorporating individual choices and positioning the market as the final judge; a providential expression of divine will. Combining detailed social-policy analysis and theological sources, this chapter is perhaps more challenging, but it is the key to our thesis, and also to our recommendations, which are summarized in our conclusion, that reform can be excessive and welfare would be better off wholly unconditional, especially in the face of contemporary challenges.

2

Archaic Anthropology: The Presence of the Past in the Present

Our work is easier to know by its fruits than by its roots, and readers may wish to skip forward to later chapters to see our methods in action. Here we outline an approach which is not quite a methodological procedure nor an abstract theory but a mode of recognizing the present in the past: archaic anthropology. Herein, 'archaic' is not antiquated and superannuated, nor do we adopt the Greek sense of 'arché' as an origin or a source, but the 'archae' of archaeological. The 'archaic' is always another sedimented layer of times past which forms the site we investigate today. We are formed by the cascade of history – our society, our thoughts, our approach, our idea of ourselves has come to us from the past. We are digging less to find the origin – because there are always further layers – than to understand why the world has the shape it does today. While etymologically arché means 'beginnings', today it denotes ancient, and this collision of meanings expresses our sense that the present is alive with the past.

Our approach is interdisciplinary, combining ideas from anthropology, sociology, history, philosophy and beyond in an attempt to reconsider the present as decisively shaped by theological ideas from the past, often unrecognized, yet pervasive and significant, animating our world. Our focus is not the religious beliefs of modern people, whether policymakers or jobseekers, but how their ideas about the economy, choice, work and so forth are at least partially and unknowingly drawn from Judeo-Christian ideas. Of course, there are other historical influences – Greek philosophy and Roman law and beyond – but for various reasons religion is most neglected, despite being the most influential inheritance, for good or for ill.

Recognizing the past in the present is an approach which combines at least three elements: an anthropological immersion in our topic, through interviews with the unemployed, analysis of policy documents, media and politics, and ethnographies of the physical and digital spaces of welfare; a historical awareness of key religious ideas, from popular beliefs and practices like purgatory and pilgrimage to theological ideas of providence, sin, salvation and redemption; and the final element, reflexivity, which cannot be supplied simply by extensive research or intensive reading – it is the practice of examining our own ways of thinking, and recognizing them as part of a wider culture, a tangled inheritance.

Rather than arid logical analysis or introspective navel-gazing, reflexivity here means a reflection upon ourselves as formed by our culture and society. Archaic anthropology calls for reflexivity around our complex intellectual inheritance, our culture, a sociology of ourselves as historically formed. Such reflexivity is challenging when much of what we think of as reflexive thinking focuses on individuals philosophizing, often biographically, about themselves and their experiences. It is also challenging because the potential and possibility of our thinking is, in and of itself, also a complex cultural inheritance, and so we have to think, to be reflexive, from within the tensions and traditions of a historical inheritance, not a fixed tradition but a series of tensions between complex ideas.

However, culture or discourse is not 'settled dogma', but a way of seeing the world, interpreting data and 'producing truth' in an attempt to understand ourselves. Reflexivity has many meanings in academia, and it is not a shortcut to insight or objectivity (Lynch, 2000). Rather, reflexivity is reflecting upon our culture, which is part of our culture, and we end up interpreting how others interpret their culture: inescapably, culture is a slippery fish, tending to slip out of our grasp just when we think we have it! (O'Carroll, 1987)

Our archaic anthropology draws upon Nietzsche, Weber, Foucault and Agamben, each of whom diagnoses modernity as reflecting neglected historical transformations. Academically, this approach is known by the strange moniker of 'genealogy', which here does not refer to family trees of kings or biblical lineages of 'begats' but to the attempt to write the history of things which appear to be outside of history; for instance, morality or individuality or reason. Against essentialism or claims about human nature, or that 'there is no alternative', or that 'it has always been thus', genealogy suggests that the present is created by a complex of intertwined and unrecognized histories.

Genealogy has become increasingly well recognized within contemporary scholarship, perhaps not widely practiced, but respected as a way of interrogating contemporary problems from a longer perspective. Broadly, genealogy is expected to be critical, although as we shall see critique itself has a religious inheritance. Additionally, genealogy has recently branched into economic theology (Dean, 2019), demonstrating the longer religious inheritance of ideas as diverse as debt (Stimilli, 2017 and 2019), money (Singh, 2018) and markets (Schwarzkopf, 2020). While economics and theology seem to sit uneasily with each other, both concern how life should be conducted, how society is organized and states governed.

Like most genealogists, we begin in the present with contemporary problems: why is welfare reform interminable yet so repetitive? Why does a secular state attempt to reform its people? Why is the economy the test through which the worth of people is discovered? In this reflexive meditation on the contemporary, we make use of historical sources – biblical passages, ancient theologians and dusty philosophers – but we do not pretend to discover new historical evidence. What makes our archaic anthropology a distinctive genealogy is the breadth of our engagement with the contemporary field. Our work explores the present, anthropologically, in depth, at length – by engaging with the lives and experiences of the unemployed, and taking welfare policy as a wider culture which shapes society to be explored, not simply a technical exercise of governance. Strikingly, the religious ideas that matter here are remarkably well known and enduring ones; purgatory, pilgrimage, redemption, confession and so forth.

Archaic anthropology also grasps the connection between religion and economics: this reflexivity means an examination of thought itself, an interrogation of the very categories we use to think; it means refusing to rely on concepts and theories from academic disciplines such as economics and sociology as simple descriptions of reality. Instead, following Foucault, we take these as 'discourses', cultural ideas and models which themselves have a history and exist as modes of 'truth-production' in modern society. Both theology and theory are discourses, ways of thinking and categorizing the world. Thus, before we outline our method and review the insights of Nietzsche, Weber, Foucault and Agamben; why religion?

Why religion? Iconoclasm and critique

This book is neither for nor against religion in general or Christianity specifically, but suggests that theology is hidden in plain sight throughout the modern world. Hidden because we choose not to look. Indeed, our theological inheritance even forms part of our modern uneasiness about religion, how uncomfortable we are with belief or ritual or anything which smacks of superstition. Remarkably, this attitude replicates Protestant antipathy to Catholic church practices, or Judaic condemnation of idolatry. Furthermore, our sense that religion is a special set of beliefs separate from culture in general and preferably independent from politics is also a Christian inheritance (Holland, 2019) – partly a reaction of Jewish peoples to being a colony of Roman imperialists with their own state cult. For millennia, religion was effectively indistinguishable from life in general; for instance, colonialists imposed the category of religion upon the vast landscape of Hindu which they found within Indian culture, interpreting a diversity of world views and practices in terms of belief and ritual as they knew them within Christianity.

What of the place of religion in modernity? Critics sometimes use the terms religion or cult as criticisms, to denounce the 'work cult', expose 'faith in progress' or decry 'capitalism as a religion' (Benjamin, [1921] 1996; Beder, 2000). Others point out the persistence of organized religion despite secularization, particularly in America where church attendance remains high and faith permeates politics and society (Davies, 2000). Despite this, modernity broadly understands itself as secular, having incrementally left Christianity behind since the scientific revolution, the Enlightenment of Voltaire and Diderot and in the growth of liberal democracies. Of course, many historians have argued that, contrary to stereotypes about feudalism, Christian religion actually drives technological progress, free markets, colonialism, human rights and many other elements of the modern world (McCloskey, 2004; Stark, 2006).

Perhaps the most vocal commentators against religion today are the New Atheists, led by celebrity scientist Richard Dawkins, who insist that religion is an antiquated version of reason, incompatible with the modern world. Dawkins even extends Darwinian ideas about the survival of the fittest to assert there are 'selfish genes', but more importantly, that ideas try to reproduce like 'memes' (Dawkins, 1976). Considering religion in this fashion – 'Western culture is the bible's way of making more bibles' – religion appears as a sort of parasite on the thriving scientific culture of modernity, an impediment to rationality, selfishly reproducing itself but ultimately unfit to survive and likely to become extinct.

The irony here is that the New Atheists are distinctly evangelical; proselytizing around the world in favour of rationality and the scientific method, debating and haranguing religious figures in public, preaching largely to the choir but always hoping for new converts. More specifically, their denunciation of other people's beliefs as fantasies is iconoclasm, the breaking of idols, the condemnation of ritual, found centuries before in Puritanism and millennia ago in Old Testament prophecy (Boland, 2019). Claiming others are blind and need to be awakened to the truth, that false prophets or ideology leads people astray, and that delusions lead to oppression and injustice is a religious inheritance. While the religious speak in the name of God, or proclaim the Bible 'revelation', contemporary critics invoke the 'voice of reason' which speaks to them.

Famously, it is easier to see the splinter in the eye of someone else than the beam of wood in one's own! Our archaic anthropology inevitably partakes somewhat of this urge towards revelation – less a prophecy predicting the future than a diagnosis of the forces at work within society. Recognizing our own thought as not being an internal mental creation of pure cognition – if that exists – allows us to reflect upon it as culture, to understand the models we use to describe the world and the distinctions we make – even concerning categories as technical as the labour market or welfare reform.

Rather than paradoxically accusing modernity of being a secular ideology, we follow Nietzsche's insight, 'We knowers are unknown to ourselves' – modernity fails to recognize how religious thinking constitutes us as subjects. This is partially because the tradition of Judeo-Christian thought is to take oneself as seeing clearly, seeing things as they really are, not being deceived by false idols but knowing the truth directly. More importantly, religious thought is not a single dogma but a series of tensions between multiple ideas and competing imperatives all of which inhabit us and animate our thought. For instance, there is the idea of individual choice and freedom, yet also the explanation of society as a providential order; or equally there is the punitive attitude to other's failings, demanding redemption through suffering, balanced by the impulse towards forgiveness. Rather than dogmatism, there is tension in thought here. As authors and as readers we have all felt these things intensely, experienced them as 'the truth' rather than as 'culture'. Indeed, we actively use these ideas to interpret the world, and they become self-confirming; we see the world as we are, not as it is.

Importantly, the activity of historicizing is not neutral or simply factual. Rather, all models of history have cultural sources. For instance, there is the dialectic, taken from Hegel and made famous by Marx, which describes history as the constant battle between different forces to produce a better future – the revolutionary utopia. This idea is inspired by obscure Gnostic and Manichean cults, but familiar as the battle of good and evil unto the end of the world. Similarly, the idea of history as a series of crises which are solved by charismatic leaders who institute a new order is recognisably the story of Israelite prophecy, most famously Moses and the Covenant – a divine 'social contract' – but in Isaiah and Ezekiel and other prophets, it recurs as the hope for salvation from decline and chaos through a New Jerusalem. Even contemporary accounts of the history of struggles or 'hidden histories', wherein subjugated groups resist power, can be traced to a vein of 'counter-histories' inspired by salvation narratives. 'Its method is the perpetual denunciation of the evil that has been done in history' (Foucault, 2005: 135). Conversely, histories which celebrate the state or modernity or democracy or capitalism express the idea of a providential or even 'divinely-ordained order' where 'what is, ought to be', in Alexander Pope's phrase – acclamations of power (Agamben, 2011; Dean, 2017). Our work is unlike any of these, instead drawing from the millennia-old practice of exegesis, interrogating the meaning of things, partially a matter of biblical interpretation, then of the examination of conscience, and now the interpretation of society (Taylor, 1989).

The recurrence of older ideas is grasped at in phrases like 'history always repeats itself', or in more ominous tones, 'the return of the repressed'. However, ideas do not persist in pure form, as though they had some core or essential element, rather, they are adapted to new contexts; our aim is to demonstrate the influence of religious thinking on labour markets and welfare, which is historically relatively recent. So, the peculiar enigma we must explore is why crises and transitions are resolved through the reworking of older ideas rather than genuinely new thinking. Tracing these ideas through history involves genealogy as we shall see, but more importantly, a reflexive interrogation of these ideas in the present.

Archaic anthropology

Understanding modernity requires a deep anthropological engagement with contemporary practices; not just in the sense of a deep ethnographic immersion in unemployment and jobseeking but dwelling anthropologically in the 'given' world of data (Ingold, 2011). Partially this means extensive empirical research, interpretative and qualitative, which we have pursued continuously since 2012, a project of tracing the experience of unemployment, a governmental concept but also a category lived out by actual people in time and place. Our ethnographic inquiry is approached through multiple, extensive large-scale datasets;

around 130 interviews with jobseekers, autoethnographic accounts of social welfare offices, digital ethnography, media and social policy analysis. This is less a scientific method than an anthropological immersion in the worlds of unemployment, jobseeking, the labour market and welfare reform. In the following chapters we cite the words of the unemployed and describe their worlds at length.

Rather than studying objects across a distance as scientists do, this is a reflexive approach, as recognizing historically significant ideas in the present is possible mainly because we participate in them; we are part of the culture we are attempting to understand. These influences can neither be measured decisively nor dismissed as mere irrelevances – these are elements of culture which are too central and pervasive to be ignored – any coherent interpretation of modernity simply must take them into account. The inescapability of meaning does not make the book 'merely subjective' – the authors are Irish but do not pretend that Ireland's myths or cosmology have remotely shaped the modern world. Rather the method is to dwell upon cultural fragments, words, phrases, documents, practices and institutions, and to recognize the presence of theological ideas within them, styled 'sociological impressionism' by Frisby (2013).

Archaic anthropology is inspired by two main traditions. First, Weber's interpretative sociology, which is focused on the meanings given to social action, basically the study of culture. Second, Foucault's governmentality studies, which focuses on the 'production of truth' through power relations which form individuals and society. Both place a strong emphasis on history, not just the study of the past but the presence of the past in the present, the continued influence of older ideas, unrecognized, in shaping the contemporary world. A key precursor to this was Nietzsche, who argued that supposedly secular modernity was, in fact, deeply Christian, even after the 'death of God'. These thinkers addressed distinctive topics: Weber is famed for his Protestant ethic thesis and work on bureaucracy, while Foucault is best known for his historical works on prisons, asylums and sexuality. However, there is significant overlap between them: Weber is concerned with the 'meanings of social life', and Foucault with the 'production of truth', and we draw their ideas together to observe the production of meaning in society. To these, Agamben adds a particular approach to economic theology whereby religious ideas operate as 'signatures' allowing the adaptation and adoption of ideas over time. Without judging veracity or values, we focus on how people interpret society, the models and metaphors they use to make sense of it and the meaning they ascribe to their experiences.

Consider the word 'welfare': today this generally means state support for those in need, but this usage is only really about a hundred years old in English, with the phrase 'welfare state' only becoming widespread in the 1940s (Edling, 2019). For centuries beforehand, the term welfare referred mainly to individual welfare in the sense of health, or occasionally hinted at in the idea of a collective 'common wealth'. Yet, no history of the welfare state starts in 1900 as though from ground zero, because the longer history of welfare in the poor law, the work house and the medieval institutions of charity must be acknowledged. Nothing springs from nothing in society – ideas, words, concepts, institutions and organizations always have a longer history. Yet, there is no 'essence' of welfare, no universal and unchanging idea or definition, waiting to be discovered somehow 'beneath' the various instances we find, as though it existed outside history.

Archaic anthropology entails taking words and other symbols as 'discourses', a loose term which covers a whole panorama of concepts, classifications and categories, from technical terminology to narrative stories, all of which are produced by society about society. Adopted from Foucault (1972), the term discourse is not special, indeed, we will also discuss 'culture', although this implies shared belief and values, which cannot be presumed – often we will examine dry, technical documents. Thus, welfare is not just a system, but a discourse, both the word itself and its symbolic meaning, how it is interpreted by society at large, and the surrounding set of policy documents and debates, from media reports down to benefit application forms. While we have interviewed dozens of people who have been on welfare, we really have no direct, unmediated access to their experiences, so we must try to understand it through discourse, simply, by what they say.

Are we drifting into relativism – the idea that there is no objective reality? This is a false dichotomy, because there is nothing unreal about discourse. Indeed, the problem with many analyses is the exaggerated distinction between 'reality' and 'appearance' or 'truth' and 'ideology' – a dichotomy which unsurprisingly has a religious history. This idea appears in archaic form in Zoroastrianism, enters into Judaism in the figure of prophets railing against iniquity and delusion, and inspires peasant rebellions with apocalyptic thinking, then influencing modern philosophies of Enlightenment, Marxism and more (Cohn, 1971). While politically or rhetorically it may be exciting or even effective to declare that there is a 'deeper reality', which other people's words and ideas obscure, deliberately or otherwise, it serves the purpose of interpretation and analysis less well. Thus, we avoid using the term 'social construct', because that term is now implicitly a critical unmasking: saying, "that's only a social construct" basically means, "that's only an illusion". Of course, the term discourse can also be used in this way: "That's only a discourse", implies that the words and ideas people have are misleading, delusional and possibly oppressive.

Rather than suggesting that there are 'false' discourses which misrepresent the 'true' reality, our approach recognizes that there is nothing 'unreal' about the way things are spoken about. Of course, there are multiple ways of talking about ideas in society at any one time, describing a complex social world in different ways, full of tensions, elisions and complications. Discourses are open to contestation and culturally specific to a time and place. Yet, it is sterile and arrogant to simply criticize and correct other people's discourses, as though we had direct access to the truth. Our words are discourses too, and will be criticized in turn! Instead, our method focuses on understanding discourses and observing their effects, how they interpret reality, the world and experience, how they direct action and shape behaviour, how they give meaning and value, how they are institutionalized in policies and organizations. Rather than describing our materials – documents, interviews, words – as a series of delusions about the world, we attempt to understand them as 'things of this world'.

Our archaic anthropology means observing how discourses constitute reality – how the terms and evaluations used to describe something contribute to shaping it. This has limits – a beetle or a virus continues to be itself no matter what people say about it. However, it makes perfect sense whenever we turn to social or cultural things – a workplace or a welfare office are both largely created by people saying things about property, labour, the state and so forth, and these places are changed and transformed when people say different things about them. Quite where the dividing line between the hard facts of nature and the changeable social world lies is a matter of debate – certainly, being human is more than a biological experience, and is shaped by discourses, from philosophy to psychology. What matters is to recognize that discourses constitute the things which they describe, and that these ideas do not remain abstract but are implemented, shaping relationships, creating organizations and forming institutions (Boltanski, 2011). This occurs from a micro scale to society-wide, from the discourse of friendship shaping relationships to large-scale phenomena like the welfare state (Hansen, 2019).

While focused on discourses, this approach is not an idealist philosophy wherein ideas and concepts exist separately from society, powerfully shaping the world. Indeed, for Foucault, alongside a plethora of terms for discourse there is an equally inexhaustible list for discussing power relations; tactics, strategies, apparatuses, etc. Sometimes the word 'etc' should simply be added to all of his sentences as he attempts to cover a vast range of things. Importantly, power and knowledge are inextricably linked, expressed in the phrase 'power/knowledge', which implies that all truth is produced socially, and there is no space or place in society which is free of power relations (Foucault, 1984). Furthermore, truth or knowledge or discourses have consequences; they are powerful in that they classify, categorize and define, shaping the situations in which they are produced.

While the phrase 'power/knowledge' is relatively well known – not to be confused with the slogan 'knowledge is power' – Foucault's work supplies some more intriguing and relatively clearer expressions of this relationship. Rather than accept the veracity and authority of academic disciplines or philosophical schools of thought, Foucault takes them as 'regimes of truth', discourses which resemble systems, classifying data, verifying facts, offering models of reality and giving rules which govern the possibility of making a true statement. Obvious examples are psychology or economics, but equally theology – and clearly all of these ideas have consequences in the 'real world'. Within a 'regime of truth', Foucault identifies 'truth-games'; interactions and power relationships which produce and determine truth – for instance, the psychoanalyst's couch or the confession box or a CV workshop.

Evidently, Foucault's work generates conceptual innovation, a plethora of words – disciplinary power, bio-power, governmentality, for instance – in an attempt to interpret the world anew, which he describes as an 'analytic of power' (Dean, 2013). More metaphorically, he describes his work as an 'archaeology of knowledge', invoking the image of sifting through the sediment accumulated by centuries of 'truth-production'. His terminology shifts rapidly over his career, because his aim is not to provide a series of pristine theoretical categories but to diagnose how truth is produced in our society today – which inevitably means unsettling existing theories and academic disciplines. Indeed, the term 'truth' here becomes quite strange, as it is not idealized truth nor a critical account of 'truth' in scare quotes denounced as false and ideological. Truth is produced, but has consequences; it is situated socially, changing historically, but situationally effective. Crucially, these regimes of truth enable us to think in certain ways, and various truth games constitute us as individuals. Nevertheless, there is something dry and technical about this use of the term 'truth', which was perhaps appropriate to Foucault's work on academic disciplines and useful for our analyses of welfare and active labour market policies, yet lacks a recognition of culture, somewhat neglecting the level of meaning.

Our work addresses the production of meaning, that is, the interpretation given to society and individual experience by certain discourses. Perhaps it is over-wrought to speak of a regime of meaning, a circumlocution which means culture, that is, ideas which interpret and evaluate life and society, thereby ascribing meaning. For instance, there is workplace culture with its emphasis on effort and labour, individual discipline and professionalism, career trajectory and ambition and even marketing and entrepreneurial culture. Equally, the phrase 'truth games' could extend to 'meaning games', a phrase more simply rendered by the existing term 'practices', that is, regular institutionalized routines in society whereby people create meaning – for instance, writing CVs, applying for jobs or accounting for themselves to welfare officers. So, the terminology is not as important as the method of analysis, joining the Weberian concern with culture and meaning to the Foucauldian insistence on examining how truth or meaning are produced socially, over time, historically.

Our method follows how words, terms, discourse and culture shape and constitute society in powerful ways. Knowledge is powerful, but not in the dystopian sense that it dominates or manipulates hapless individuals, because all truth games are created and used by people, indeed, discourse actually *empowers*, making people capable of defining reality, asserting values, interpreting situations and contesting other discourses. Furthermore, discourses allow events and experiences to be interpreted and given a meaning, howsoever contested, and direct future action. However, individuals cannot use discourses simply as handy tools, mere instruments; rather, they are 'constituted as subjects' by discourse – we know ourselves and shape our lives through ideas: for instance, detecting one's interests and talents and therefore forming life into a career. Such discourses should not be considered as illusions or ideologies but as 'real in their consequences'; every bit as real as any discourse which seeks to criticize or unmask them. Discourse is not a covering over reality but a representation of it which becomes part of it, producing truth and meaning, and this applies equally to all discourses – including our own. Thus, discourse matters, from the shaping of states to the behaviour of individuals, to the way critics interpret and analyse the words of others.

Clearly, discourses change over time, through contestation and different uses, becoming intertwined with other ideas. Nothing emerges out of nothing, which turns our attention to the history of discourses – or genealogy.

Nietzsche: modernity as Christian 'slave morality'

Genealogy is the difficult interrogation of ourselves, how we are constituted as subjects and how we think. At its best, genealogy allows us to recognize elements of our constitution which have been neglected or occluded, not necessarily hidden but so densely intertwined with other elements that they become unnoticed. Yet, there is a shock of recognition in genealogy, as though we are brought face to face with the uncanny. It holds out the possibility of being critical, as the method disrupts assumptions in the present and challenges existing discourses and practices (Koopman, 2013; Folkers, 2016), but for us, in our approach, such externally oriented polemic critique is a by-product of some genealogies rather than its purpose (Allen, 2017). Genealogy is inescapably reflexive. This is most clearly the case with Nietzsche, the 'first' genealogist.

Whatever and whenever 'modernity' is supposed to be, without getting into the confusions of 'postmodernity', our society distinctly understands itself as having left the past behind. Ironically, the post-religious quip 'God is dead' is taken from Nietzsche, who suggested that modernity was inextricably Christian, particularly because of its commitment to human equality, personal liberty, empathy with suffering and ideas of progress or revolution. Rather than accept that contemporary morality – ideas about good and evil – was simply a matter of basic human feeling and natural reason, Nietzsche insisted that it derived from religion, which permeated modern culture all the more thoroughly because its effect was unrecognized.

Particularly, the idea that suffering could be ennobling or that the weak were holy struck him as peculiar, and he attempts to account for this in *On the Genealogy of Morals* (1876) as a 'revaluation of values' which occurred in Judaism and Christianity. He characterized these as 'slave morality', which reversed the ancient interpretation of strength and power as signs of divine favour, making weakness, poverty and humility into virtues. Asceticism, deliberately denying oneself comfort or pleasure, became a way of purifying the self. Nietzsche polemically interpreted this discourse as nihilism – not just relativism, but a radical denial of life and rejection of the world.

Reconstructing Nietzsche's intellectual milieu is not our focus; suffice it to say that he disagreed with virtually every philosopher, including Socrates. New fields of psychology and sociology, or developments in moral philosophy or historiography, seemed bogus to him, because they assumed things about human nature which he considered cloaked versions of Christianity. Famously, he described these self-deceptions as the 'will to truth', which only served to disguise the 'will to power' which he assumed to underlie everything – the hunger for life and the struggle with others. Indeed, the extraordinary impact of the Darwinian theory of evolution cannot be ignored in Nietzsche: first, it implies that 'God is dead', as man is nothing but an animal; but second, because it removes all plans or goals – teleology – from history, life is nothing but a struggle for survival. Whatever beings or ideas or societies attain dominance in the present are largely accidents of history and a product of past struggles – whatever succeeds will be succeeded in turn.

Rather than adopt Nietzsche's overly polemical assessment of modernity and Christianity, what matters is his method, the strangely named 'genealogy', most commonly understood as a family tree, for instance, in medieval kingship or in Biblical lists of 'begetting'. Such records served to assert the lineage and legitimacy of figures of authority, asserting sovereignty through connection to holy precursors, even establishing a divine right to rule. Yet Nietzsche reverses this procedure by pointing out that anything which exists in the present came to be through a series of conjunctions; every lineage is promiscuous, not pure, an interwoven tapestry of discordant elements. Rather than being concerned with individuals and their biological heritage, Nietzsche is interested in the history and generation of ideas, and insists that there is no pure essence of anything in the present, only an entangled tapestry of past influences. Furthermore, there is no single source or origin of anything, no universals, only an almost infinite multiplicity of hybridized elements.

Methodologically, Nietzsche's genealogy involves diagnosing the whole of contemporary society as being derived from the past – refusing all claims about 'human nature' or 'essences'. It means critiquing commonplace assumptions, not simply as illusions but as deeply historically conditioned modes of thought, particularly ideas which seem merely practical, pragmatic common sense. Wherever social life appears merely natural, history is unacknowledged or unknown: genealogy challenges us to rediscover and recognize the contingency of our present world, created through the 'promiscuous couplings' of multiple ideas, and the present as a contingent moment in an uncertain and disorderly procession of struggles.

> There is a world of difference between the reason for something coming into existence in the first place, and the ultimate use to which it is put, its actual application and integration into a system of goals; that anything which exists, once it has somehow come into being, can be

reinterpreted in the service of new intentions, repossessed, repeatedly modified to a new use by a power superior to it. (Nietzsche, [1887] 1998: 57)

This position is known as anti-foundationalist because it disputes all universal or essential claims, and even disputes the interpretation of ideas as 'functional' – like religion as a salve for social injustice.

Crucially, in his efforts to overcome nihilism, Nietzsche recognized himself as an inextricably Christian thinker – he cannot help feeling pity or seeking to transform the world. Explicitly, he suggests that he is best positioned to understand nihilism because he has been an utter nihilist, yet passed through it, and is thereby able to comment upon it. Thus, from the start, genealogy is a reflexive endeavour.

Weber: spirits and ethics in history

Initially, Nietzsche was a feted professor, but through illness and idiosyncrasy he fell out of the German academy, although his influence was considerable. Indeed, Weber explored his topic of the continued influence of religion, unacknowledged and unrecognized in society, most famously in *The Protestant Ethic and Spirit of Capitalism*, and also built on Nietzsche's method.

In a key essay, 'The Social Psychology of the World Religions', Weber refutes both Nietzsche's interpretation of Christianity as mere nihilism and Marx's denunciation of religion as mere class ideology. Instead, he emphasizes the diversity of religions and cultures, and suggests that these derive from different interpretations of the world and suffering within it. Human society inevitably encounters death, suffering, pain, sickness and sometimes ecological crises. Typically these are given meaning through rituals, yet, the world religions responded to the emergence of empires, which created unprecedented warfare and disruption, inequality and oppression. Imperial religions asserted their rule was divinely ordered, yet empires rose and fell, creating devastation on a global scale.

In Weber's reading, these extraordinary events strained the capacity of existing culture to give meaning to existence. Evidently, they involved suffering on a chronic and massive scale: enslavement, dislocation of populations, cramped cities, standing armies, sudden conquests and massacres, famines, floods and plagues through the overreach of agricultural systems, and then sudden collapse into chaos and anarchy. Older agrarian religions, which asserted that the world was ordered by the gods, were insufficient. Society and culture entered into a crisis of meaning, whereby justifying life and giving it a meaning became difficult. In response to this, world religions offered new charismatic visions which gave new meaning to experience – which Weber describes as 'world-images' that 'have, like switchmen, determined the tracks along which action has been pushed by the dynamic of interest' (Weber 1991: 280). Well-known examples of 'world-images' are karma (what goes around comes around), dualism (the world is the scene of a struggle between good and evil), and 'salvation' religions, wherein life is a trial set for each individual to purify and test them. These ideas are pronounced by 'charismatic prophets' – not soothsayers who predict the future but compelling visionaries: 'Behind them always lies a stand towards something in the actual world which is experienced as specifically "senseless". Thus, the demand has been implied: that the world order in its totality is, could, and should somehow be a meaningful "cosmos"' (Weber 1991: 281). While Weber is particularly concerned with world religions and diagnosing the 'economic ethic' which guides behaviour within historically shaped civilization, this idea supplies key suggestions for a genealogical method which is concerned with meaning.

By linking the emergence of new ideas to crises, Weber points out that while there may be no origin points in history, certain moments matter decisively, as the breakdown of existing order makes it possible to propose new ideas. Such 'world-images' are not entirely new, as they inevitably recombine older ideas, but if a charismatic prophet is successful, then their vision becomes crystallized, not permanently fixed, but substantially influential thereafter. Thus, rather than an endless entangled mess of genealogical promiscuity, Weber suggests paying attention to key crisis moments, the sort of suffering they encounter and the meaning they give to life, which becomes institutionalized thereafter. The famous Protestant ethic thesis – discussed in Chapter 4 – is a paradigm case; the Reformation was a crisis of meaning, and charismatic thinkers like Luther and Calvin appear, giving a new interpretation of life as individual striving for salvation, which becomes institutionalized thereafter – even motivating those in modernity who espouse no religious beliefs. Thus, moments of crisis create charismatic ideas, which thereafter are routinized, often losing something of their original spirit – a neat model for historical change – although Weber stresses that there are differing sorts of crisis, environmental or political, and that the 'carrier strata' for the new ideas also matters greatly.

Older ideas persist – consider the idea of transforming the poor into better workers through exercising surveillance over them: typical histories suggest that as the welfare state emerges, the Poor Law of 1834 disappears, gradually. Parish-based Poor Law guardians are replaced by actuarial social insurance and the state bureaucracy of claims. Symbolically, the Poor Law is abolished in 1948, yet the new welfare state takes on many of the characteristics of the Poor Law, for instance, public works or household means tests (Fraser, 1992). Ideas around preventing any disincentives to work were one of the main concerns of the 1834 Poor Law reform; the principle of 'less eligibility', whereby the workhouse was made a last resort for the poor because conditions there were worse than for those on the very lowest wages outside the workhouse. Any charitable subvention of those outside the workhouse was ruled out, officially anyway. Thus, the great transformation of the welfare state is effectively from institutionalization to 'outdoor relief', the provision of Poor Law charity outside the workhouse.

Thus, the birth of the welfare state is not simply a matter of the replacement of the Poor Law but of its adaptation and continuance. Economic crises allow the more puritanical and punitive ideas of 1834 to be adjusted to more charitable ways of thinking, the continuous 'reformation of welfare'. This suggests three key characteristics of historical transformations: first, that temporary crisis measures allow for new ideas but that these are made permanent, or at least chronic in the form of institutions, becoming a perennial problem for social policy. Second, small-scale or self-contained institutions or situations can become generalized throughout society; The workhouse as a container for parish poverty becomes generalized into a welfare state to manage unemployment across the population. This idea is anticipated in Weber; through Protestantism the whole world becomes something of a monastery. Thirdly, older ideas are transformed and given new life – nineteenth century ideas of giving people choices and reforming the destitute through purifying labour are reinstated in the form of welfare policy.

To the critical impulses of Nietzsche's genealogy, Weber contributes an orientation towards culture and meaning, the reflexive art of recognizing older ideas as informing contemporary practice. Elsewhere (Boland and Griffin, 2018), we have suggested this is a 'spirit and ethic' model, with an emphasis on the impact of ideas, charisma and world-image in history providing a 'spirit' for life thereafter – in an economic ethic. More widely, Weber's approach is known for the 'routinization of charisma', how explosive ideas become institutionalized – as prophets give way to disciples and then priests. This approach allows our analysis to move beyond the detail of welfare reform and the minutiae of unemployment schemes to consider the ideas which animate them.

Foucault: historicizing government as pastoral power

Ironically, Foucault was strongly inclined to disrupt the truth production of academic disciplines, and so he might have considered Weber's crisis-charisma-routinization model of history as just another discourse. Rather than claiming a special status for any philosophical position or academic discipline, Foucault suggested that disciplines construct the things which they purport to describe; 'Discourses systematically form the objects of which they speak' (Foucault 1972: 54). Thus, philosophies and disciplines are just ways of describing and thereby shaping the world: if we believe in psychology or economics or sociology, we interpret the world and act in it in specific ways.

Occasionally, Foucault is considered as a 'theorist of power', yet he consistently asserts that there is no such thing as 'Power with a capital P', only concrete 'relations of power' between people. He offers no theory of power beyond the simple definition that power acts relationally, reacting to other acts (Foucault, 1984). What matters is to understand the specific relations of power in certain societies, in periods of history. Through his 'archaeology of knowledge' and 'genealogy of truth', he analyses ideas and systems, and especially academic disciplines, as ways of producing definitions and classifications of reality. However, such abstract 'power/knowledge' relationships are also grounded in the 'subject' or the 'self', and in his later work, Foucault declares his oeuvre actually concerned the production of subjectivity through relations of power and knowledge. Thus, ideas matter, but principally because they exert power through defining reality, creating institutions and organizations which shape individuals and thereby society. Like Nietzsche, Foucault disputes any essentialist or universalistic account of the self: there is no stable human nature, even our 'inner' experience of ourselves is shaped by ideas and institutions.

Following Nietzsche, Foucault's genealogy of truth tends to emphasize discontinuity, struggles, entanglements of discourses rather than the model of a clear idea emerging at a singular crisis point. Many commentators consider Foucault's work as distinctly critical in the sense that it challenges the contemporary status quo or 're-politicizes' issues which seem be settled or merely technical (Hansen, 2016). Certainly, the insistence that human nature is not fixed but shaped by society, and that knowledge is produced by power relations, has a critical edge, as almost any conception of truth is placed in scare quotes, considered an idea produced by society. Making all knowledge into the target of investigation – including his own perspective – may seem like a step into relativistic postmodernism, yet actually Foucault's approach is a flat realism, which insists there is nothing but 'words and things', *Les mots et les choses* as per his earliest title (1966). Yet, within these critical interrogations – the archaeology of knowledge and the genealogy of truth – there is also recognition at work, of the presence of particular historical ideas in the contemporary world.

Much of Foucault's early work tends to historicize academic disciplines, particularly psychology and economics, but equally history, politics and sociology, by tracing the diversity of elements which contribute to their truth production. A subtle shift in emphasis emerges in his later works. Rather than undermining contemporary theory by 'revealing' historical influences, the effort is to *recognize* the roots of our current modes of 'telling the truth' as rooted in history. For instance, the persistence of Greek philosophy in how we reflect upon ourselves or speak the truth to power, which is demonstrably still influential in modern society. Identifying these complex hybrids is far more difficult than asserting that 'everything changes' or that all current 'essences' are actually the product of history.

Yet, Foucault's genealogy is not oriented towards setting the historical record straight in the style of revisionism, the work of official state historians or museum curators of artefacts of the past. Instead, his work is a 'history of the present', a contribution to current social and political debates, because inevitably his truth production is contemporary – as is ours or any academic, national or critical history; 'History does not simply analyse or interpret forces; it modifies them' (Foucault, 2003: 171). Histories of the present focus on elements of contemporary society – whether controversial or unremarkable – and reconsider them as temporally specific articulations and institutions of older or even archaic ideas. While ruptures, discontinuities and cross-fertilizing promiscuities are emphasized in his earlier methodological descriptions of genealogy, Foucault's later essays pick out the transmission, adaptation and persistence of certain ideas – for instance, the notion of life as a test or trial, or the relationship of self-transformation and telling the truth about oneself. Drawing attention to the presence of history within the present serves the inescapably political element of scholarship, the art of 'problematizing' the present – not just commenting on things which are already 'problematic', but equally observing how society 'poses the problem' and recognizing the historical legacies involved in all modes of thinking (Bacchi, 2015). Much of this book concerns how religious thought influences how the 'problem' of welfare or unemployment is posed as a moral and individual problem rather than an economic, political or social issue.

While Foucault sometimes offered erudite studies of the exotic and unusual, his method does not consist in revealing hidden evidence or overlooked clues in history. Just as frequently, he analyses well-known sources – Socrates or Hobbes, or banal records and texts. Whether described as the archaeology of knowledge or the genealogy of truth, his method is a history of the present, a thorough rumination on the contemporary as a specific articulation of discourses which are derived from the past and which shape society today in ways that are either acknowledged or not. Recognizing supposed 'human nature' or 'merely practical' ways of organizing life, or even 'scientifically established' assertions about society or politics, as the products of history – locating even partial legacies from the past – allows us to rethink the present.

Foucault's early work on disciplinary institutions such as prisons is probably best known for the 'panopticon': this was an eighteenth-century design for a prison where inmates were continuously under surveillance from a central tower; they cannot see their overseers who demand certain behaviour, motivating them with rewards and punishments, until the prisoners internalize the gaze of the prison guards. Beyond this ornate apparatus of control, what really matters are the minutiae of power, from architectural arrangements to procedures, processing, forms and paperwork with their classification and categorizations, the endless 'microphysics of power'. Crucially, he recognizes that the techniques used to control and reform the inmates of prisons, asylums and hospitals are derived originally from monasteries, and that the sixteenth century onwards saw the 'colonization of an entire society by means of disciplinary apparatuses' (Foucault, 2006: 68). These were initially enclosed institutions for marginal populations – the mad, the criminal, the sick – but became routine, in the forms of the school, the factory, the office – places of surveillance and control which we all pass through in modernity, which shape who we are. Strikingly, the demand that inmates tell the truth about themselves to authority figures, wardens, doctors and teachers replicates the religious logic of confession.

From enclosed 'disciplinary power' Foucault moves to 'governmentality', which is the exercise of power across whole states, and then to 'subject formation', investigating the 'techniques of self' whereby individuals are formed and constituted by 'subjectification'. This strange term 'governmentality' can be understood as a specific rationality, a way of thinking about a population. Knowledge, particularly disciplinary knowledge, governs by knowing the population and producing interventions and policies according to 'political rationalities' which inform 'how administrators and authorities make judgements' (Miller and Rose, 2013). Beyond fascination with historical detail, Foucault attempts to 'diagnose' the character of this power, variously describing the growth of institutions as disciplinary power, overstating his case by calling it 'bio-power', then turning towards the more culturally specific formulation of governmentality.

Foucault's last years were also marked by a sustained interest in religion, with specific analyses of monastic discipline, early Christian confession and medieval 'counter-conduct'. However, what is most significant for our purposes is his theological genealogy of governmentality. In brief, governmentality covers the whole assemblage of exercises of power and ways of knowing a population in order to transform the 'conduct of conduct'. It is not violence or coercion but more subtle and insistent, an elaborate apparatus of interventions arrayed in an attempt to govern others by encouraging them to govern themselves in specific ways. The aim of the state is to constitute individuals who strengthen the overall aims of the state. Clearly, welfare activation is an exemplary case of governmentality.

Interestingly, for Foucault, 'the state is nothing else but the mobile effect of a regime of multiple governmental actions' (Foucault, 2008: 77). Yet the state is also sovereign, deciding on matters of justice, deriving legitimacy through the exercise of power – the king has power over life and death. Modern states decreasingly exercise sovereign powers which threaten life, deciding who is protected by the law, or demanding sacrifice in war, but increasingly govern life itself, managing people from the cradle to the grave, as individuals and as aggregate populations. However, since the emergence of liberal democracy, we have increasingly seen 'a state under the supervision of the market rather than a market supervised by the state' (Foucault, 2008: 84). Thus, the state becomes secondary to the market, legitimized by the efficacy of its actions according to market reactions – the economy reveals the 'true' effect of the state's governmental actions.

Foucault's approach is not an attempt to define the essence of governmentality, but to write a history of state power relations which traces the strange entanglements, continuities and ruptures that create the present, which implies that the present is contingent and therefore open to change. This enables a critical orientation towards contemporary political struggles, but also implies multiple transformations in the past. In particular, Foucault identifies how the modern state adapted its governmentality from the medieval church – as we shall see in Chapter 5, provisions for the support of the poor, sick and elderly, which we now think of as the welfare state, were once provided by parishes, churches and religious communities.

For Foucault, the metaphor of the shepherd and the flock emerges partially from Greek thought, but more strongly from Judaism: the Athenian statesman was implicitly a citizen, whereas 'the Lord is my shepherd' implies a hierarchical and sacred distinction (Foucault, 1981). Importantly, the flock are more important than the Promised Land – the population is more important than the territory, and in modernity security of borders is secondary to the management of population. Following the flock metaphor, the shepherd – the governor – is concerned for all and one – *omnes et singulatum* – and thus cares for lost sheep, bringing them back to the fold. In our analysis this occurs through processes of confession, purification and redemption, in psychological 'sciences' and in disciplinary institutions.

Yet, Judeo-Christian-inspired governmentality does not mean treating the state as a farm, nor imagining the population as a herd. Perhaps occluded by this metaphor is the centrality of individual choice to Christian religion and modernity. Any decision or choice is interpreted as expressing or articulating something 'within' the individual, and every person is judged by their choices, creating their own destiny in part at least –'by their deeds you shall know them' (Matthew: 7:16). Thus, after his more famous 'Governmentality Lectures' of 1977, Foucault turns towards 'liberal governmentality' to demonstrate firstly the different varieties of neoliberalism, secondly how liberalism runs deep in our culture, and thirdly how modern states characteristically generate spaces for the possibility of choice, for instance in the market, the public sphere or in 'civil society' each of which constitute places of choice which gives rise to legitimacy and even sovereignty (Schwarzkopf, 2016).

Agamben: signatures of theology

A key figure in the shift from genealogies of governmentality to economic theology is Giorgio Agamben, who took up Foucault's thesis on political power relations in his *Homo Sacer* project (1995–2014). But of interest to us here is his companion work, *The Kingdom and the Glory*, which has been taken up by Dean (2012, 2013) and (Singh, 2018), to analyse contemporary economic governance. This important reformulation is the point of departure for economic theology studies (Leshem, 2016; Heron, 2018; Dean, 2019) and Schwarzkopf's authoritative *Routledge Handbook of Economic Theology* (2020), which aspires to rigorously define the emerging field. Expanding beyond Foucault, Dean's 'What is economic theology?' (2019) makes Agamben's work central to an authoritative articulation of a distinctive method.

Effectively, Agamben's approach takes Carl Schmitt's pronouncement on political theology; 'All significant concepts of the modern theory of the state are secularized theological concepts', and extends it to the economy (Agamben, 2011).

Contemporary critics often highlight the Greek etymology of the word 'economy', *oikos nomos*, meaning the law of the household, which imputes a moral order to production and consumption. Indeed, for most of human history trade and markets were limited as almost all communities were self-sufficient or, in another Greek phrase, autarchic – producing all they needed. Long-distance trade was only in non-perishables and luxuries. Even in Socrates' Athens, the emergence of markets in the city *agora* were viewed with suspicion and tightly regulated (Agnew, 1986). Yet rather than criticizing the economy for having lost its implicitly moral character in modernity, the point is to trace how it was transformed. Indeed, the word 'economy' is only applied to markets in the seventeenth century (Szakolczai, 2019), and connecting the labour of production, the marketplace of exchange and domestic consumption of goods is a modern discourse. Whereas the Greek oikos nomos existed to support political engagement in the city, philosophical thought and self-development, in modernity economics is at the heart of contemporary politics.

Agamben traces how early church figures and theologians used oikos nomos to represent the organization of the church, but most especially to model the Trinity (2011). By being translated into Latin as *dispensio* – the divine dispensation – the more metaphorical connotations of oikos nomos are somewhat neglected. The oikonomia or dispensio of God was a mode of organizing the rule and provision for the world he had created, redeemed through the crucifixion and cared for through the Holy Spirit. By splitting the divine into a Trinity, a wholly determinist world where the omnipotent deity was responsible for every human action was avoided, as was the dualist vision of a battle of good and evil, as envisaged by many competitors to Roman Christianity. Instead, error and evil entered into the world through the absence of God, through the failings of individuals who had not yet turned to Christ for salvation; evil is not the wrath of God, but his absence, indeed God's punishments and trials are always purgative tests. Within this model, the possibility of grace by the providential intervention of the Holy Spirit attends all human actions, making redemption continuously possible, despite the sinful, fallen nature of humankind.

This sounds like mere cosmic superstition, yet Agamben suggests these archaic ideas are embedded in contemporary social institutions, most particularly the economy and the state. Counter-intuitively, this theological position allows for a 'disenchanted' vision of reality: bar the crucifixion and a few miracles, there are no signs of the divine father who is a *deus abscondicus,* more distant than the stars. 'God has made the world just as if it were without God, and governs it as though it governs itself' (Agamben, 2011: 286). The divine is invisible, except to those of faith who construe his handiwork in all things, yet his plans remain inscrutable; the economy is a mystery to be interpreted, 'conferring a hidden meaning on every event' (Agamben, 2011: 50). So, rather than markets being seen as chaotic affairs open to the whims of chance or zones of illusion or even oppression, they are rendered as 'economies', reflecting the will of God and rewarding and punishing human choices. In effect, the economy is 'providential', not just a fixed divine plan but allowing for each individual to be tested, and always providing another opportunity for redemption – for the faithful at least.

Joining economy to state, Agamben traces the emergence of a 'double structure of providence' (Agamben, 2011: 135–6), which accounts for the world in terms of divine will, human choice and the intervention of the Holy Spirit. While most famously captured by Leibiniz's thesis that God's omnipotence means that we live in the best of all possible worlds, the idea that the world reflects an omnipotent will and omniscient plan is very old. Yet, this will is not deterministic but is tempered by the possibility of choice for all humans, allowing them to err, sin and be redeemed. 'Modern Governmental reason reproduces precisely the double structure of providence' (Agamben, 2011: 119) This first order of providence explains events in the world, from political and military to economic outcomes. However, within this order, churches and states are created – surely the will of God – which subsequently dispense goods to the poor, widows and orphans, to mitigate the impact of the economy. This palliative ministering is akin to the work of the Holy Spirit, a secondary providential redemption for those who are not favoured by general providence. Over time, the work of ministers becomes the bureaucracy of administration and the providential order becomes governmental machinery: 'The administrative apparatus through which the sovereigns of the earth preserve their kingdom becomes a paradigm of the divine government of the world' (Agamben, 2011: 71). Thus, the modern liberal state respects the economy by allowing market freedoms, yet in itself embodies providence by providing the welfare state.

Lesham (2016) develops Agamben's work by attempting to recover this prehistory through a detailed exploration of pre-Christian economy (the oikonomia) and its transformation and institutionalization (in the *ecclesia*) in early Christianity. Before Christianity, in ancient Greece the economic concern of the household was to satisfy life's necessities and generate a surplus of time and means that could be spent on the higher activities of philosophy and politics. Thus, the economy addressed prudent management, the desire for surplus and the idea that politics and philosophy were built upon the economy and so were the ultimate accomplishments of the economy. Lesham traces the story forward into examining Apostolic brotherhood, St. Paul's church and ultimately Christian Rome, through to Augustine's reframing of the church, thereby taking the issue of economic salvation to the core of life. There is a theological tension which informs how the political has gradually been subsumed to service the economy, even though these two 'realms' are mutually constitutive (Heron, 2018). Dean goes further, suggesting that secularization is a signature rather than a concept (Dean, 2013), whereby signatures serve to displace concepts without ever redefining them systematically; thus, breaks in continuity such as the reformation are restored into a continuum of history.

Conclusion

Broadly, our archaic anthropology approach involves a number of steps, often faltering or repeated: first, it starts from a deep and practical anthropological engagement with our own present, exploring the mundane and quotidian elements of culture, society and practice – for instance, writing CVs or jobseeking. Secondly, the lineage of these ideas and practices in history is traced, not in a search for a single or hidden origin, but from multiple sources, in recognition of the multiplicity of ideas and the tensions between strands within our culture. For instance, the idea of the self as having an essential character, yet being malleable and capable of transformation. Thirdly, the presence of these archaic ideas is recognized in the present, a recognition of how they constitute our society, politics and economics, but moreover, our selves – our ways of thinking and being, our values and the meaning we give to our lives.

Yet, this is not a navel-gazing or merely subjective perspective exploring 'personal feelings' but recognizes the presence of a larger social history shaping individual experience. In this way, archaic anthropology opens itself up to uncanny recognitions, understanding the presence of the wider and long-term within everyday life. This is not the surfacing of a singular 'other' history or origin, one that flattens difference and plurality, but rather the effort of recognizing multiple shared cultural ideas which animate our lives; for instance, the idea of work as giving meaning to life – for good or for ill. In this approach, culture is not taken as a simple coherent philosophy but as a multitude of different ideas and imperatives in tension with each other. Finally, we recognize limitations; our illuminations of contemporary culture as reincarnating religious ideas always exist *inter alia* – there are multiple strands of any idea, adapted to different contexts and alloyed in different forms over time. Such a method is intrinsically incomplete; there are many ways of reflecting upon the present, and more connections to be made to the past – perhaps emphasizing other historical influences.

Most importantly, this approach is oriented towards fruitful analyses, pursuing a generative contribution: it does more than simply critiquing the present as ideological, offering an understanding of the current, interminable project of welfare reform. The animus or urge to govern people and reform them appears less as a project of power for its own sake than a cultural pursuit of reformation – of the state and its people, to redeem them, even to create a 'better world'. This broad impulse towards reformation does not have a single origin or 'spirit', but is composed of multiple elements: purgatorial purification, vocational work, penitential pilgrimages, confessions and conversions; the theological urge towards the 'reformation of welfare' significantly precedes and exceeds Protestantism. In the following chapters we will concentrate on distinctive elements of the contemporary world: unemployment, welfare policy, work, jobseeking, CV writing and so forth. While these elements from religion, history and economics may seem vast and disparate, the key component of our archaic anthropology is a reflexive openness to seeing the past in the present.

This returns us to our problem: the interminable and stagnant world of welfare reform, the incessant tinkering with unemployment in the name of activation. 'When policies fail, they are evaluated as a behavioural problem fostered by passive governing that requires more active and intense measurement, including sanctions' (Hansen, 2019: 189). Why is this? Our next chapter answers this in detail by examining two dimensions of 'reform'.

3

Reform: Policies and the Polity

Welfare policy reform is widely researched, but culturally unexplored. In public policy and political science, welfare policy reform is a cacophony of research and recommendations, plans and evaluations, cross-country comparisons and longitudinal studies, all tied to particular places and times, with perennial problems in want of solutions. Such work involves complex compromises between competing imperatives, and what is actionable by a government in the policy mix is invariably a tried and trusted upcycling of existing approaches. Our book is not a contribution to policy, nor a critique of contemporary welfare policy as neoliberal or paternalist, important as such work is, nor is this chapter a history of policy reform. Rather, our ambition is to explore how the idea and practice of 'reform' encodes a distinctive theological inheritance, *inter alia*.

Broadly we argue that considering welfare policy as a 'governmentalizing' power, with an assemblage of definitions which classify individuals as unemployed (Boland and Griffin, 2015), explains much of how welfare policy works, but does not explore its whys and wherefores – or what it means. In this chapter we explore the deeper formulation of problems that foreshadow their solution, as a theological impulse to reformat people and the polity at large.

Welfare is broadly an anti-revolutionary construct (Ewald, 2020), an insurance against unrest that guarantees the state's existence, maintenance and adaptation. This idea follows in the footsteps of Machiavelli's originality as a prophet of policymaking with a deep understanding of instrumental, managerialist political thinking, and his general concern for political continuity through internal stability (Berlin, 1974). In his lesser known *Florentine Histories*, he dispassionately considers the Ciompi Revolt, an insurrection of the lowest stratum of Florentine working classes (1378), which led to revolution, the overthrow of the elite and instituting of a radical democracy. Machiavelli departed from the historical orthodoxy of Bracciolini, who suggested the insurrection was God's wrath on the city, and Bruni who had little sympathy for the violent criminals or for treating the revolt as a political movement (Winters, 2012). Machiavelli retells the story as a lesson: an excess of poverty can spill over into political violence which can even topple the Medici dynasty for a while, something every leader must keep under a keen eye.

From medieval peasant rebellions met by dispensations for the poor, to post-war opportunities for reconstruction, the state frequently prescribes welfare as a salve to inequality and suffering, without systemic change. This is evident in the post-1968 era which saw the final evisceration of the radical left after the supposedly 'history-ending' coup de grâce of 1989. Creative destruction, chaos, the ex nihilo impulse to rise up and revolt are irreconcilable with policy reform. Although the birth of the welfare state in the post-war era is often presented as a new perpetual settlement, it is an amalgam of older concepts from the 'poor law' pensions, old age and child care, universal healthcare, poverty alleviation schemes and income protection that are assembled together. Importantly, it is also an explicit gesture towards rapprochement in Europe, an armistice to the continent's repeated state of fratricidal war. Welfare is a salve to moderate rather than address inequality (Pickett and Wilkinson, 2009; Piketty, 2020), to do enough to keep people off the streets, and welfare is thus most compelling when those with wealth and power fear for their position and lives, and welfare recedes when they are comfortable.

Revolution is animated by ideologies that announce their ambitions. The current intense epoch of welfare reform (Esping-Andersen, 2002) has rippled out from the Scandinavian shift towards more activation, taking hold in the USA under Regan and Clinton, Germany in the Hartz reforms, France under Sarkozy, and Britain from Thatcher, Blair and Cameron. Yet, these reforms are just as political as revolutions, seeking to transform society in line with ideal horizons: not a revolutionary apocalypse, but an earthly 'City of God' where individuals are tested, judged and reformed.

To ground these diagnoses of welfare reform, we will examine specific welfare reforms, from crisis, through politics, to policy, concentrating on the recent EU Youth Guarantee. Later we argue that welfare processes put the unemployed through trials, in an attempt to transform them. But first, we must clarify the matter of reformation.

Reformers

Famously, Esping-Andersen (1990) divided 'worlds of welfare' into three, based on their current disposition: conservative systems of Spain, Italy and France; Social Democratic states like Germany and Scandinavia; and Liberal systems such as the UK, US, Netherlands and Australia. The root of this commonly accepted taxonomy, in our analysis, is buried in Catholic, Lutheran and Calvinist religious histories that reside in the cultural heritage of these nation states and still persists. Church and community-based charity endure in Mediterranean countries, whereas state-based entitlements and public works appeared in Lutheran states, and harsher regimes for the poor appeared in Calvinist states. 'Indeed, Calvinists simultaneously asserted that poverty was predestined and that the poor are responsible for their plight' (Kahl, 2005: 117). Strikingly it is the Calvinist reforming instinct that has come to dominate the global policy imagination, lying beneath the 'punitive turn' in welfare policy (Wacquant, 2009). Although such sharp distinctions may be exaggerated, there is a broad relationship between national religion and the development of the welfare state.

The term 'reformation' evokes the Protestant Reformation of 1517, Luther, Calvin, Knox and a host of puritans who split from the Roman Church into a series of reformed churches. However, 'reform' has a much longer history in theology – most obviously in the 'reformatio' of Pope Gregory VII (1073–85), but also throughout the fifteenth century with Christian scholars such as Desiderius Erasmus, John Colet and Thomas More and others. Indeed, since before the fall of Rome, the church has continuously engaged in self-reform through synods, meetings and debates, despite the aura of dogmatic continuity which it exudes. More importantly, the church continuously works to reform its flock, the *ecclesia*, the people, by preaching, monastic rules, sacraments of confession and the care for and regulation of the poor. These two dimensions of reform – of the institution by the institution *and* of the lives of the flock – are the twin foci of this chapter.

However, the urge towards reformation is not simply Calvinist, nor exclusively Protestant, but suffuses the Christian and Jewish tradition. Indeed, the transformation from the pantheon of gods of Egyptian, Greek and pre-Christian Rome, from polytheism to monotheism, is also a transformation of the interests of God in reforming man's conduct. Ancient Israelite prophecy – from Amos, Isaiah and Ezekiel to Jeremiah – was not just an excoriating critique of society but also a demand for reform, of rulers, priests and ordinary people. In a similar vein, St. Paul's many epistles to early Christian communities, Corinthians, Thessalonians, Galatians, Romans, Ephebians and so forth are expressions of faith in the miracle of the crucifixion and resurrection, but also practical instructions for how to organize and administer the church community, directions as to how to live a good life. Thus, the impulse to reform appears to emerge from the 'world-image' of Judaism and Christianity: life as a trial of redemption set by God for the chosen people or each person.

There is a central tension between the urge to reform and revolt in these texts; ancient prophets proclaim that the final judgement is fast approaching, which has inspired millenarian religions and revolutionary movements from medieval to modern times (Cohn, 1993). By contrast, the letters of St. Paul promise the second coming, but warn individuals against resisting authority and condemn libertinism. Each letter, whether to a specific community of believers or the whole world – the ecumene – dampens down any revolutionary sentiment and calls for a disciplined life.

While contemporary scholarship broadly recognizes the influence of theological ideas on contemporary political culture, by contrast, the policy machinery of 'reform' is considered 'apolitical', as though state interventions were a purely scientific, disinterested, evidence-based governance of society in order to optimize individual and collective life – and always in balance with individual choice. Within this chapter, we will attempt not only to re-historicize the impulse to reform as firmly theological, but also to demonstrate that it is manifestly political.

The politics of history

Sequential history is ill-suited to consider the welfare state or the concept of unemployment, as its boundaries oscillate between the abstract category and the individual experience, key moments dissipate into mundane revisions, and rapid recent reorganization antecedes research quickly. By contrast our genealogical approach begins in the present at the contemporary scene of welfare activation and then casts backwards scouring for important precursors and discontinuities. Evidently, most histories of welfare and unemployment also tend to be histories of politics, identifying strands of ideology, usually the enduring struggle between liberalism and socialism. Of course, all history writing is political, a contribution to contemporary debates, and many contemporary writers are open about their allegiances and generally announce their 'critical history' as a revelation of the forces at work in the past and present. By contrast, our attempt here is not to unmask the historical workings of ideological forces, for instance, neoliberal ideology or state control, but to recognize the presence and persistence of religious ideas in shaping the institutions of today.

Starting in the present poses its own problems, because any moment in time in policy has its own minutiae – the rate of unemployment, existing welfare provisions, international labour markets, political and geopolitical demands, currents in policymaking and so forth. Yet, contemporary social policy is also relatively stable, with decades of near consensus that unemployment and welfare are problems which should be addressed by Active Labour Market Policies (ALMPs). These are government programmes that intervene in the labour market to help unemployed people find work. Many ALMPs are work-first policy interventions to increase 'labour market participation' – either by providing jobseekers with employability-orientated training or education or by forcing them to seek work actively and accept any job offers by the threat of cuts to their welfare entitlements. ALMPs reform in two ways, intervening in individual lives to reform conduct, but equally intervening in existing, 'passive' welfare institutions that rendered the unemployed 'welfare dependent'.

Starting with ALMPs is not to neglect critics or ignore revolutionary alternatives, such as the idea of universal basic income – curiously popular across left and right. However, within the circles which actually contribute to the formation of policy and therefore shape the lives of individuals, ALMPs are dominant; the question which matters is how to design and implement these policies, not whether or not these are the right policies. Recent unemployment crises such as the global financial crisis and the COVID-19 pandemic have deepened the reformists' commitment to ALMPs, suggesting that the concept of welfare as anti-revolutionary technology of society becomes more visible when the economy experiences difficulty.

Standard histories trace ALMPs to post-war Scandinavia, particularly in the 1950's Swedish Rehn-Meidner policies, where extensive social provision was popular and activation policies were seen as important means of 'social inclusion'. The idea that welfare reform plays an important role in preventing 'labour market exclusion' is still current. These policies were adopted by the US, with a considerably harsher emphasis on conditionality, then spread to Australia, the UK and became adopted by the OECD in the 1990s, becoming EU-wide policy by the end of the century. Notable examples include welfare reforms under Blair's Labour Party, the Hartz reforms in Germany, the erosion of the rights-based French welfare state under Sarkozy (Hansen, 2019). Since then ALMPs have spread and diversified; for instance, conditional-cash-transfers, particularly in Mexico and Brazil, whereby welfare benefits depend on individuals complying with norms around health or education (Peck and Theodore, 2016). The social policy process of ALMPs involves designing measures to reform individuals, assessing whether this has been effective and then returning to the policy drawing board for further reform. Both individuals and state policies must be optimized continuously, through whatever means, and today algorithmic targeting of interventions and 'nudge' methods from behavioural economics are increasingly deployed to hone the effectiveness of interventions (Friedli and Stearn, 2015; Desiere and Struyven, 2021).

Welfare reforms assume the provision of welfare entitlements; the logic of ALMPs assumes there is something passive that needs to be 'activated'. These policies clearly emerge in response to the provision of universal state-funded benefits to the unemployed, outside of systems of contributory 'social insurance', what is today termed the welfare state. The persuasiveness of ALMPs, particularly in America, is underpinned by the critique of the welfare state articulated by Von Hayek even as the Beveridge report was being published in 1942 and popularized by Milton Friedman in the post-war period. Amid these various neoliberal critics attempting to 'dismantle the welfare state' – as the standard left-wing critique phrase goes – there are perhaps a very few who are in favour of eliminating actual welfare payments. Primarily, ALMPs accept that welfare payments are necessary supports to a volatile economy and unpredictable labour market. Thus there is a tension inherent within ALMPs, between providing monetary support and extracting jobseeking behaviour to support 'labour market participation'. Paradoxically, it is only through the provision of support which is made conditional on behaviour – turning up to meetings, making a CV, applying for jobs, retraining – that welfare offices can exert influence over the unemployed.

While Hayek and Friedman criticized the welfare state drawing on classical liberalism – that it interfered with the individual right to choose and the responsibility to face the consequences – more academic discourses have been instrumental in ushering in ALMPs, obviously from economics, but perhaps surprisingly from sociology. This is most evident in US critics who demand welfare reform in the sense of reforming the welfare state because it supposedly creates perverse incentives to refuse work: the welfare trap or the poverty trap. Simultaneously, welfare recipients are also morally condemned as having low ambitions or poor understanding of the rewards of work, but they are nonetheless presumed to be strategic actors. For instance,

Charles Murray (2006) suggests that some young men 'prefer' doles to work, or that some women use pregnancy as a strategy to assure welfare support. More recently in the UK Andrew Dunn (2014) described the 'choosiness' of welfare recipients who would not accept simply any work whatsoever, echoing the political discourse of generations of Conservative Party politicians, but most importantly Ian Duncan Smith and David Cameron, architects of welfare reforms which introduced harsh conditionality and activation, leading to unprecedented levels of sanctions (Watts and Fitzpatrick, 2018; Dwyer, 2019).

A key figure here is Lawrence Mead (1986, 1993, 1997), a prominent politically active researcher whose well-argued yet polemical books became welfare policy in the United States and beyond. His work offered a more polished political rationale for the work-first reform of his precursors Charles Murray and George Gilder. Echoing American president Reagan, Mead argued in the *New Politics of Poverty* that the old economic questions the welfare state addressed were obsolete, replaced by the new problem of the 'dependency of the poor': individuals enfeebled by the post-war welfare state. Supposedly 'government' was the problem and the absence of a work ethic amongst the poor threatened the legitimacy of all anti-poverty programmes (Mead, 1997). The reforms Mead sought were authoritarian work-first policies underwritten by punitive sanctions to jolt people into any form of paid employment however menial, dirty or low paid as a necessary prerequisite for escaping poverty (Wacquant, 2009). Mead came to these views from his experience as a policy advisor on welfare issues for the Nixon administration, and he appeals to evidence based in social policy, but also political polling. The combination of a scientific approach to data and clinical disdain for the subject of his surveillance is particularly evident in his practical experiments in Wisconsin and New York. Simultaneously he articulates a zealous personal commitment to identifying the welfare state as a political failure and poverty as an individualized moral failing.

Strikingly, right-wing critics of welfare have begun to adapt the vocabularies of the left-wing to their own purposes, talking of 'learned dependency' or the 'culture of poverty'. These ideas can be critically described as 'psy-science' or pop-psychology (Friedli and Stearn, 2015), but even more uncomfortably, they are recognizably sociological. Indeed, Mead's phrases 'underclass' and 'non-working poor' focus welfare politics around a problem of *conduct* habituated by social conditions. For Mead, the growth of the welfare state simply multiplies problems because it corrupts people's work ethic, making them dependent upon the generosity of others, supposedly leading to a downward spiral of indigence, incompetence and even criminality. Thus, rather than simply rearranging the system of incentives – making work pay and so on – these reformers envisage a system which totally transforms people: "*In progressive-era politics the issue was government control of the economy; in dependency politics it is government supervision of behaviour*"(Mead, 1993: 112, italics in original). In particular, Mead envisages the state managing the young, intervening in cases of passivity and weakness. Furthermore, he positions the left as defending the 'status quo' of the welfare state, while the right 'ushers in a new political age' (Mead, 1993: 114). Strikingly, this echoes Jeremiah, condemning the present and harking back to an imagined past (Bercovitch, 2012).

While ALMP is a neologism, this tension between giving support and demanding compliance with economic and social norms has a long history. Roosevelt's speech introducing comprehensive welfare in the face of the 1930s depression explicitly addresses the fear of welfare dependency. The end of the Great War in Europe in 1919 necessitated direct welfare payments, wholly funded by the state, regardless of the 'social-insurance' principle; during the 1920s these temporary emergency measures proved hard to withdraw, and the 1920s saw multiple attempts to introduce time limits and conditionality until the Great Depression led to the 1934 Unemployment Act made more or less temporary provisions permanent (Fraser, 1992). Before the war, policy wrestled with abolishing the Poor Laws and associated institutional workhouses for the destitute through the introduction of Bismarkian social insurance and labour exchanges. Indeed the debates that surrounded the introduction and multiple reforms of the Poor Laws, particularly the Poor Law reforms in 1834, all addressed the politics of universal welfare and individualizing conditionality and behavioural reform.

Much research explores the governance structures, policy formation and evaluation of ALMPs in different countries (de Graaf et al, 2011). For their proponents, ALMPs are a given, considered as effectively the only option in an austere economic context to expand interventions into the lives of the unemployed, as passive benefits are not considered viable (Bonoli, 2013). Following critics of welfare, ALMPs pose the 'problem' of unemployment in terms of the individual – requiring training on the 'supply side' of the market if not explicitly blaming claimants (Bacchi, 2015). Evocatively, activation policies have been equated to a 'trampoline' rather than the 'safety net' of older modes of welfare (Giddens, 2013). Critics of activation policies abound, and allege that not only do they push individuals into precarious work, impose cruel psychological punishment and stigmatize individuals, but they also are ineffective at reducing unemployment, especially for youths (Leschke et al, 2019; Tyler, 2020).

Our interest is not focused on contributing to these debates about the effect or efficacy of these ALMPs. Of course, the outcomes of these policies matter immensely –'by their fruits you shall know them' (Matthew, 7:20). But here we argue that it is not enough to know a system by its fruits; instead we have to understand how these policies and systems think. So, from our bird's-eye view of history we descend to the thickets of policy, to examine the contemporary EU-wide *Youth Guarantee*, the ALMP which sought to heal the last crisis, whose diagnosis and remedy for unemployment will no doubt be prescribed again in the near future.

Back to the future

Formally adopted by the Council on 22 April 2013, the Youth Guarantee (YG) aspires to offer good apprenticeships, training, education or employment opportunities to all unemployed young people within four months of their leaving employment or education. The guarantee is a strange hybrid of the modern and the archaic: archaic in its formulation as a promise from the sovereign power, and modern in that it manifests upon implementation as a pragmatic platform of various improvised or ad hoc local structures and technical ALMPs. YG is a modification to ALMPs in four distinctive ways: it offers a guarantee (Bussi and Geyer, 2013), it imposes a metricized objective on the state (Besamusca et al, 2013; Bussi and Geyer, 2013), including long-form human capital development as well as immediate employability responses to unemployment and economic inactivity, and finally, though incompletely, it transforms the national problem of youth unemployment into a continental issue that cannot be solved by national economies.

YG's radicalism is a reaction to high levels of youth unemployment – cresting 23 percent across the EU, but as high as 58 percent in Greece and 55 percent in Spain – and the fear that an entire generation of Europeans was being left behind or permanently scarred which if left unaddressed might endanger the European model (Scarpetta et al, 2010). Parallel to ALMPs the concept of a Youth Guarantee had emerged in Scandinavian countries, but in the 1990s, targeted at marginal groups of youths who might suffer 'labour market exclusion', quite distinct from the case of mass youth unemployment across the EU. Crucially, these YGs are ALMPs as they focus on 'activating' the individual, promoting labour market participation rather than directly creating jobs or instituting job-sharing. Whether work-first or oriented to 'building human capital', these policies are all oriented to getting individuals to work, turning them into jobseekers, making them participate in the economy.

Mass unemployment resulted from the great financial crash of 2007–8, and the ensuing recession was marked by austerity policies across Europe especially (Coulter and Nagle, 2015; Springer, 2016). Remarkably, despite general cuts to spending, states increased investment in activation policies during this period. As job losses during recessions take longer to recover than economic growth and capital investment, international institutions took the initiative by focusing on employment. Supported by the UN, the International Labour Organization (ILO) promoted a 'Global Jobs Pact' in 2009 – which offered specific policy recommendations alongside rhetorical declarations: 'The world must do better ... The world should look different after a crisis'. The 'relevant stakeholders' for this policy included states, businesses, unions, politicians and citizens, envisaged as acting in unison to achieve a common goal. Importantly, while commitments were made towards protecting the vulnerable, equalizing access to jobs and environmental sustainability, the policy also recommends the use of activation policy and the extension of Personal Employment Services – a mixture of measures which certainly includes monitoring, compulsion and sanctions. The cooperative amalgam of stakeholders consulted does not include the unemployed, who are targets of activation.

The YG was trumpeted as a great success by Jean-Claude Juncker as president of the European Commission in his 'State of the Union' speech in 2016. The missionary fervour for employment is palpable: "I cannot and will not accept that Europe is and remains the continent of youth unemployment. I cannot and will not accept that the millennials, Generation Y, might be the first generation in seventy years to be poorer than their parents" (Juncker, 2016). However, while youth unemployment certainly fell during this period, statistical assessments by the OECD and the ILO highlight that this probably would have happened anyway, given that unemployment fell overall for all age groups – making the Youth Guarantee 'economic deadweight', state expenditure wasted on things that would happen anyway in the economy (see Eichhorst and Rinne, 2017; Escudero and Mourelo, 2017). What the policy did do was institutionalize activation more strongly, by extending it to youth via early intervention, rather than waiting for the twelve-months threshold which marks long-term unemployment. Early intervention, algorithmic profiling, monitored job searching, threats and implementations of sanction become routine: these are the actual labour market activities which are generated in the aftermath of political rhetoric. Even after ILO statistical analyses suggested that activation may be ineffective and that sanctions may have negative impacts on job quality or even push people out of the labour market, the policy continues, an interminable attempt to restore 'full employment', harking back nostalgically to the past as a prescription for the future.

This is not to suggest that the YG had no effect or that it was 'irrational' in the sense of being an ineffective ideological project. Certainly, ALMPs do impact individual lives, forcing people into more extensive jobseeking, training and self-scrutiny, forcing them to accept unsatisfactory or unfeasible work and even imposing sanctions on them – with negative consequences. However, our aim here is not to decry this 'irrationality' but to understand this particular form of 'governmental rationality', how the state imagines its citizens and the economy more broadly.

The YG is inspired by the policy term NEET – 'Not in Employment, Education or Training' – coined by Istance et al (1994) to describe young people in Glamorgan, Wales, who had failed to get a footing in the labour market. Echoed in the media, this term became common parlance and a key organizing concern of research and policy around young people, a problem to be tackled by individuals through responsible self-management, at the state level through Government action to responsibilize young citizens (Wrigley, 2017), and at the supra-national level most manifestly in the EU YG but also in the UN Secretary General's Envoy on youth 2015 focus on youth unemployment.

NEET adds to a longer discourse wherein young people are considered as a troublesome population, fragile or already damaged, who need guidance through the inherent vulnerability of the complicated transition into adulthood in the labour market (Furlong and Cartmel, 2007). Effectively, the transformation of children through education and training into participants in the labour market and good workers is rendered a governmental concern (Roberts, 2004). Healthy labour markets, elsewhere or in the past, real or imagined, supposedly had a linear and seamless transition into industrial apprenticeships, employment training schemes with paternalistic employers who set people on a course for a job for life (Willis, 1977). A phalanx of youth activation schemes – in the UK, the Youth Opportunities Programme (YOP), Youth Training Scheme (YTS), Youth Training (YT) and Restart Programmes – emerged in response to the decline of such employers, in the form of the state standing in, albeit without the offer of secure meaningful employment, and thus resulting in undirected training (Furlong and Cartmel, 2007: 41–4). The form of gendered work envisaged or, perhaps more accurately, imagined or dreamed up in these schemes was aggressive, masculine and unpredictable (Simmons et al, 2014; Roberts, 2018).

Like the negative definition of unemployment – not in work, but available for and seeking work – NEET refers to what the individual is not: not in work, not in education, not in training, defining youth as incomplete or even failing individuals. The construction of NEET relates any alternative use of time to paid employment (Batsleer, 2008: 34). NEET exists as an acceptable policy term for 'chav' (Jones, 2012), a key term in the fabric of moral underclass discourse (Levitas, 2005) associated with delinquency, anti-social behaviour, crime, early or chaotic parenthood and dangerous political questions (Wrigley, 2017), referring to people who need to be held accountable, controlled and subjected to intervention so that they learn the hard lessons of responsibility (Gillies, 2016). Indeed, Istance et al's (1994) Welsh study, which became New Labour's policy, explores the transformation of 'status zero' people into NEET. This, in turn, reflects a subtle but over time meaningful transformation in the understanding of the good character of young people outside of education, employment and training (Gillies, 2016).

How can we see the wood for the trees here?

All discussions of welfare policy are interminable; there are innumerable thickets of studies and data, an apparent superfluity of data. Yet across this diversity there is continuity, most obviously in the idealization of work and full employment. Beyond this, the idea of a free and 'functional' labour market is crucial, implying social mobility, flexibility and so forth. Occasionally, 'reducing labour market rigidities' is emphasized which in practice involves curbing trade unions or deregulating employment law. However, the targets of ALMPs are the unemployed, like the problematic figure of the NEET, considered as raw material to be reshaped, reformed and even redeemed. Long-term unemployment is considered to lead to 'subjective deterioration', 'therefore, it is essential to intervene early, at the beginning of the unemployment spell' (Fuentes, 2007: 14). Taken from an EU-level briefing on unemployment – addressing the existence and experience of literally millions of people – a singular remedy is offered: 'Benefit recipients are expected to engage in monitored job-search activities and improve their employability "in exchange" for receiving benefits' (Fuentes, 2007: 10). Whereas this recommendation appeared polemical in the works of Mead and Murray, by now it has effectively become 'evidence-based policy', a matter of statecraft and careful management of individual lives.

There are several components to these policies: they react to crises or problems, provide diagnoses of society and individuals and suggest remedies or reforms. Both individuals and institutions are considered capable of transformation, which gradually renders them more perfect – a highly political project.

The politics of policy

Broadly, politics and policy are concerned with the same matters, yet approach them differently. The former is concerned with values and aspirations, contestation and struggle, transforming society through legitimized leadership. The latter is concerned with evidence and data, compromises and collaboration, optimizing individual lives and social institutions through careful tinkering. Indeed, while policy shapes lives immensely, more people are aware of political discourse about welfare than the actual content of the YG or other ALMPs.

Policy is formed, within its own set of logics, by objective, rational evidence, a tradition nestled in the British empiricism of Bacon, Locke, Berkley and Hume. Policy requires impeccable evidence as a precursor to understanding the problem at hand. Over centuries of 'governmentality', states have increasingly collected data about their citizens, particularly the unemployed, numbers and trends which inform policy (Foucault, 2007). Yet, the original and literal meaning of data is *a thing given* from the natural world, a gift that entangles us in cycles of generosity and reciprocity (Ingold, 2011). Contemporary social policy aspires to be 'evidence-based' science and therefore eschews this entanglement as data must be extracted clinically without contaminating the field. This usually means numerical data that is severed from context, meaning and the web of social relations, which means this data is extracted rather than given. Indeed, these disciplines of knowledge are modes of truth production that depend on state power.

The limits of state power to govern society and the economy by sovereign fiat were manifest in the violent wars and utopian impulses that generated revolutionary political regimes. An accommodation of sorts emerged in various approaches to welfare capitalism (Esping-Andersen, 1990) of Nordic social democracy, European conservatism and the neoliberal anglosphere. Since the 1970s, as with many policy domains, a common approach to welfare has emerged across Europe and beyond (Lind and Møller, 2006). The homogenization and pasteurization of national social policies around activation (Van Berkel and Møller, 2002) has reduced the sense of alternatives, the possibility of doing things differently (Fisher, 2009).

Over the course of the 1970s, the golden age of welfare capitalism ended, ushering in the start of the end of welfare diversity and innovation. The continual process of opening up markets to competition, in particular the logic of recrafting supply chains to areas of location-specific advantage, lead to the rapid collapse of entire, labour-intensive sectors of national economies in many industrialized countries. Against this backdrop, from the 1980s capital asserted itself politically with the rise of the New Right in many countries (Hall, 1988), evoking a doctrine of a minimalist, 'night watchmen' approach to government (Nozick, 1974), albeit one that was destined to repeatedly fail. Similarly, the welfare state was critiqued as an overly ambitious failure: perhaps it liberated society from extreme poverty, but at the price of permanent subjugation, thereby robbing individuals of their autonomy and sense of personal progress and potential (Ewald, 2020).

In short, the welfare state was portrayed as a machine for fabricating rights without demanding responsibility; it deprived individuals of the need to act responsibly, while sharing their risks with multitudinous others. Furthermore, critics argued that welfare was increasingly unaffordable; there were limits to financial solidarity in society, to what the economy would support, particularly against the backdrop of preserving nationally competitive economies with globally mobile capital (Hansen, 2019). These political sensibilities led to welfare being curtailed, as governments introduced ALMPs to push the unemployed into work, particularly focusing on making even unattractive work pay, reducing welfare traps, and using cynical insights from behavioural economics to govern the vulnerable through sanctions and workfare (Tyler and Slater, 2018).

Supposedly, 'it is easier to imagine an end to the world than an end to capitalism', a quote attributed to both Fredric Jameson and Slavoj Žižek (Fisher, 2009). This is usually understood to be a call to arms, for revolutionary action. Clearly, the 'end of history' pronounced prematurely by Fukuyama in 1989 is a post-revolutionary process of endless reform. Yet, the urge towards reform is historically entangled with the demand for revolutionary transformation.

Sceptics often rhetorically describe ideals as 'utopias', and within a Western context these are often 'millenarian', in the Judeo-Christian orientation towards the apocalyptic end of the world. Such 'end-time' visions are close to socialist dreams of revolution – an eschatological vision of sudden total transformation, whereas ALMPs and the YG are more incremental and mundane goals, horizons to be pursued relentlessly. Interestingly, millennial hopes within the Christian tradition equally can refer to the anticipation of a 'thousand-year reign' of a near perfect 'heaven on earth'. Such an 'intra-mundane eschatology' means the attempt to establish a perfect or pure society – traditionally in the form of the ecclesia, but now in the form of a perfectly free and open market (Schwarzkopf, 2020). In this sense, contemporary reform of welfare through activation pursues the horizon of a perfect labour market: a place where consensual actors with perfect information make decisions and enter into contracts continuously. This modern 'city of God' entails continuous tests of each individual, who makes choices and develops themselves continuously in a constant pilgrimage of 'self-realization'.

The political horizons of ALMPs, the quest for full employment and flexible labour markets, are clearly non-revolutionary, or presumes that the necessary revolutions have already occurred. They carry the hope that governmental activation will shape individuals to better participate in society so that they develop their 'inner' potentials and talents; as per Adam Smith's vision of economic man: 'Every man lives by exchanging or becomes to some measure a merchant and the society itself grows to be what is properly a commercial society' (Smith, 2003: 31). Government seeks to produce a properly commercial society where there is relatively perfect information and choice so that individuals can sell their labour actively; it hopes to create an integrated society through collective and individualized responsibility for economic activity and the provision of institutional supports for human capital. Everyone will work, in multiple jobs and contracts, and be investors, shareholders and consumers in a perfect market which generates optimal outcomes for all. Rather than prophesizing the imminent arrival of the apocalypse, it preaches a good life, personal redemption, salvation – perpetual reform.

These political horizons have an ambition parallel to the church: the salvation of souls. Within ALMPs, salvation is by way of work; work is a vitamin that has behavioural, psychological and cultural goods (Warr, 1987), but work is also imbued with so much more inexplicable meaning. In Foucault's formulation of pastoral power, the pastor exercises careful jurisdiction over the bodies and souls of his flock to assure their salvation, and in return members of the flock each must comply and thus the pastorate operates through salvation, obedience and truth-telling. The duty of the pastor is the salvation of the entire flock, so that the overall system is being saved when an individual is saved, as per the parable of the lost sheep (Matthew 18:12–14 and Luke 15:3–7).

Agamben in *The Coming Community* extends that articulation of the cycle of revelation, obedience and salvation. Following Kafka he suggests that 'innermost character of salvation is that we are saved only at the point when we no longer want to be' (Agamben, 1993: 102). In this theological formulation, the unemployed jobseeker is understandably ambivalent about being the target of the state's efforts at salvation, ambivalent about accepting an identity that is both excluded and parasitic. In this reading, ALMPs aspire to save the system by insisting on the salvation of individuals.

Reformation as transformation

Theology and theory intersect and intertwine; the history of ideas constitutes the range of possibility for our thought. Inescapably, the psychological, social or human sciences are a product of history like any other discourses and are entangled with theological modes of thought. This is not to deny their efficacy – economics, sociology, psychology, political science and so forth are powerful, and not only in the production of truth, but in the creation of institutions – not least the welfare state and ALMPs. Yet, these modes of thinking do not reflect the natural internal workings of the brain but cultural legacies. This is not to say that they are ideological blinkers; rather than constraining the potential of our thinking, they constitute the possibility of our thought. Without this heritage of discourses – not a dogma but an internally diverse tapestry of ideas in constant tension – we would think very differently.

The key theoretical tenet of Western thinking is the idea of reform, in the sense that individuals can be reformed – they have fallen into sin and error in theological terms, or into ideology in contemporary parlance, part of the machinery of oppression and ideology, yet they can be redeemed, saved, transformed. Governmental and pastoral power require obedience, demand confessions and promise salvation (Foucault, 2005). Encoded here is a balance between two models of individuality – on the one hand the idea of an innate character, and on the other the shaping of the self through circumstances or culture. Within this model, being 'reformed' is redemption, salvation or liberation, but not a total metamorphosis, as something of the individual persists, described as the 'core/real/authentic self' in modern times or the soul in religion (Taylor, 1989). Reforming the self is in part a matter of discipline – governing the 'conduct of conduct' in Foucault's studies of the minutiae of institutions, but it goes beyond modifying behaviour to a distinctive transformation of the self.

In early theological models there are two main metaphorical models of subjective transformation – *epistrophe* and *metanoia* (Hadot, 1953). Epistrophe meant awakening or enlightenment, drawn from philosophical models of self-mastery through knowledge. Metanoia meant a transformation through purification, effectively suffering through the death of one part of the self, to be reborn as a better person. Clearly, within modern culture reformations are not simple modifications, not just adding to the self, but a painful transformation through suffering, related to knowing the truth about the world but also the truth of the self. Enigmatically, the means of transforming oneself is telling the truth about the self, yet the price of this truth is also personal transformation. The genealogical conjunction of Greek philosophy and Hellenic spiritual exercises as translated unto the early Christian monasteries is still crucial to modern thinking about individuality. 'This notion of conversions, of the return to the self, of the turning to oneself … is one of the most important technologies of the self the West has known' (Foucault, 2005: 208). Turning 'inwards', scrutinizing the self, yet transforming that self are practices which suffuse our culture, from self-help to active labour market policies.

The key biblical example of conversion is Saint Paul. As a sinner, Saul is blinded by light on the road to Damascus as the Lord speaks directly to him, and after three days of prayer, he regains his sight: 'The scales fell from his eyes', after which he leads the spread of the early Christian church, as a proponent and symbol of conversion. Saul is both changed into Paul and unchanged with the same body and memories. Conversion is a form of suffering, reflected in his blindness, relieved by his eventual baptism. The Lord clearly chooses him, making him a 'vessel', making him 'suffer for my sake' – yet not just to be changed, but to take on a mission of action within the world, preaching the word. Told again at intervals (Acts 22, 26), the story presents a model of an overwhelming and difficult experience of encountering the divine, leading to a defining break in personal identity, the start of a new life.

Evidently metaphors abound around the reformation of the self – awakening, blindness, contrasts of dark and light, being purified or purged, freedom and slavery, dying and being born again. These metaphors are replaced by more technical-sounding terms in modernity, from academic and popular psychology: 'self-transformation', 'self-work', 'changing your internal dialogue', 'discovering your true identity'. These comingle in biblical accounts of transformation; for instance the prophet Ezekiel describes the 'heart of stone' being replaced by the 'true heart' (Ezekiel 36: 26). To be converted is not just to acquire new beliefs but to be personally transformed:

> The hour has come for you to wake up from your slumber, for our salvation is nearer now than when we first believed. The night is nearly over; the day has drawn near. So let us lay aside the deeds of darkness and put on the armor of light. (Romans 12:11–12)

> Do not lie to one another, for you have taken off the old self with its habits and have put on the new self. (Collosians 3:9)

This proliferation of metaphors implies that conversion was a subjective internal experience which was difficult to narrate. Judith Butler's work on subject formation similarly describes the modern idea of the new self emerging from the old as a paradox: the impossibility of a 'self-inaugurating agency' (Butler, 1997: 16). Furthermore, it could be suggested that the process of conversion is itself constitutively produced by descriptions of it – the model of Paul, the metaphors of conversion – these inspire narratives of self-transformation which become self-fulfilling. These parables and their modern echoes imagine the individual in Western culture as malleable, open to endless transformations and reformations by governmental power that assesses, judges and imposes changes upon its subjects. Crucially though, transformations cannot be entirely enforced from the outside but require the self to work upon itself.

Perhaps the most famous account of conversion is Augustine's *Confessions*. Before Rousseau's *Confessions* (1782), this was hitherto the most extensive autobiography, and exemplifies the retrospective inquiry into one's own self which permeates contemporary society. For Augustine, the sins of the flesh were particularly troubling, and *Confessions* recalls his lusts and desires repeatedly. These are represented as poor choices, made in full knowledge of immorality, both intuitively grasped and as articulated by his pious mother. Yet Augustine also offers an account of sin as socialization: 'For the rule of sin is the force of habit, by which the mind is swept along and held fast, even against its own will, yet deservedly, because it fell into the habit of its own accord' (Augustine, 1961: 8:3, p 165). Everyone is continuously tempted to sin, and transgressing becomes a habit, harder and harder to resist, and even warps the mind, developing hypocrisy and ignorance. Here sin is not just transgression but a morally culpable form of socialization or self-formation. Yet, within the self the possibility of choosing differently always resides, indestructibly: 'One thing lifted me up into the light of your day. It was that I knew that I had a will, as surely as I knew there was life in me. When I chose' (Augustine, 1961: 7:1, p 136). Like Descartes, who was only sure he has a mind, a millennium beforehand Augustine was sure of his will, and therefore of his responsibility. Resonant with the prophets or the epistles, individual choice is always affirmed, even facing an omnipotent God.

How is conversion achieved? In part it is a matter of turning around, as in the contemporary cliché 'turn your life around'. To 'convert' etymologically means to turn around, which resonates with the Greek word *periagoge*, which Plato used to describe those who turned away from illusion to face reality in the famous cave allegory. This metaphor is certainly used by Augustine: 'O Lord, you were turning me around to look at myself.' (Augustine, 1961: 8:7, p 169), or in contemporary parlance, 'take a good look at yourself'.

Confessions is a paradigm of confession, in that Augustine relentlessly examines his own life and experiences, his conduct and choices, and admits to culpability for all the sins and errors within it. From the opening pages the narration depicts a high emotional intensity, representing a repentant sinner who considers their salvation recent, tenuous and precious. After narrating youthful robbery, debauchery and heresy, eventually Augustine is 'converted', an event marked by difficulty, struggle and self-sacrifice: 'My inner self was a house divided against itself. ... I was beside myself with madness that would bring me sanity. I was dying a death that would bring me life' (Augustine, 1961: 8:8, p 171). The self is metaphorically split in two here, the sinner and the soul longing for salvation. Part of the self must be excised in order to redeem the whole: sinful habits, tastes for iniquities, indulgence in heretical errors. These sinful tendencies are cast aside – shriven, in later medieval language. Yet, paradoxically, they are also retained, as part of a narrative; even sins renounced must be remembered, as admitting culpability is crucial to redemption. For Augustine, confession must be continuous, not a single ritual of purification, even though conversion is a definitive event in life; yet given mankind's fallen nature, sin will recur, and to pretend otherwise leads only to pride – another sin.

Even after this moment of conversion, the *Confessio* is quite relentlessly self-excoriating, which reflects Augustine's ethos of continuous self-analysis, confession and reformation: 'Day after day without ceasing these temptations put us to the test, O Lord. The Human Tongue is a furnace in which the temper of our souls is daily tried' (Augustine, 1961: 10, p 37). Thus, the singular act of conversion, confirmed by a ritual of baptism, becomes transformed into a continuous struggle with temptation. It is a continuous test, and here again the human tongue is central, the 'truth' told about oneself forms the self decisively.

Notably, this reformation of the self is transformative, but requires chronic work: 'Salvation then is an activity, the subject's constant action on themselves' (Foucault, 2005: 184). Of course, there are many differences from contemporary society – particularly belief in supernatural forces, absolute moral commandments, the immortality of the soul and so forth – but there are also key continuities: first, the self can be reformed and redeemed, but only through difficulty and suffering. Second, this transformation involves a sort of turning; away from the world or against the self, rejecting previous poor conduct or behaviour acquired by habit – socialization in modern parlance. Thirdly, some outside force prompts this conversion, whether it is divine intervention, extreme experiences or the words of others in preaching or confession. Fourthly, the individual is transformed by telling the truth about themselves, usually to others, yet simultaneously, the price of knowing the truth is also a transformation of the self.

Beyond the religious resonances of salvation and conversion, the underlying idea here is that individuals are malleable – shaped like clay in biblical accounts, socialized by circumstance and environment in sociology. Indeed, even 'high theories' such as Foucault's maintain this ontology: that the subject can be transformed, externally by governmental intervention and internally by what he describes as 'techniques of self' (Foucault, 1988). Whatever moral or political value is placed upon particular transformations of the individual, the idea that the self can be reformed is the central model; it is a powerful idea which makes it possible to analyze different societies as shaping individuals – basically the key idea of the human sciences. For critics, this is sociology's 'heart of darkness', because it makes academic disciplines complicit in state and corporate projects of transforming society – many of which are morally dubious (Bauman, 1989). Equally, this idea of reformation also makes it possible and worthwhile to invest time and effort in educating and enlightening individuals, empowering them, which may sound patronizing or even colonizing, yet it is the warrant for universal education as much as for ALMPs. Indeed, the idea that individuals are partially products of their society and capable of change also informs an ethic of forgiveness, always holding out the possibility of redemption. Yet, rather than supporting individuals unconditionally, modern welfare gives an endless series of second chances at the same test – of finding work in the labour market – but implicitly of reforming the self.

Antecedent to our contemporary idea of socialization as a mixture of individual choice and social structure are theological ideas: choice and free will are central to individual salvation in Christianity – even though God is presumed to be omnipotent and to have created the world according to a divine plan, each individual is responsible for themselves: 'For God will reward every person according to what he has done' (Romans, 2.6) – or as expressed by the prophet Ezekiel centuries earlier in Judaism. This balance between individual choice and divine will is reflected in centuries of philosophical hairsplitting between 'free will and determinism' or more recently 'structure and agency' or 'power and resistance'. All of these imply the possibility of reform, both in the sense that the individual is shaped by their environment and culture and that they have the individual capacity to make choices and better themselves: 'For the rule of sin is the force of habit, by which the mind is swept along and held fast, even against its own will, yet deservedly, because it fell into the habit of its own accord' (Augustine, 1961: 9:3, p 165). Thus, the work of transforming or reforming the self is interminable, but it cannot take place without individual involvement – as expressed earlier by the classical theologian St. Augustine and repeated in the 'great medieval synthesis' of Thomas Aquinas: 'God indeed causes the things we do but not without our acting, for he works in every will and nature' (Aquinas, 1961: 660). Rather than a theological dogma which requires faith in mystery, this theology is a theory of human existence, with a tension between circumstances and choice, which informs how we think today – in sociological theory, in everyday life and within governmental policymaking, which seeks to reform individuals. Dystopian visions of states that attempt to create people like machines through social engineering miss the point that contemporary governance inherits pastoral power – which holds individual choice sacrosanct. Thus, no-one is reformed from outside, but must participate in their own transformation; within liberal governmentality, 'freedom is something which is constantly produced' (Foucault, 2008: 65).

These seemingly abstract theories inform welfare institutions by providing explanatory schemes of how individual characters may be changed and redeemed by governmental interventions, such as ALMPs. Among these there are those which attempt to govern using incentives and the threat of sanctions or 'sticks and carrots', which assume that individuals are calculating economic agents. This train of thought goes back through Charles Murray's insistence on economic self-responsibility to Jeremy Bentham's utilitarianism which insisted that all individuals follow their self-interest, and attempt to minimize pain and maximize pleasure (see Chapter 5). This economic 'science' has a narrow conception of human nature – treating people like donkeys by using sticks and carrots – and attempts to transform behaviour by 'making work pay' and making welfare ungenerous and dependent on labour market engagement.

Tests and trials

Transformation of subjects is at the heart of governmentality and pastoral power (Foucault, 1981): the attempt to redeem and reform individuals through subtle interventions, from exerting pressure, through the processes of welfare claiming, to discourses which incite and entice them to be good jobseekers. Detailed studies of the 'microphysics of power' in welfare offices suggest that there are a myriad of different elements, from required meetings to monitored job searches, compulsory participation in training, one-to-one case officer meetings, psychometric assessment and so forth (Brodkin and Marsden, 2013). Simultaneously, welfare recipients are also engaged in the labour market – beyond the reach of the welfare office – but judged on their performance within it, assigned more training or coaching depending on their experiences. Thus, the broad mode of transforming individuals that emerges here is that individuals are tested, they are subjected to certain trials, put to the test until they succeed, and repeated failure only leads to further tests.

Tests are central to modernity in a number of ways: most clearly, the market process of liberal economies 'tests' the value of goods and services, verifying their value in the form of price (Foucault, 2008). Such market tests are also used to scrutinize governmental action – interventions are only justified if they produce actual benefits in economy or society. Thus, welfare policies have testing built in, they are designed to be assessable, even attempting to create scientific experiments, for instance, by randomized selection or by ensuring a representative sample, and even creating a 'control group', that is, a sample of the population upon whom no intervention is made, thereby creating a baseline against which the effect of interventions is measured (Peck and Theodore, 2016). Indeed, Boltanski (2011) argues that modern institutions, particularly those involved in education and employment, continuously test and assess individuals, so that the task of sociology is 'to describe the social world *as the scene of a trial*' (Boltanski, 2011: 25, emphasis in original). Notably, this phenomenon predominates in modernity; not that 'traditional' society was a static world of unchanging custom and uncontested status, but modernity has made life itself into a trial.

This is a distinctly religious interpretation of life: 'Every Christian will be called upon to regard life as nothing but a test' (Foucault, 2005: 446).

An individual career is interpreted as a test or a trial, wherein suffering and difficulty serve to purify the self and allow jobseekers to learn about themselves. Without challenges, supposedly, no one can know the truth of their character. Equally, society learns about itself by undergoing crises and challenges; it becomes stronger by responding, learning about itself and transforming itself: 'My Christian brothers, you should be happy when you have all kinds of tests. You know these prove your faith. It helps you not to give up. The man who does not give up when tests come is happy' (James 1:2). Thus, adversity and challenges are to be welcomed as edifying, to be endured faithfully. Here, to 'prove your faith' both means to demonstrate belief but also to strengthen or refine, like iron proved in the furnace. Again, personal choice is central – the individual determination not to give up in the face of tests – and yet these tests are also interpreted as 'godsends', as is the strength to endure them; a paradoxical coupling of free will and a providential order: 'God keeps his promise and he will not allow you to be tested beyond your power to remain firm; at the time you are put to the test, he will give you the strength to endure it, and so provide you with a way out' (1 Corinthians 10:12–13). For the faithful, there is no test which cannot be endured, no suffering which cannot be rendered edifying, and moreover, these tests serve to reveal the true character of individuals. Now, everyone must endure something like the 'trials of Job'.

Again, this is a cultural interpretation of life, or a discourse which produces the objects of which it speaks. Clearly, how suffering is interpreted is central to religious thought, as argued by Nietzsche's polemic against Christian sanctification of suffering, and in Weber's more nuanced exploration of world religions as specifically creating new interpretations of suffering. Beyond the broad brushstrokes of theology, each individual is directed to interpret their own suffering in specific ways: 'Suffering is actually a test that is recognized lived and practiced as such by the subject.' (Foucault, 2005: 443). For instance, there are subtle differences between Roman stoics, who took all apparent evil as a source of education to prepare the self for life through the exercise of rational self-control, and Christians, who take suffering as a test which proves their faith and purifies their sinful tendencies.

So what? All of this may seem like 'mere' culture, a set of strange beliefs about experiences and selfhood and society. However, beyond being an intellectual philosophy, these ideas are institutionalized, most especially in the institutions of the welfare office and ALMPs, and policy gestures such as the YG. State institutions, from schools to policy think tanks, presume that people are malleable, formed by their circumstances, but capable of making choices, which serve to transform them alongside the exercise of pastoral power, with 'its zeal, devotion and endless application' (Foucault, 2007: 127). Our society is set up to test people, from education to workplaces, and how they respond to and react to these trials is supposed to reveal the 'true' character of the individual. In times of trouble – for instance, unemployment – individuals are not just supported, but subjected to further trials, whereby they must show their mettle, because transformation or redemption is neither automatic nor a foregone possibility – there are an infinite number of second chances. In effect, states take the place of providence, both in that they offer charitable assistance to the destitute, but more importantly in that they array a series of opportunities for choices and self-reformation for anyone and everyone. And increasingly, support is contingent on compliance with reformation and transformation.

What emerges here is not only the model of the individual as malleable clay, to be tested and transformed, but by extension, a version of government modelled on the divine. Implicitly, the state must be involved in judging individuals, particularly the unemployed. Whereas the Epistle of James exhorts its readers, 'Do not criticize one another. ... Who are you to judge?' (James 4:11–12) – phrases which resonate today: the welfare state takes on this role, perhaps not quite a 'stigma machine' (Tyler, 2020), but at the very least a 'judgement machine'.

Contemporary processes of welfare activation impose secular adaptations of pastoral power upon the unemployed, first by requiring that they establish membership of society – the ecclesia – through a name, a birth cert, a PPS number, but more importantly in an oath expressing their commitment to the work cult by swearing that they are lacking, available for and actively seeking work. Effectively, that they are willing to undergo tests, both that of the welfare office and the labour market. Beyond this, the unemployed must tell the truth about themselves, they must account for their lives and choices in interviews. These proceed on the assumption that the individual is responsible for their situation through their choices and behaviour, that these stem from their inner characteristics, and that there is some form of personal deficiency – low educational attainment, poor work ethic, pickiness or even criminal tendencies – or sloth, pride and avarice in religious terms. Individuals are encouraged to identify their weaknesses and flaws for the purposes of self-improvement and personal transformation, by reforming or even redeeming their character.

Conclusion

Contemporary states attempt to incarnate something akin to the 'City of God' in its welfare institutions, to 'immanentise the eschaton' in Voegelin's terms (1969). Endless tests and trials, help, advice and opportunities for self-transformation are offered. Rather than escape, there is no end to the work of reformation; even to the stubborn and recalcitrant or backsliding, endless second chances are offered. Perhaps forgiveness is offered, but only at the price of penance and reformation. For the unemployed there are few alternatives to the model of life as a trial of self-transformation. Within this model, the state also deliberately administers suffering of various sorts, from pressure through scrutiny, to threats, to actually implementing welfare cuts, with the obvious impact of poverty, hunger, anxiety and the possibility of debt, homelessness or suicide. These dangers are justified because suffering is implicitly the only route towards transformation; if the jobseeker fails the 'labour market test' by being unable to secure work in a competitive world, then welfare provides alternatives – career days, confidence training, work-readiness courses, all a series of trials oriented towards self-work, conversions from passive unemployment unto active jobseeking. These 'providential' offerings may be inadequate to actually create a job or genuinely build a CV, yet their purpose is to maintain the possibility that the individual can be redeemed.

Effectively, the truth of an individual, their worth and character, are considered as revealed by tests and trials – occasions which offer the possibility of transformation but also impose reform, demanding faith in the self and the labour market. And while these are only discourses, they effectively work, not necessarily to create jobs or transform people through training, but by imposing an interpretation of life in the labour market.

4

Vocation: Doing God's Work

While we are primarily concerned with welfare, unemployment and jobseeking, work is nevertheless central to these experiences. Dozens of people we interviewed over the past ten years who were currently 'out of work' stated unequivocally that they wanted to work, often that they enjoyed work, or even that they were a 'worker' unlike some of the 'shirkers' or 'spongers' who they imagined to populate the dole queue. When they spoke about their family background, many described how their parents had instilled a strong work ethic in them.

Regarding attitudes towards work, the greatest contrast was not between men and women, urban and rural or any class divide, it was between those who had work and those who didn't. People were relieved to have found work, even if it was temporary, part-time or precarious, but weren't slow to criticize the difficulties, indignities and inequality of work – they complained about their bosses, colleagues, working conditions and customers. But for those who currently had no paid employment, work acquired a sort of ideal status, seen as an unarguably good thing and always better than unemployment.

Perhaps this is unsurprising: people often want what others have and they do not (Girard, 1977). Yet in the longing of the unemployed for a job, the ideal or even magical qualities ascribed to work appear. For instance, Darren had worked manufacturing windows after leaving school early and had been unemployed for two years due to the collapse of the construction industry. He only watched television at night-time, because otherwise it felt bad: "There is nothing sweeter than slobbing in front of crap TV after a hard day's work. There is nothing worse than slobbing in front of crap TV after a hard day's nothing!"

Somehow, work transforms crap TV into a "sweet" experience; if he watched it during the daytime he would feel like a "waste of space". What Darren describes here is a peculiarly religious balancing of accounts, wherein indulgences must be justified by hard labour. Darren had moved back in with his mother and described a day of avoiding her while jobseeking in the morning, mainly online, working on his car in the afternoon and staying up late watching movies and spending time on social media. The absence of a job haunted his everyday life, and even though he deliberately maintained a facade of happiness, he declared he had "zero faith" that he would get a job.

Clearly, Darren worked. He was a jobseeker, an amateur mechanic, did household work and constantly engaged in 'impression management'. Yet those labours did not count. His increased free time, something he longed for while employed, was now a burden. There is something mysterious about work, which we can glimpse even in his very ordinary complaints about unemployment: "God I hate it. This is no existence; I keep saying it's only temporary! But two years is far from temporary ... I was leader of my line and can't believe I went from that to nothing!" For Darren, his current way of life is not an alternative, but a non-existence: in the factory he was a leader – now he is nothing. This is far from unique. Many of the individuals we interviewed described the lack of work as an absence, like cold storage or limbo. Perhaps this is just the moment at which words fail, because some experiences are very difficult to convey as a story. Yet, even from this everyday talk, it becomes apparent that work cannot be simply equated with physical tasks or mental effort, but is part of our culture with far deeper meanings which need to be explored culturally and historically. Why is work both a burden yet also a redemption? Why is freedom from work sometimes a curse rather than a blessing?

The ethos of work

'Work' means many things, not just effort or different jobs but monumental works or poetic works. Interestingly, this idea of a 'great work' in the sense of an achievement carried out by skilled humans who autonomously and creatively generate something admirable is actually considerably older than the idea of work as labour or toil (Arendt, 1989). Historical linguists speculate that new words reflect new experiences, and it is possible that the word 'labour' emerges from agricultural civilizations, where toil in the fields was a relentless and repetitive duty, distinct from the glorious activity called 'work' which might range from hunting to architectural works to philosophy. Today, these distinct versions of work are becoming blurred, so that burdensome toil like cooking, gardening or even cleaning and 'decluttering' is presented as some kind of art which makes us into better human beings and produces something special.

Certainly, in modernity work is highly valued and we look back at the aristocratic disdain for work with incomprehension. Nobles who deliberately avoided the sun and cultivated a pale complexion to flaunt that they never worked outside seem like frivolous wastrels. The lives of the independently wealthy for most of the last millennia simply do not make sense to contemporary eyes, whether we view them fondly as relics of a different age or are appalled at their wasteful luxuries. Curiously, in our times, those who are rich and successful are intensely busy; even when they do not have to work they are engaged in new projects – for instance, incessant work for philanthropic foundations or obsessive desires for interplanetary travel. Consider the high rate of depression of lottery winners, victims of sudden abundance, who often waste their good fortune or worse, as relationships and communal moorings are disturbed by their changed status.

Rather than a straightforward word for effort or an employment contract, 'work' is strange. On the one hand it is toil, the means to an end, and on the other it is the ultimate purpose of life, an expression of identity and creativity.

Unsurprisingly, religion shapes how we think about work: when Adam and Eve were expelled from Eden, not only were they doomed to die, but they had to work in order to eat, in the absence of the luxuries of paradise. Their sons, Cain and Abel, became farmers. Aside from this, the Bible also grants man dominion over all the other animals, and tells him to 'go forth and multiply'. The wilderness is there to be tamed and made productive, the world is effectively given by God to man in stewardship as a giant farm. The consequences of these ideas don't just effect the modern age, but are visible in the development of medieval agriculture according to historian Lynn White, who suggests that the roots of our contemporary ecological crisis stems from the Bible. Western man has been on a quest to expand farming, territorially and technologically, since the fall of Rome, all for the glory of God.

This is most famously expressed in Paul's Letter to the Thessalonians which exhorts the new Christian community to live a disciplined life, and they commanded: 'If any would not work, neither should he eat' (2 Thessalonians 3:10). Strikingly, this command was echoed by Lenin – the religious worship of work belongs to socialism as much as capitalism. However, early church figures admonished the community not to expect the Second Coming imminently – a proto-socialist revolution – but to live a disciplined life of work and spreading the Gospels. Indeed, they recommended a prudent economic life: 'Make it your aim to live a quiet life, to mind your own business and to earn your own living ... and you will not have to depend on anyone for what you need' (1 Thessalonians 4:10–12). Balancing this, it is important to recall that the early apostles practiced collective ownership, so that their new converts shared all their possessions, and none went without. Yet, already in the early church, the work ethic was clear, whereby labour could be a sacred task: 'Whatever you do, work at it with all your heart, as working for the Lord, not for human masters' (Colossians 3:23).

However, in medieval times, work was still seen as a burden, imposed upon peasants, engaged in by merchants and professions in order to make a living and scrupulously avoided by aristocrats. Work was a duty or a means to an end, not a way of life or a source of identity. This is particularly evident in early capitalism, wherein incentives to work harder rarely succeeded: a ploughman offered an increased piece rate did not work longer and earn more, but preferred to work less and keep on earning the same amount (Thompson, 1967). For medieval peasants, time was definitely not money, the day was divided up into periods of dark and light, tasks and rest, not abstract hours which could be exchanged in the form of labour for remuneration.

Here we turn to Max Weber's *The Protestant Ethic and the Spirit of Capitalism*; taught to undergraduates for decades, debated by critics, the 'Protestant ethic' is part of popular parlance – a widely recognized 'economic theology'. The 'work ethic' basically means a zealous dedication to work, a frugal lifestyle, a pursuit of earnings or profit even when they are surplus to requirements. Weber started from the puzzle of explaining why Protestants outnumbered Catholics among German businessmen, and argued that their religious beliefs caused them to pursue their vocation and enterprise unrelentingly. This ethos provides the impetus to work without need, which is a hugely important ingredient in capitalism. Despite secularization, the work ethic spread beyond Christian groups, animating capitalism across the globe. Crucially it provides motivation for individuals to work beyond providing for their basic needs, because work acquires a meaning in itself rather than being just a means to an end.

In Weber's interpretation there are a number of elements within Protestantism that strongly influence the emergence of capitalism. For Protestantism, salvation is a personal matter: the individual must read and interpret the Bible for themselves and take care of their own soul by pursuing ethical conduct rather than relying on rituals such as confession to cleanse their soul. No collective rites could intervene in divine judgement of the individual. As per the next chapter, the rejection of purgatory along with other such 'second chances', such as giving alms and pilgrimages of penance, is central to why charity is displaced by workhouses in the aftermath of the Reformation. However, more important to Weber is Luther's sense of work as a 'calling', a vocation, bestowed upon the individual by God. The idea of Providence for Luther suggested that God had assigned a place and position to each individual, and that it was their duty to pursue that vocation as a divinely ordained task. Interestingly, Luther was a monk but then rejected monasticism as a withdrawal from the world; his Protestantism demanded constant vocational work in this world, a systematic ethical conduct – as though the world were a monastery. By hard toil the believer was doing God's work, they were manifesting the divine will in the world, which made idleness or relaxation a sin.

Beyond Luther, Weber analyzed Calvinism and related Puritan sects, smaller in number perhaps, but historically strongly influential in the Netherlands, England and America – via the Pilgrim fathers. Brushing aside the idea of salvation through good works or by faith alone, Calvin insisted on God's omnipotence and omniscience, so that the individual soul was already predestined to salvation or damnation. Nothing an individual did or chose could affect the divine will, which divided humanity into two; the elect, who would join God in heaven, and those who would not, implicitly bound to hellfire. Weber shrewdly points out that this was an immense and intense psychological burden: unless they could utterly resign themselves to their fate, the Calvinist necessarily sought for signs of favour which indicated that they were saved. Particularly, they were oriented towards economic signs – a secure vocation or success in business seemed credible manifestations of divine favour. Evidently, this was a strong motivating force to ensure that the faithful worked constantly and attempted to create the signs of their own success.

These were strong religious motivations towards work and enterprise, making work into a holy mission rather than toil, and making success in business an indicator of divine judgement rather than a strategic risk. Within early modern Europe this gave rise to a new capitalist spirit, not just the pursuit of gold and gain for the purpose of enjoyment or status, but a constant, disciplined, sober ethic of steady, even relentless work and reinvestment of profit. Interestingly, this religious distinction between the elect and the damned – between the 'brethren' and the 'worldly' in English Puritanism – also tends to map onto the moralizing distinction between imaginary strivers and shirkers (Kotsko, 2018). Evidently, this persists after considerable centuries of secularization, after the discarding of the idea of divine providence or predestination, so that this cultural model of hard work and profit seeking underpins how we think about economic outcomes today. Indeed, the whole idea that our success at work or in the market really indicates something about ourselves is always doubtful, yet we continue to pursue projects and promotions zealously – even to the point of personal burn-out or environmental unsustainability – and without theological warrant for our behaviour.

This religious dedication to work is often easiest to identify in American examples, a country which is still considerably religious, where Protestant sects were historically central to business, and where the idea of the economy as a providential test is still ingrained. Consider, for instance, Bardwick's warning about the laxness of the US economy of the 1990s, *Danger in the Comfort Zone:*

> People with a psychology of earning know they're winners, but they know they're always being judged.
>
> People prefer accountability; they want to be rewarded when they work hard and they want those who don't to be punished.
>
> They want their work to be judged because it is the only way they know their work is significant. (Bardwick, 1993: 56)

Obviously, Bardwick is a cheerleader for hard work, but what are most interesting here are the theological dimensions to how she presents hard work. When she refers to a 'psychology of earning' in which people 'know they're winners', she replicates the advice of Puritan pastors: believe you are among the elect and behave accordingly. Work becomes an abacus of reward and punishment, dividing the world into the saved and the damned. Indeed, 'accountability' implies a sort of all-seeing judgement, the all-seeing eye of God. In our era of anxiety around mass surveillance, the benevolence of this overseer seems questionable, evoking digital monitoring rather than a guardian angel! Yet, in a world of performance targets, online profiles, digital reviews and constant audits, we are effectively encountering an earth-bound place of divine judgement, where work is an end in itself, an inescapable metric of individual worth.

The work–ethic

While Weber's famous thesis clearly demonstrates how a religious interpretation of the world motivates an economic ethic of diligent work and unrelenting enterprise, it is somewhat incomplete. This is not an attempt to criticize the theory, or disprove it – Weber clearly stated that religion was only one factor among many and subsequent historians have pointed out that work-ethic permeates Christianity, particularly monasteries (Szakolczai, 2000; Stark, 2006). Yet perpetually seeking success seems distant from real-life experience, a cliché usually attributed to others: to workaholics and killjoys, to fathers in Disney films who eventually learn that their family are more important than the office. Occasionally we may catch ourselves in the moment of relentlessly seeking achievements or making sacrifices in the pursuit of gain, yet the meaningfulness of our work and careers is neglected. Among academics, Weber's Protestant ethic thesis is often weaponized into a critique of capitalism as an ideology of limitless acquisitiveness or as the 'iron cage' of relentless self-discipline.

Thus, the Protestant ethic often seems abstract, not just because of its outdated religious trappings but because its stakes are distant. Like Pascal's wager – the philosophy that one should believe in God just in case he exists – the Protestant ethic seems like a continuous bet, seeking for signs of one's own good fortune as surety of salvation. Occasionally this may ring true; for instance, when doing a job interview or awaiting the annual sales figures. Generally, however, work is a more complex experience which rarely delivers a clear signal that one is a member of the elect. Indeed, the actual emotional experience of doubting oneself and seeking salvation needs to be recognized: something of the everyday experience of work is neglected in Weber's thesis, or more precisely the 'spirit' of work.

Illustratively, Weber used an actual historical figure to exemplify the work ethic, Benjamin Franklin, who espoused an ethic of constant labour to demonstrate one's diligence. Here we turn to Abraham Maslow, a key figure of 'humanistic psychology', who views work as a means of constant self-development. His idea of the 'hierarchy of needs' is one of the most frequently cited ideas in psychology and management literature; from motivation textbooks to guides for the unemployed, Maslow's name is ubiquitous. Ironically, his actual work is rarely read, and tellingly, most proponents of his ideas misrepresent him as having created a 'pyramid' with a hierarchy of needs – there is no pyramid diagram in his published work. Indeed, this may suggest that Maslow's ideas chime with modern culture so well that there is little need to read them – they surround us in everyday phrases like 'fulfil your potential' or 'be your best self'. This is not quite the same as saying that Maslow's ideas are actually common sense dressed up in psychological jargon and therefore wrong. Instead, these are discourses which culturally shape our experience of work.

The idea of the hierarchy of needs is that human beings have multiple needs: physiological needs like sleep or water; safety needs for security or health; social needs for love or belonging; esteem needs for status and recognition; and 'self-actualization' needs – a term which needs some elaboration, yet is resonant and familiar. For Maslow, this hierarchy goes upwards from the survival needs to higher motivations; once basic needs are fulfilled the person is more free to concentrate on loftier aims – but even if there are problems at the lower levels, a person can still pursue social esteem or self-actualization. Beyond asserting that shelter and food are necessary before status matters, Maslow's work has more subtle implications about motivation, even amid welfare offices that use sanctions to compel individuals to comply with jobseeking regimes. Indeed, Maslow represents a distinct alternative to Frederick W. Taylor's attempts to make the worker a perfectly functional cog in the machine (Taylor, 1919), but does so by putting the whole person to work –'body and soul'.

Self-actualization basically means that a person uses their innate potential within the world, thereby becoming the person they are capable of becoming: 'What a man *can* be, he *must* be. This need we may call self-actualization' (Maslow, 1998: 261, emphasis in original). For Maslow, every person self-actualizes to a greater or lesser extent, and those who are highly self-actualizing tend to become leaders or otherwise highly successful. 'One's deepest nature cannot be altogether denied' (Maslow, 1998: 315). Obviously, this conception of the self employs a 'metaphor of depth', whereby the person we see is described as the result of inner potentialities rather than a product of circumstances. This has been criticized for its individualism, that is, how it supports social and economic hierarchies by implying that current fate is based on merit rather than structures. Interestingly, there is no definite end to this quest for self-actualization, because Maslow's hierarchy of needs defines man as a 'perpetually wanting animal. ... A want that is satisfied is no longer a want' (Maslow, 1998: 256).

In Maslow's thinking, self-actualization cannot take place on a blank slate or empty stage but takes place throughout the life course, primarily through work. Indeed, work is positioned as a central dimension of human life: 'If work is meaningless then life comes close to being meaningless' (Maslow, 2000: 39). Thus, work here is not mere labour or drudgery but an exciting arena of challenges and projects: 'Life is a continual series of choices' (Maslow, 2000: 35). So, self-actualization happens through the exercise of choice, autonomy, self-expression and other higher virtues in any scenario, but most especially work, so that work and play become almost indistinguishable. The highly self-actualizing person becomes fused with their task, dedicated to performing excellently, in concert with others, whose self-actualization they mentor: essentially, work becomes a vocation, not just a project but a quest for self-transformation.

What really matters for our purposes is to recognize the distinctly religious qualities of self-actualization. Most obviously, the idea imagines an interior self or soul to the person, a religious hangover which pervades modern psychological ideas about human beings. Maslow's account resembles the biblical parable of the talents – wherein the king leaves servants 'talents' or money to be invested, and the servant who takes a high risk and invests wisely and gains a return is praised, whereas the fearful servant who simply hides the money until the king's return is admonished. In modern psychologized readings, the currency of 'talents' is now inner potentials, which must be used to assure salvation or economic success.

More importantly, Maslow's account positions life as a series of challenges and trials, as though ordained by a divine overseer, whereby 'one must permit oneself to be chosen' (Maslow, 2000: 14). Finding a fitting line of work or a vocation is the key to self-actualization, which requires self-scrutiny, careful choices and dedicated work. The labour market is not a random or contingent assembly for Maslow, but a sorting system for finding our destiny: 'We are all called to a particular task for which our nature fits us' (Maslow, 2000: 316). As an individual increasingly identifies with their work, the more they subsume their being in that task, the greater their self-actualization – yet, as noted earlier, this is an interminable pursuit, no 'vocational' accreditation can complete the 'career'. Here, the older meaning of 'career' is relevant: before meaning an employment history, career was simply the turning of a wheel during a journey.

Beyond this religious sense of work as a mode of salvation of the self, Maslow's idea of self-actualization implies a particular orientation towards the world around us. Work here means taking up the challenge laid down by the world, implicitly by the divine creator, and thereby doing God's work. As an individualistic version of 'Go forth and multiply', self-actualization implies that individual choices and self-expression are consubstantial with the will of God; the worker is figuratively the Hand of God, doing his will, manifesting the divine plan or creating the City of God on earth. Maslow is explicit about this: 'Enlightened management was a way of limited human beings trying the best way they could to produce the good life on earth or to make a heavenly society on earth' (Maslow, 1998: 83). For an individual life or for the management of a firm, the promotion of self-actualization is not just proposed because it is more effective, but because it provides a meaningful working life. Indeed, for Maslow, management was not simply a technical task but a psychological experiment in which economic outcomes would demonstrate the truth and efficacy of theories. More than that, it was a utopian experiment in transforming individuals by guiding them towards self-actualization; productivity was a mere 'by-product' of all this human development. Management for Maslow was a patriotic endeavour to transform society as a whole.

While phrases like 'self-actualization' and 'hierarchy of needs' sound relatively academic, these ideas pervade the culture of work in modernity so thoroughly that they have become proverbial wisdom: 'Find a job you love and you'll never work a day in your life'. The well-known poem by Marianne Williamson, 'Our Deepest Fear', is an exhortation to self-actualization: 'Our deepest fear is not that we are inadequate. / Our deepest fear is that we are powerful beyond measure. / It is our light, not our darkness / That most frightens us'. The poet is an evangelist preacher, and insists to her audience that they can be special because they are one of God's children. Interestingly, these words are often misattributed to Nelson Mandela, for instance, in the 1990s self-help bestseller *Chicken Soup for the Soul*, full of inspirational stories for business and work.

Similar ideas animate the bestselling *Man's Search for Meaning* (Frankl, 2006), wherein holocaust survivor Victor Frankl expounds the idea that the 'meaning of life' is not a philosophical secret but something located and created by each individual as they explore their world and choose a form of work or quest to change the world, help others or any form of action in the world. Like Maslow, Frankl invented a minor version of psychoanalysis called 'logotherapy'. These versions of the 'talking cure' are a twentieth-century adaptation of the religious confessional – see Chapter 7. Typically they endorse the idea that humans have innate dignity and potential and are defined by their capacity to make choices. Unsurprisingly these ideas make intuitive sense to students, readers of self-help guides, jobseekers or entrepreneurs; self-actualization or salvation through work and choices is a core tenet of modernity's Christian background.

Whereas Weber's Protestant ethic focuses on competitive individualism in the relentless search for success, the 'spirit of capitalism' which emerges from Maslow involves people attempting to find an identity in a form of work. They find a vocation, discover themselves, unfold their potential and effectively 'do God's work.' Indeed, Boltanski and Chiapello's *The New Spirit of Capitalism* (2005) notes that the demand for meaningful work means that motivating workers is a key management concern. They examined management texts from the '60s and '90s, which revealed a clear contrast: older, custom-based, dutiful ideas about the work ethic in obedience to superiors were displaced by a new focus on projects, whereby workers could express themselves creatively and autonomously, continuously fulfilling their potential in new and exciting ways. Existing hierarchies within business were flattened in favour of networks of individuals who collaborated temporarily in changing configurations of talent. Of course, this exciting vista of projects and networks for many actually means precarious work, but what is interesting is how the ethos of individual self-actualization was harnessed – co-opted even – in order to motivate workers (Petersen, 2011).

Of course, this career of finding work and vocation can be subject to multiple twists and turns, self-actualization being an endless journey for Maslow. Thus, as Pecchenino argues, the contemporary logic of economic life replicates the Christian idea of life as a trial of self-discovery:

> Thus, the individual, through living, discerns his preferences, possibly suffering numerous setbacks where those preferences discerned turn out to be false or experiencing epiphanies through which some aspect of his true preferences can be, or is believed to be, discerned accurately. (Pecchenino, 2011: 241)

Work is thereby not just expending energy in outer-worldly labours but an inner-directed exercise of self-discovery, provoking 'epiphanies', as the person comes to know themselves and creates the truth about themselves. Hence the endless search for meaningful work: 'Work to live, don't live to work', as per the popular fridge magnet. Yet, being without work appears as an extraordinary deprivation, not just financially, and so this curious experience called 'unemployment' deserves further scrutiny.

Deprived and depraved

Even critics of capitalism are champions of work and lament its absence. For instance, Orwell's *The Road to Wigan Pier* describes the amazing capacities of miners who athletically negotiate a journey to the pit which leaves him breathless, all before a long shift literally at the coal face. Like many, he describes how unemployment ruins the working-class man, disrupts the order of his household and destroys the pride of working-class communities. Similarly, French existentialist and socialist Simone Weil positioned work as sacred: 'Nothing in the world can make up for the loss of joy in one's work' (Weil, [1952] 2003: 78). For Weil the proletariat were 'obsessed by the fear of total uprootedness, that is, of unemployment' (Weil, 2003: 49). Thus, work becomes being, and unemployment nothingness.

More concrete experiences of unemployment are described in Walter Greenwood's veiled autobiography *Love on the Dole* (1933). The narrative follows a young working-class lad, Harry, through redundancy to an interminable unemployment ending in poorhouse charity. While unemployed, the worker is relentlessly 'killing time': 'Nothing to do with time ... stand transfixed at a street corner, brain a blank' (Greenwood, 1933: 170). Men even take amusement in watching others working, as spectators to the labour market: when the siren marking lunch time at the factory blows, 'he felt icily alone' (Greenwood, 1933: 160). Here, we see a fictional embodiment of Joan Robinson's counter-intuitive quip that 'the misery of being exploited by capitalists is nothing compared to the misery of not being exploited at all' (Robinson, 1964: 46).

Simultaneously the unemployed are oriented to any future employment, with a constant refrain of 'wait till I get a job', in a tone mixing resolve with resentment at the current lack. The question 'Have you found a job?' awaits the protagonist and his friends on returning home to disappointed wives or mothers, creating avoidance and alienation to compound gendered divisions between masculine labouring and feminized caring work. A bright future is imagined in the much-desired job, which makes its absence almost unendurable. Each individual constantly seeks work, offering themselves as hired hands anywhere, everyday, but routinely fail, and become discouraged, looking at cohorts who lost their jobs years ago and have deteriorated into a chronic tramp-like status, almost devoid of hope, but always available for work.

This experience of enduring unemployment and longing for work is poignantly captured in Harry's prayer for a job: 'Aw God, just let me get a job, [I] don't care if it's on'y half pay', he found comfort in this conversation; kept it up: ... [I] mean, that if [I] don't get a job t'day let me get one soon' (Greenwood, 1933: 159). Hope and despair mingle here, supplicating to providential power for the benediction of employment, pleading, bargaining, even for half pay, if not now, then soon. Thus, the unemployed person not only lacks work but is desperate to escape their current state into a transformed future.

Attentive readers will notice that many of the foregoing sources are derived from the 1930s, a decade inextricably linked to the image of unemployment after the Wall Street Crash and the ensuing Great Depression. In this decade, unemployment as an extended experience becomes crystallized as an absence of work, as a deprivation which leads to subjective deterioration. To an extent this simply follows from the long-term historical idealization of work: idleness is a sin, and in the phrase of Benedictine monks, '*Laborae est orare*' – to work is to pray. Yet in the 1930s this model becomes more explicit, perhaps surprisingly, through sociology.

The main sociological theory of unemployment is known as 'deprivation theory', whereby work is conceived of as providing not just economic benefits, but key social goods, specifically:

- social solidarity
- esteem and status
- collective purpose
- time structure
- regular activity

'Deprivation theory' conceives of unemployment as the absence of these social goods. This theory specifically emerges from *Marienthal*, a study of the collapse of a textile factory in 1930 by the Austrian Research Unit for Economic Psychology led by Paul Lazarsfeld and then Marie Jahoda, both socialist authors who published extensively on unemployment after the end of World War II. The study itself was reprinted in 1960 and first published in English in 1971, feeding into the emergence of 'activation policy' as a 'cure' for the ills of unemployment.

Marienthal concerns a very distinctive case. The surrounding area was almost wholly dependent for employment on a single factory and unemployment there was prolonged and visible in the shape of ex-factory workers lingering on street corners. Almost all families were touched by unemployment, and so it became an everyday topic of conversation, indeed the whole community, from leisure to politics, was affected by it. For Lazarsfeld, in retrospect, it appeared that high unemployment was one factor which contributed to the rise of fascism. For Jahoda, it seemed that unemployment undermined socialism, leading to resignation rather than revolution.

Yet, Marienthal is not a typical case; it is a small rural area where a single factory provided most jobs, suddenly struck down by the Great Depression. By contrast, most unemployment occurs in urban centres and only impacts a small sector of the whole population; thus, generalizations from this study should be treated cautiously. While it often has a scientific and technical tone, *Marienthal* also exhibits a melodramatic style – depicting workers as 'deprived' of their character as workers: 'Nothing is urgent anymore; they have forgotten how to hurry' (Jahoda and Zeisel, 2002: 37) – or an elegiac lament for the once busy factory: 'Silence has come to the factory. Somewhere across the empty courtyards one can hear at times the thud of a hammer knocking old bricks out of a wall. That is the last job the factory has to offer' (Jahoda and Zeisel, 2002: 37).

Our aim here is not to minimize the difficulties of unemployment, especially the economic impact which reduces people to the breadline. However, what matters here is to understand precisely why unemployment is interpreted socially as deprivation, as deterioration. The idea that work provides specific social goods is the first claim which requires attention. Of course, critics have pointed out that many jobs are exploitative rather than bestowing 'social goods'; but rather than 'deconstructing' the idea of the social goods of work, we should understand them more thoroughly. Deprivation theory is not an ideology to be unmasked, but a mode of valuing and interpreting work which deserves deeper consideration and interpretation.

By focusing in on the social consequences for the individual of the absence of work, the deprivation theory reflects the paradigm of governmental power as described earlier; governmentality is a subtle modern form of power which attempts to maximize the qualities of every individual in line with various state and economic priorities. Governmentality sets out a sort of life ethos which implies work and the cultivation of individual flourishing through social goods.

Of the five social goods, the most straightforward is probably regular activity; work provides exercise and activity, which ensures workers maintain their skills, both manual and mental, being able to concentrate on assigned tasks and the labour process. Similarly, the way work provides a time-structure for live, ordering the day in terms of work and rest, times to eat, socialize and celebrate is clearly a way of managing the lives of workers so that they are oriented towards work. Even the focus on the provision of a positive identity through work, the social status of work, can be seen as governmental, in that it provides the psychological stability which underpins the technical completion of work. Understandably, deprivation theory focuses on the importance of social solidarity and collective purpose, given that the Austrian Psychological Unit for Economic Psychology was essentially run by socialist thinkers, most notably Lazarsfeld and Jahoda. For Marxists, the collective work of the proletariat united in solidarity is idealized, and is even considered the precursor to a communist revolution. Yet, even these could be considered as a form of governmentality, binding workers together with *esprit de corps* so that they work as a team, pursuing a collective purpose of industrial production. Thus, solidarity and collective purpose appear as forms of motivation, employed by firms to boost productivity. Work is central to life here, in the governmental sense of 'life' as 'bio-political life', that is, a form of life cultivated by the state and by firms. Jahoda claims that work is 'a person's strongest tie to reality', which is a startling claim; more important than family or community or politics, work is the secure ground of personhood. Partially this may be because socialist thinkers position work as the solidaristic basis for the revolutionary proletariat, but also because through becoming a worker, people are governmentally shaped into citizens.

Considered in this manner, deprivation theory reflects how workers are governmentalized generally in industrial capitalism. Through education, training, apprenticeships and the disciplinary forces of the factory floor, human beings are transformed into good industrial workers or office clerks or salespersons. Indubitably, the deprivation theory of unemployment is implicitly modelled on industrial work; some of its elements cannot apply to peasant agriculture, like the time structure of the clock, not present in feudal farming which worked according to custom and exigency. Similarly, solidarity is diminished in contemporary internally competitive professions, from stockbrokers to taxi drivers. So, deprivation theory is really a theory of work, modelled on the industrial factory, with unemployment figured as the absence of this worker self. It idealizes work and suggests that its absence leads to subjective deterioration, which needs to be remedied either by finding work as quickly as possible or by the supplementation of welfare by various ersatz work activities: jobseeking, internships, training and so forth. In terms of the history of welfare policy, deprivation theory makes the individual rather than the economy the target of governmental intervention.

As Foucault noted, there are extraordinary parallels between prisons, asylums, hospitals, schools and factories. Governmentality is not simply a new subtle and wholly secular exercise of power which proceeds to transform the citizens of a state until they are 'fitter, happier, more productive' – in Radiohead's phrase. Rather it is the inheritor of a complex apparatus of pastoral power, how the church attempted to shape its congregation, individually and as a group. So, before the factory, the model of the good worker actually derives from the monastery.

Laborae est orare: to work is to pray

Monasteries play a curious and paradoxical role in the history of work. Early Christian monasticism was typically oriented towards the desert as an escape from worldly distractions and cares, and eventually spread across Europe to the remotest parts of the landscape. During the fall of Rome, monks became missionaries, attempting to spread the word of the gospel everywhere as the end of the world was apparently nigh. After the decline of the empire, early medieval monks sometimes took on an evangelical role, confronting pagan kings with the demands of Christianity. As we shall see, monastic institutions also became part of pilgrimage networks, and some monks were akin to perpetual pilgrims among the poor, particularly Franciscan friars. However, the key characteristic of the monastery is that it is a closed order, an institution with an abbot and a hierarchy, which admits novitiates from the community but stands separate from the family or tribal ties. Differences exist between different orders, Dominicans, Benedictines and Cistercian being the best-known and most influential orders. What is most important here for our purposes is that monasteries generate a very specific work discipline which corresponds strongly with deprivation theory.

Historians of work, Weber notable among them, acknowledge that the time structure and regular activity of the monastery are very distinctive, breaking the day up into hours of prayer and work, with regular times for waking, sleeping, eating and resting. Ironically, these arrangements were highly productive, making monasteries into centres of wealth because of their efficient management of agriculture and their frugal disposal of profits. This also turned them into sources of funds for feudal lords, including crusaders, who turned to them for mortgages: loans against sureties which reverted to the monastery upon death (*mort*). Of course, monasteries also were engaged in charitable offices, helping the local poor, providing work and thereby food for the landless and giving succour to roaming beggars – monks washed the feet of beggars in a gesture of humility designed to ensure the salvation of the monk rather than the hygiene of the beggar.

Evidently, monks worked together with a very distinctive sense of social solidarity, as they called each other 'brother' and were supposed to entertain no pride or rivalry. As to collective purpose, they were doing God's work, tilling the earth which had been given to man to make fertile, helping the poor who were identified with Jesus, so their work was literally a mission. The status of a monk as a man of God was unquestionable – and retreating to an order of nuns was one of the few routes to high status for women in medieval society. Similarly to Maslow's quip earlier about enlightened management as an attempt to create a heavenly society on earth, a monastery was the closest equivalent to the hosts of ministering angels.

Early monasticism instituted work as a mode of shaping conduct, not just as valuable in itself as labour or a punishment but as crucial to the transformation of subjects: 'Work became a fundamental activity – of course, with a spiritual value, since work reduced up to a certain point the dispersion of thoughts that was one of the conditions for contemplation, work also imposed a necessary humility on the individual' (Foucault, 2014b: 174). Monastic discipline required obedience to superiors, patient, unquestioning humility, most easily demonstrated by diligent labour. Such obedience was considered a guarantee of truthfulness in confession, which made salvation possible (Foucault, 2007). Indeed, the unemployed are often forced to 'confess' their personal story through unequal power relations (Skeggs, 2004: 119–27). This relationship of telling the truth about the self – to an abbot or a welfare officer – as a route to self-transformation will be explored in greater detail in Chapter 7.

Historically, monasteries were economically productive and technologically innovative; their influence on modern factories is complex, and very often the requirements of machine production overrule any ideal version of work. For instance, many industrial factories paid at a piece rate, so that workers were competing with each other. Yet, from Robert Owen's utopian factory experiments of the early 1800s with their compulsory education, to Frederick W. Taylor's 'time and motion' studies a century later, it is clear that the factory tried to transform ordinary people into a specific kind of industrial worker. Peasants had to be remade into workers: rather than following customary and time-honoured ways of working they had to exert their minds and bodies in machine-like ways, in confined spaces at set times, with constant concentration and attention to their work.

Deprivation theory clearly idealizes work as providing social goods beyond the economic benefits of work: rather than labour being a burden, it is ennobling, making workers into better persons. Within this apparently dry academic idea of psychological well-being there are resonances of an older religious idea of work. Indeed, encoded within the deprivation theory is the Protestant work ethic, but curiously inverted, expressing the contrast between the disciplined ranks of monks and the rabble of beggars.

In modernity, those without work are *imagined* as a mass or even a mob. The rabble of those deprived of work lack solidarity, constantly struggling with each other: they have no collective purpose, but wander aimlessly, like scavengers; they have no status, no fixed identity, connections or abode; their time is not structured, they roam abroad at night at unexpected hours; they have no regular activity, but pass their time in idleness and dissolute activities. Contemporary scholarship argues that welfare institutions serve to stigmatize the unemployed even while supporting them with cash benefits (Tyler, 2020). However, the contemporary 'punitive turn' is not just a pointlessly cruel neoliberal ideology. Rather, those without work are not just 'demonized', by tabloid press and political rhetoric, but also rendered responsible for their own fate within the market by welfare systems (Kotsko, 2018). Those who are deprived of work are implicitly depraved. This may seem extreme, yet contemporary media and politics still stigmatizes welfare recipients in broadly these terms, as scroungers, idlers, fraudsters, dependents, useless, quasi-criminal mobs who at best deserve sympathy for their chaotic lives but more likely deserve condemnation and need reformation. Indeed, they are 'sinners' according to a moralizing diagnosis wherein their character faults explain their unemployment.

Just as Weber identified how Protestantism spread a monastic work discipline throughout the world, here it appears that even non-workers are novitiates for the work cult. Yet the institutions of the welfare state are not simply charitable, but seek to purify claimants through creating a purgatory on earth.

Conclusion

Critics have long alleged that the 'ideology of work' is used to exploit people. Before the advent of social science there were Romantic critics like Wordsworth and Blake who described rural and urban poverty, or Rousseau who critiqued inequality and greed. These informed Marxist and socialist ideas of how work was rendered exploitative and alienating by capitalism. Work is criticized as making people into numb worker-drones devoid of human sensibilities, or into competitive and selfish individualists without communal solidarity but with a limitless appetite for consumer goods, and finally work contributes to the destruction of the environment. Yet, even for the Romantics, 'work' in the sense of the 'great work' was the centre of life, and they often idealized the craft worker who created traditional goods in a beautiful manner. Similarly, Marx idealizes work as the source of all value, from hunting and gathering through agriculture to industry. For Marx, the 'labour-process' generates 'species-being' provided the 'mode of production' is not alienating – a complex way of saying that work is life.

In considering the meaning of work, it is important not to presume that capitalists are in favour of work and critics are against it. On the contrary, socialist writers have an extraordinary reverence for work. However, rather than pursuing this through the often arcane texts of Marx, which are less frequently read than referenced, let us consider *The Grapes of Wrath* – the 1939 novel for which John Steinbeck won the Pulitzer Prize, and subsequently the Nobel prize in 1962. The work was composed in the '30s, reflecting the migration of the 'Okies' from the dust bowl to California during the Great Depression. The novel is partly an epic family journey of migration, hardships, dangers, temptations and the pitting of hope against despair. However, interspersed with the narrative chapters are overviews of economy and society, still in the tenor of folksy storytelling, but clearly articulating socialist critiques of capitalism.

Variously Steinbeck gives elegiac overviews of the effect of finance, technology and specialization in disrupting existing agriculture, the wastefulness of market commodification and overproduction, the problems of greed and competitiveness. For instance, farmers tell managers that the land is theirs because they were born on it, work on it and die on it, which positions life as work between the cradle and the grave, and makes work the essence of possession and identity. Of course, the titular 'grapes of wrath' refer to the biblical grapes of wrath, invoked in the 'Battle Hymn of the Republic', and Steinbeck broadly implies that revolution is imminent, although clearly historically what actually comes to pass is the New Deal, that is, the emergence of the welfare state.

Central to Steinbeck's socialist vision of community, migration and the economy in general is the idealization of work. The migrant family are depicted in the midst of skilled communal co-operation, and even when they become proletarianized as day labourers in the cotton-picking and fruit mega-farms of California, their work is still a source of pride and identity. Work is primary, essential to humankind in Steinbeck's vision:

> Muscles and mind aching to grow, to work, to create, multiplied a million times. The last clear definite function of man – muscles aching to work, minds aching to create beyond the single need – this is man. To build a wall, to build a house a dam, and in the wall and house and dam to put something of Manself, and to Manself take back something of the wall, the house the dam, to take hard muscles from the lifting to take clear lines and form from conceiving. (Steinbeck, 1975, p 160)

To work is *to be*, ennobling the worker, expressing their mental and physical being. Furthermore, work is a way of being which transforms the worker and the world itself. Steinbeck's vague formulation 'Manself' unites the individual and the collective, implying both the chosen people and the struggling single soul. Beyond the simple effects of effort to complete tasks, work is special. Beyond being transformative, it also is an end in itself, an insatiable need for self-actualization, in Maslow's terms.

Clearly, socialists embrace the work cult of the Western world just as much as capitalists. Whereas capitalists imagine a 'city of God' wherein everyone is continuously working and self-actualizing through the market, socialists anticipate a revolution which will generate a form of non-alienated work: autonomous, creative, equal but still work nonetheless. History has worked out compromises between capitalism and socialism or the market and the state which have lead to welfare systems which position work as central, as a means of transforming individuals. Even if it means suffering, work is the route to salvation; indeed, administering suffering productively is a distinctive focus of contemporary welfare systems. Beyond vocation, this requires a purgatory for jobseekers.

5

Purgatory: The Ideal
of Purifying Suffering

Doing nothing is a paradox: nothing is not an amount to be used up
or an activity which can be completed. The unemployed who we
spoke to repeatedly emphasized that they found time a burden. Here
we might well turn to philosophers to unravel the conundrum – like
the unemployed they often have a great deal of time on their hands
but somehow do not enjoy it. In the late seventeenth century, Pascal
opined that 'all of humanity's problems stem from man's inability
to sit quietly in a room alone'; indeed our interviewees stressed the
difficulty of sitting quietly in a room alone. More recently, Wittgenstein
said, 'If we take eternity to mean not infinite temporal duration but
timelessness, then eternal life belongs to those who live in the present'.
Yet jobseekers often describe their day-to-day existence as a sort of
infinite time, where hours seem like an eternity. This is not an eternal
bliss of present satisfaction but an undefined period of waiting to escape
from an interminable predicament.

There is something perplexing, curious and enigmatic about the
experience of doing nothing, feeling time slowly passing. However,
there is no natural or neutral human experience of 'doing nothing';
what matters decisively is how people think about the absence of
defined activity. For the unemployed, what matters is how they are
governed by the welfare state, that is, by the form of pastoral power
which is exerted upon them. This is not just a personal problem, but a
social issue. Contemporary states and international organizations such
as the EU and OECD are concerned that long-term unemployment
produces 'subjective deterioration', that is, decreased health, diminished
future earnings, or lower educational attainment for children in 'jobless
households'. Their solution is to increase 'activation': more advice,

training and pressure on the unemployed to attain work. This may have some effect, including increasing in-work poverty, but what it really does is intensify the negative experience of unemployment. Problematically, states react to an economic or social problem with measures that are only marginally effective in reducing the numbers of long-term unemployed and really make the experience worse.

Our answer to why unemployment is such a puzzling experience and governed in such a paradoxical way is to point to the persistence of a religious idea: purgatory. This idea is a relative latecomer in theology, a medieval addition to Christian ideas about the next world which was rejected by Protestantism and eventually abandoned by Catholicism. Basically, purgatory is an interim space between this world and the next, where the soul can suffer for their sins until they are sufficiently purified to enter heaven – or if they are insufficiently penitent, be cast into hell. Enduring time, waiting, completing remedial tasks is positioned as a sort of transformative suffering. This peculiar idea informs how the unemployed experience their lives, and how the state organizes welfare.

There are two main critiques of contemporary welfare activation: that it is ideologically capitalist or neoliberal, cheapening and commodifying labour, generating precarious work; and that it is cruel, putting people under pressure, cutting off their supports, driving them to destitution and desperation. Beyond outrage at these injustices, this chapter will show why states do these things, even why making people suffer appears an expression of righteousness. Supposedly suffering purifies people; this uncomfortable but familiar idea requires sustained attention.

Doing nothing

In Western culture, being forced to do nothing is used as a punishment. Children are given time out as a reprimand. Prisoners 'do time'. Having to wait is a sign of lower social status. Without activity, choices or distraction, time seems like a heavy burden. Yet, we all crave free time, holidays or at least a break! Our culture seems beset by conflicting interpretations of free time, but really the crucial thing is to 'do' something, even if that is leisure or a holiday or consumerism. To be is to do in modernity: make choices, explore, face adversity, overcome challenges and achieve the potential inside yourself –'search for the hero inside yourself', even.

For many commentators, this idea should be exposed as an ideology, a form of propaganda which protects the status quo and keeps everyone else working hard. For our purposes, the most important thing is to recognize how it encodes religious ideas – a person is defined by their choices and constant effort, and challenges are a chance to learn and transform yourself: life makes sense as a sort of pilgrimage through this world – as we will explore in our next chapter. Within that 'design for life', having nothing to do becomes a challenge or predicament, a form of purgatory.

Over the past ten years, we have interviewed many different unemployed people in a variety of circumstances: male and female, young and old, with various levels of education and different family situations, past careers and lengths of time unemployed. All of them said that their free time was a burden, even that they wished they had less of it. Frequently, they would tell us that they were 'doing nothing', employing metaphors like cabin fever or cold storage to try to explain their state:

> 'Filling the time is the killer. It is now … I'm available now but I'm sitting on my fucking arse, ya know what I mean, what's the difference, you can get caught in an absolute rut, and find yourself doing nothing day after day, because you're so demoralised. You have nothing to do.'

Conversation often returned to this nothingness over an hour or so, and while it was a commonplace experience, it was nonetheless difficult to explain. Not only did the unemployed think that others didn't understand their predicament, they themselves found it perplexing. Paradoxically, their excess of free time provoked boredom, tedium and frustration rather than relaxation and satisfaction. Most of those we spoke to had once been employed and admitted that they had thought unemployment was an easy life of enjoyment for 'slackers' and suchlike, something which they envied mildly while in hard work. The reality was that unemployment was almost unbearable.

Many of them used the metaphor of 'madness' to describe how they felt, saying, 'You'd go nuts sitting at home', or, 'You'd go insane'. Partly this reflects people reaching for a comparison, but in other cases they related clinical mental health problems, which are statistically increased by unemployment. For instance, one older man said: "But then it hits ya, getting up every morning sitting on your arse. Cause I, I had to go to the doctors now for depression, I got so bad, I was on tablets. … If you've got nothing to do yourself, to keep yourself occupied you'll go round the twist."

Initially this seems like a confirmation of the deprivation theory of unemployment whereby the absence of the social good of work leads to 'subjective degeneration'. Yet simply noting this correlation is not sufficient to explain it: for instance, retirees, children or the independently wealthy do not experience their spare time as an abyss that needs to be filled – unless they already equate life and work. Indeed, the words 'mad' or 'insane' here do not refer to a clinical problem but falteringly attempt to convey an inexplicable experience.

Beyond being an economic problem, unemployment seems to spoil everyday enjoyments. For instance, one young man tried to enjoy the life of the 'slacker', but found the reality far from his expectations: "I was waking up playing games all day, eating microwave food and generally living pretty badly ... but I wasn't enjoying it. Or at least not enjoying it much; it lost its charm really fast and after it did I had to do other stuff to stop myself from turning stir crazy." Without the activity of work to justify it, indulgence in leisure and junk food is neither pleasant nor meaningful. This contravenes the bald economic logic that people work only in order to procure the consumer goods they desire; somehow, unemployment ruins the very free time it provides. This was starkly articulated by a father of three young children who described how he did not enjoy parental duties since he had become unemployed: "It gets monotonous; you're only there, you know you have to be there with your kids, thing, but you're only there, it's not because of choice, I mean if I had my choice, I wouldn't be there. You have to be there, it's not by choice, like." Obviously, this response reflects gendered expectations of a male breadwinner, yet what is remarkable is the capacity of unemployment to sour relationships and experiences.

Aside from their efforts to find paid employment, many people described how they filled their days with tasks:

> 'I'm like "Oh My God". I need something to do like. There's only so much housework and that that you can do before you start to drive yourself mad, so.'

> 'Some days are as long – like two years in a day, like. I'd be good, I do try and ehm, I couldn't just get up and sit around and do nothing; I'd have to get up and do something so that when I do sit down, I do feel like – well look it; I can sit down now, I'm after doing something you know that way?'

Several elements are captured succinctly in the latter quote: first, time seems to stretch elastically so that a single day seems like two years. Unemployment is akin to a twilight zone where clocks tick more slowly, days drag on and there is no end in sight. Second, in the absence of employment, the interviewee created her own standard, where she cannot simply rest or 'do nothing', but must 'do something', anything, from housework to jobseeking, in order to justify herself in sitting down. Our interviews were carried out in Ireland, initially under a relatively 'passive' welfare system, whereby the unemployed were encouraged but not compelled to seek work. Over the last decade, more 'active' welfare measures have been introduced, monitoring and pressurizing people to seek and accept any job whatsoever. Compliance is assured by the threat of sanctions, a cut of about a quarter of benefit allowances for a period of up to nine weeks. These policies certainly intensified the jobseeking activities of the people we spoke to and made their everyday lives feel overshadowed by their lack of work.

The cruelty of these sorts of systems has been well documented, ranging from pushing people into debt, subjecting people to hunger, to forcing them into homelessness or even into suicide. These extreme cases are the tip of the iceberg of an experience which is already unpleasant for anyone. For instance, one young man described being forced to apply for jobs online as a banal experience of being ordered about by the office: "At that time it was more kinda tedious more than anything else … I was just … I was just working away doing my nothings and getting paid for it." Being threatened with sanctions and forced to seek work at an office computer, under surveillance, had become relatively normalized, tedious. While each person we spoke to fervently wanted a job, even looking for work became an endless, Sisyphean task of constant effort and repeated failure. Furthermore, the case officer assigned to each person prescribed further tasks at each meeting, implying that unemployment was the fault of the individual not the wider economy. 'Goin' in and lookin' at these things being pulled down and lookin' at DVDs, wasting two or three hours questioning ya and you're goin', "I already answered that six or eight weeks ago." Then they'd wait for two or three months, "Do you wanna do a computer course, do you wanna do this, do you wanna do that?"' Clearly annoyed at such constant low-level harassment, this man particularly noted the ineffectiveness of the activation services. Contemporary sociologists often seek to give voice to the small acts of resistance against power, and we certainly found cases of individuals circumventing the demands of the office, or, quite frequently, the kindness of case officers who found loopholes or excuses for leniency. Yet, for each case of resistance, there are just as many cases where the unemployed individual becomes almost a mouthpiece for activation, hard work and even the deprivation theory: "Well, when you're unemployed for a while you become, you kinda stagnate, y' know, and your job should be looking for work. When you're at home from nine to five, you should make that your looking-for-work time." Remarkably, the unemployed people we spoke to distanced themselves from 'the unemployed' – a finding reproduced consistently (Shildrick and MacDonald, 2013). Many described themselves as 'not really unemployed' and stigmatized the idleness of 'real scroungers' and 'welfare spongers'. This may be disappointing, but it is unsurprising; most people we spoke to had recently been made redundant. Their attitude to unemployment was the same that prevails throughout society – make the idle work, for their own good, and at any cost.

Welfare before welfare

Historical records of how societies have responded to those in need go back very far (Tilley, 2012). There are also many hunter-gatherer tribes who share everything in common, so that no one is needy, and if slackers exist they face mild ostracism at most. This sets up 'irrational' disincentives to work in economic parlance, but letting other people suffer makes no sense, not just because the hungry may become desperate, but because they are part of society, sharing culture, space and relationships. Interestingly, economic textbooks routinely describe economics as the management of 'scarce resources', but for pre-agricultural peoples, resources generally are not scarce. The average working day is five hours, often characterized by playfulness and enjoyment of the 'work' of hunting and gathering (Sahlins, 1972).

By contrast, after the emergence of agriculture, 'work' becomes labour: strenuous and repetitive. Generally, agriculture leads to a growing population, more mouths to feed, but worse health and life expectancy. Surprisingly, this 'agricultural revolution' makes resources scarce (Scott, 2017). Of course, there are many different agricultural civilizations, but the most historically influential became Mesopotamian and Mediterranean empires: Egypt, Persia, Assyria, Greece, Rome. While some provision is made for the poor in these empires – the 'bread and circuses' to keep the Roman plebeians in line – the principle institution for managing the poor is debt slavery (Graeber, 2011). Such slaves are not necessarily chained, but exchange their time and labour for food and to pay off debts or acquire land. Occasionally the poor may exit debt slavery, but generally the cycle is for an increase in debts so that they are renewed constantly.

By contrast, Judaic provision for the poor was communal but voluntary after the fall of Jerusalem, and eventually Roman commentators were surprised to find that their Jewish subject peoples took care of all of the poor in certain cities. The Judaic covenant with Yahweh in exchange for liberation from Egypt made it a sacred obligation to support the poor – initially among their co-religionists, but eventually the poor in general, living under whatever empire or state prevailed: 'For there will never cease to be poor in the land. Therefore I command you: "You shall open wide your hand to your brother, to the needy and to the poor, in your land"' (Deuteronomy 15: 11). Beyond direct subsistence, there were special allowances for the poor to take part of the harvest and to be fed at synagogues, for public relief works, for hospitality offered for migrant workers and the famous debt jubilee, where debts built up were eliminated every fifty years.

Taken together this seems like an early quasi-welfare state, but these societies were very different from modernity: the poor were not socially or physically distant, nor were the institutions settled states or bureaucracies, especially after the fall of Jerusalem in 568 BCE. Decisions about how much to give, to whom, and who should pay what were very much personal and assured 'by promoting an internalized sense of obligation' (Lowenberg, 1995: 319). In short, this was charity rather than bureaucratic social policy. The voluntary spirit of this provision can be seen in the Christian tradition of 'passing a basket', a collection to support the priest and the needy of the parish.

The early Christian church took on this ethic of charity, even to the point of communism in the Acts of the Apostles, whereby new converts who accepted Jesus as the Messiah would share all their goods with the rest of the community. Regarding their relationship to God, St. Paul implies that all men are equal before God, which provides an argument against slavery as well as an impetus to relieving poverty. Thus, not only do religious ideals of charity transform the provision for the poor in the Roman Empire, medieval Christianity spreads across Europe, bringing with it an objection to slavery. Nevertheless, versions of debt slavery persist in the form of serfdom, where peasants do not own their lands and owe a tithe of their produce to their lords and the church – an economic relationship which persists right up to the industrial revolution in many countries.

However, what interests us is not the mainstream economic relationship of peasants and lords – and it is worth bearing in mind that these ranged from warrior-chiefs to robber barons to military specialists to the 'noble' aristocracy. Rather, our concern is how society dealt with the poor, the landless, the sick, the crippled: those who could not sustain themselves without aid. Of course, these problems were largely dealt with by extended family on the basis of kinship and local concern; however, where they were not, the institution of charity prevailed.

The history of medieval institutions and arrangements for charity covers a vast range – the classic account perhaps being Mollat's *The Poor in the Middle Ages* (Mollat, 1986). For instance, the seemingly simple institution of beggary was incrementally regulated across Europe so that beggars became licensed or wore badges and were only permitted to beg within certain locations. At first, monasteries were the centres for charity, with 'porters' – those who managed the doors – in charge of surveying the poor and ensuring that only worthy supplicants were admitted and that the poor did not stay in one place but travelled onwards, like perpetual pilgrims. Monasteries and churches dominated the early provision for the poor, but eventually urban centres and nobles took these duties upon themselves, with medieval workers' 'confraternities' acting to support those who had lost the means to support themselves, a precursor to trade-union 'unemployment insurance' (DeSwaan, 1988). The problem of rural poverty was addressed by mendicant friars, who exhorted parishes to give donations which they would then disburse.

What matters here is the way in which poverty was interpreted; indeed, even the words used to describe the phenomenon change over time, so that 'the poor' and 'paupers' as nouns are only slowly replaced by concepts like 'poverty' as a temporary state. Medieval ideas about poverty and charity are quite ambivalent: on the one hand there is a suspicion of the poor, that they might be idle or even criminal, and they are sometimes represented as a dangerous mob. On the other hand, poverty is sometimes equated with purity, with the poor compared to Jesus. Indeed, the rejection of all property in an attempt to follow the life of Christ was the centre of St. Francis of Assisi's mission.

Beyond this, the crucial element is how charity was imagined: giving alms to the poor was part of an 'economy of grace' – if the rich bestowed gifts upon the poor, they atoned for their own sins. As the ninth century *Vita Eligil* declared, 'God could have made all men rich, but he wanted poor men in the world so the rich might have opportunity to redeem their sins.' (Mollat, 1986: 44). Thus, the poor existed as part of God's providential plan to give people a chance to redeem themselves. This justifies charity, alms and poor relief work, including more organized church provision on a regular basis, including inspection and supervision of the poor.

However charity was administered, it was rooted in a theological concept of a voluntary gift which affected an individual soul. For the medieval church, 'True alms are by nature spontaneous, free, disinterested, discreet and habitual' (Mollat, 1986: 153–4). Central here is the soul of the giver, not the material state of the receiver. Indeed, while a spirit of benevolence and gratitude should surround almsgiving, this earthly act of alms mattered mainly in terms of its spiritual consequences, that is, the sanctification of the soul of the benefactor before divine judgement. Curiously, God is part of this 'economy of grace', even though the exchange appears to occur between the wealthy and the poor: grace or forgiveness is divinely bestowed upon the deserving; no burnt offerings or bribes can be offered to God in Judeo-Christian theology, yet charitable giving, if genuine, in the sense of 'true alms', works almost magically to conjure God's grace.

Over several centuries, there is a slow shift in the interpretation and organization of poverty. Work is perennially extolled as a Christian virtue and therefore idleness is condemned. Yet poverty can still be valuable; Mollat notes 'the purgative value of all suffering, including poverty' (Mollat, 1986: 74). As society becomes more complex, with the growth of long-range trade and urbanization, it slowly becomes necessary to reorganize poverty relief in more rationalized systems. Generally, this involves the monitoring and categorization of different sorts of paupers, giving different treatment, including training in a trade or enrolment in public works.

As modern states replace medieval churches the emphasis shifts, unevenly across Europe, with much confusion. Certainly, there is an increased tendency towards punishing the poor; for instance, the Henrican poor laws (1536) provide for the whipping of beggars found begging outside their parish, then cutting off their right ear for a second offence, and finally execution. This seems 'barbaric' or 'medieval', in historical stereotypes, yet this was part of the Renaissance: 'With humanism, contempt for the poor took a subtle and perfidious turn, becoming disdainful and philosophical, and – height of irony – invoking the dignity of man as justification' (Mollat, 1986: 255). Beyond the cruel and punitive dimension of these developments, imposing these forms of suffering, whether by privation, hunger or hard work, was an attempt to transform people. Workhouses were not simply modern versions of church or monastic shelters for the poor, but attempted to reform them by subjecting them to the discipline of hard work. Here, suffering is interpreted as purifying, as redemptive, as ennobling even in Christianity. Poor-relief shifted markedly from the 'economy of grace' in charity to the attempt to transform those stricken by poverty.

Purgatory: a religious innovation

Today, purgatory seems rather outlandish because it is mainly introduced to us as a sort of idolatrous superstition: Luther, Calvin and a host of Protestant reformers criticized the selling of alms and indulgences, a corruption of the spirit of charity which turned the 'economy of grace' into a tawdry bargain. To fund papal building projects in Rome, indulgences were sold across Europe, sometimes with the blessing of the pope, often on the part of charlatans who preyed on the gullible to sell salvation. 'As soon as the gold in the casket rings / The rescued soul to heaven springs' (Walls, 2002: 28). Aside from doctrinal differences, this was the initial spur to Protestantism, inspiring reformers to attempt to return to the true Christian spirit – iconoclasm in the literal meaning of breaking icons and other relics, and the refusal of rituals of salvation in favour of a strict or 'Puritan' life where ethical behaviour alone determined salvation. Likewise this meant rejecting ideas like purgatory, which had little justification in scripture.

Curiously, purgatory is a relatively new invention. Ideas of heaven and hell are common to Mesopotamian religions for millennia, but the idea of a third other-worldly location where souls wait, hoping to atone for their sins on earth, is a distinctive innovation. Despite that, it does not appear 'out of nothing' – many early church fathers considered life on earth a form of purgatory to test the soul: among them Clement of Alexander, Origen and Augustine. Nevertheless, the idea of purgatory as a spatial location where souls are purified after death is a distinctly medieval idea; for instance, Pope Gregory the Great conceived purgatory as a fiery redemption, based on the following scripture:

> Now if any man builds on the foundation with gold, silver, precious stones, wood, hay, straw, each man's work will become evident; for the day will show it because it is to be revealed with fire, and the fire itself will test the quality of each man's work. If any man's work which he has built on it remains, he will receive a reward. If any man's work is burned up, he will suffer loss; but he himself will be saved, yet so as through fire. (1 Corinthians 3:12–15)

This passage from Paul's epistles was used most extensively in arguments for the existence of purgatory, although the idea of purification by fire is also present in prophetic books, most prominently in Ezekiel (22:17–22). Metaphorically, the idea of fire implies a rapid transformation, testing and purifying the soul swiftly after death. Later writers conceived purgatory as a sustained burning, or a cold 'refrigerium', or as a remote mountain, for instance, the Venerable Bede, prefiguring Dante's 'Mount Purgatory' in the *Divine Comedy*. But the early Christian church eagerly anticipated the Second Coming, and so the Last Judgement for the deceased was implicitly imminent. Indeed, early Christians were often buried communally, even in unmarked graves, because it was assumed that Jesus would resurrect them, rather than the church managing their future remembrance indefinitely.

Rather than having a single identifiable author, purgatory was implied and refined by a vast range of theologians, but usually not as a central idea. Sometimes it was simply a 'limbo' space where the dead waited, but did not undergo any purification. The medieval period saw a growing concern for the dead, in prayers and masses for their salvation; for instance, the Cluniac institution of the 'Day of the Dead' on November 2nd (Le Goff, 1984: 122–5). Meanwhile, the idea of pain or suffering as salutary or redemptive is particularly strengthened in the late medieval period (Gragnolatti, 2005). For its major historian, Jacques Le Goff, the idea of purgatory as a place is mostly consolidated in debates in monasteries and in Paris from 1170–80, with Peter Comester, Tnugdal and St. Bernard as key figures. Here the idea of purgatory begins to emerge from a slew of texts and debates.

For Le Goff (1984: 222–5), purgatory is part of a broad cultural shift towards triadic conceptions within theology, inserting a 'third place' between heaven and hell. This was of serious concern to many theologians who considered any departure from dichotomy as troubling: sacred/profane, divine/human, soul/body and so forth. Western culture is often criticized for being overly 'dualistic', yet the existence of a dichotomy also makes it possible to think about the in-between, or the tension and relations between opposites. Purgatory implies a category between 'saved' and 'damned', whereby sinners were not wholly bad nor wholly good, but in-between, a sort of 'liminal' position whereby the soul could be transformed (Turner and Turner, 2011). However, purgatory was hardly an escape from penance for sins or the obligation for good conduct in this world: 'It is less harsh than hell but worse than the world' (Le Goff, 1984: 171).

As a third place outside the secular world or the eternity of heaven or hell, time operated differently within purgatory. This was possibly inspired by the account of Saint Patrick's purgatory which became a place of pilgrimage in the eleventh century, and mingled Christian theology with Irish cosmological conceptions of the 'otherworld' as places where time could pass quickly or slowly with 'past and future converging in the otherworldly present' (Carey, 1987: 10). In tales of souls returning from purgatory – often to the site of their death or sins – the ghosts describe time passing extraordinarily slowly. 'Time is marked out by the progress made by souls' (Le Goff, 1986: 353). Even as clock time rationalized the daylight-based routines of the medieval day, purgatory offered an abstract notion of time (Willis, 2008).

Purgatory involved different grades of sinner and sins: the excommunicate, the indolent and the unshriven are given special penances. Purgatory institutes a 'penitential bookkeeping' (Le Goff, 1984: 173) as a disciplinary technology within the pastoral power of the medieval church (see Foucault, 1984). Specific punishments are fitted to each sort of sin, as a remedial effort to remove the 'stain of sin', which in every case is created by an individual succumbing to temptation, a personal choice: salvation requires both repentance and the grace of God, whereby the individual must suffer to redeem themselves.

Before the popularization of purgatory, canon law had already institutionalized masses for the souls of the dead. The Lateran council of 1215 institutionalized annual confession, which implied that sins needed to be shriven, and that dying with the 'stain of sin' required posthumous contrition and penance – failure to undergo annual penance was grounds for excommunication. In 1254 Pope Innocent wrote to the Orthodox church urging them to accept the idea of purgatory on the grounds that heaven cannot receive impure souls and referencing the passage from Corinthians cited earlier, although the Orthodox church eschewed this innovation until the Council of Florence in 1439. The doctrine of purgatory was incorporated into Catholic doctrine in the Council of Lyons in 1274, with apparent popular support. The papal jubilee in 1300, whereby pilgrims to Rome could expect absolution from time due in purgatory, indicates how this obscure innovation had entered mainstream theology, church practice and culture. Perhaps more importantly, purgatory was a popular cultural idea, popping up in ghost stories and making divine judgement easier to imagine.

The appeal of the theological innovation of purgatory is related to the expanding market economy of the thirteenth century: 'It was now possible to purge sins that had not been washed away by confession. These innovations offered merchants hope for the salvation that, until the thirteenth century, the Church had denied to all usurers' (Le Goff,

2009, 117). Beyond facilitating moneylending – the medieval sin of usury – purgatory provided a model of time and the work of self-purification which would be extremely important in the development of capitalism, offering redemption for any form of sharp business practice. Of course, purgatory was not some sort of ideological trick for the smooth functioning of capitalism, rather the history of economy and religion are curiously entwined. Oddly, purgatory was important for butchers whose trade was sometimes thought to be unclean.

Interestingly, prayers petitioning forgiveness were initially communal, on the behalf of the departed, yet 'purgatory, caught up in a personalization of spiritual life, actually fostered individualism. It focused attention on individual death and the judgement that followed' (Le Goff, 1984: 233). Purgatory instituted a sort of abacus of good deeds, contrition, penance and sins – and the Aramaic word for sins and debts is identical – translated variously into Latin and vernacular bibles as sins, debts and trespass (Slok, 2020: 72–4). Purgatory implies the need to personally work to expiate sins or debts, implying a diligent economic ethic.

Purgatory forms part of a rich tapestry of religious ideas, about life, economics and attitudes towards the poor. It combines several elements: first, purgatory postpones divine judgment, so all but the most heinous sinners have a chance at redemption before being cast into hell. In purgatory they can atone through repentance and suffering until they merit admittance to heaven. Second, purgatory differentiates between categories of sinners, giving individual allotments of punishment which are tailored to redeem their sinful nature; Dante's *Purgatorio* stands in orderly contrast to the chaos of the *Inferno*, a graduated mountain of purification where the proud are humbled, the lustful made chaste and the slothful put to work. Thirdly, within purgatory, time moves differently; Le Goff relays a tale of a ghost returning from purgatory who said that 'one day seemed as long as a year to some inmates' (1984: 294), quite akin to the descriptions of time offered by the unemployed – time moves differently. Fourthly, almsgiving and masses for the dead notwithstanding, the existence of purgatory renders salvation as an individual trial, by turning life into an abacus of good deeds and sins, whereby ethical behavior, piety and contrition in this world are the most efficient means to shorten the trials of purgatory after death.

Imaginatively, purgatory is another world, yet for believers it has clear consequences for this world, operating as a sort of precursor to the Protestant work ethic. Despite rejecting purgatory, Protestantism retains crucial elements, for instance the positive valorization of suffering, whereby divine punishment 'mortifies our sinful tendencies' (Walls, 2002: 45). Indeed, the whole Protestant life ethic could be seen as a constant purifying trial, as we shall see in popular works like Bunyan's *Pilgrim's Progress*. Effectively, Protestantism offers an abacus of debt and redemption as a metaphor for sin and purification, equivalent to the penitential bookkeeping of purgatory.

By attempting to return radically to the 'original' spirit of Christianity, Protestantism peculiarly renders life itself as a continuous form of purgatory: 'The trials of life and ultimately death itself are means by which God punishes sin and brings spiritual renewal into our hearts' (Walls, 2002: 40). Within Protestantism, priests cannot claim special jurisdiction over the afterlife or extract alms or indulgences for special intercession. This makes good behaviour, but especially work, central to the lives of Protestants, giving special meaning to economic success or failure: 'A pious, or not so pious prudence commands the sinner to seek, already in his earthly existence, to atone, through an asceticism not unlike purgatory for as many of the sins on his account as he can' (Weinrich, 2008: 80). Debt is sin within this schema, and both moral conviction and practical fear of a final reckoning motivate each economic actor to constantly work to 'redeem' themselves – in both the theological and economic sense of the word. To have faith and hopes of salvation implicitly means having an active and optimistic economic attitude: 'Protestants were impelled to cultivate a lifestyle of repentance and amendment to achieve a sufficient state of purity prior to the dissolution of the body' (Throness, 2008: 66). Just like the Calvinist idea of predestination, the theology of purgatory is mainly significant because of the life conduct it inspires.

To the renewed work ethic of capitalism, purgatory contributes a transformation of time; purgatory 'created within the soul a tyranny around time: calculation, accounting and uncertainty' (Willis, 2008: 257), as individuals constantly attempt to expiate their sins or debts or even moments of idleness by renunciation, hard work and endurance: 'It induced in the soul a sense of process and development but never closure or arrival – time was linear, but the destination remained an eternal horizon – the soul was now surely on the treadmill' (Willis, 2008: 259). Here, those without work are implicitly under suspicion. Against the medieval conception of the poor as a conduit for the salvation of the souls of the rich, the early modern state gradually institutes a system of salvation by transformation, enrolling the poor in public works, training and workhouses. If economic success is equated with salvation, then poverty is a sign of sin: idleness, pride or even avarice.

Thus, purgatory informs how societies, states and social-policymakers organize poor-relief. Purgatory becomes a model for the misfortunate, the poor and unemployed to understand their fate, but also inspires welfare planners to create forms of purgatory on earth. Evidently medieval society cared for the poor through direct charity, an economy of grace which spiritually improved the benefactor. Eventually, new modes of dealing with the poor emerge under Protestant states – although the idea of transforming the poor is also a part of renaissance humanism. While not quite the same as workhouses, it is interesting that prisons are often designated as 'penitentiaries' (Throness, 2008); beyond these architectural innovations, the character of city-based poor-relief in northern Europe shifts to an attempt to categorize, supervise and redeem the poor (Michielse and Van Krieken, 1990). For Kahl (2005) there is a distinctive religious patterning to forms of welfare. Catholic countries, up until the twentieth century, maintained informal and religious modes of poverty alleviation; Lutheran countries tended to provide work for the poor as a mode of subsistence and redemption; Calvinist and reformed countries tended to create workhouses or poorhouses to punish and purify inmates.

Purgatory on earth

Workhouses emerge amid a host of other institutions within modernity, whereby the pastoral power of the church and its institutional embodiment in parochial, ecclesiastical and monastic buildings is slowly replaced by the state. From the sixteenth century onwards, barracks, hospitals, prisons, asylums, schools and factories gradually emerge, a process which Foucault describes as 'the Great Confinement'. Incrementally, more elements of life are moved from the community into specialized institutions: sickness, madness and crime and then education and work. Amid these, workhouses exist as institutions for poor-relief but also for the management and punishment of idleness, widely considered as the source of poverty, but a condition which can be transformed through the exertion of power in explicit and subtle ways.

Obviously, the rules of the workhouse impose strict discipline on their inmates, by scheduling their time rigidly – waking, mealtimes, prayer and sleep, often with weekly bathing, health inspections and religious services. Within the workhouse, inmates were forced to conduct themselves in a sober and orderly fashion, even required to be silent at mealtimes. Obviously, work was required at the workhouse, ranging from the hard labour of breaking rock to the monotonous tasks of picking hemp from old ropes. Any slacking, resistance or even high spirits could be punished, from the withdrawal of food to solitary confinement. Essentially, the poverty of the poor, their hunger, was used as a tool to extract compliance from them.

Beyond this, there were more subtle exercises of power: the very architecture of workhouses – especially purpose-built versions in the nineteenth century – was designed to separate and segregate different categories of inmates. Men and women, including husbands and wives, were separated, as were children of a certain age, the feeble and infirm. Entering into the workhouse meant undergoing assessment and categorization; humiliating submission for families who were split up, meaning this really was an institution of last resort. Admission meant accepting the workhouse rules, often donning a uniform and becoming subject to the authority of the master of the house. Leaving was not necessarily an automatic right, but depended on the permission of the governors, who preferred to release inmates to definite employment. Within the workhouse, there were penalties for climbing the high walls that separated different groups. Sleeping was in communal rooms, in rows of neatly observable single beds, and mealtimes were conducted similarly in rows of easily visible inmates who were dispensed food according to regulations – and reduced food was a regular punishment. In some institutions, religious texts were placed on walls and scripture or religious texts read during meals or the evening hour of relaxation. While partially communal and uniform, individual records of each inmate were kept; those who transgressed *and* those who wished to leave after a period of dutiful obedience were equally subject to individual interview and scrutiny to determine their fate – whether moving to the prison or the factory.

Workhouse history is immense and varied and our contemporary imagination is drawn towards the more lurid tales of cruelty, following the Dickensian imagery of *Oliver Twist*. Certainly, this is part of the story; there are reports of workhouse inmates who were labouring at crushing bone for agricultural fertiliser who were so hungry that they stripped marrow and scraps from this waste; there are masters accused and convicted of beating children viciously for minor misdemeanours; some who were classified as vagrants were placed within a cell with a hammer to break rocks until they were small enough to be pushed out through an iron grille over their window. This cruelty cannot be ignored, yet it is not the crucial purpose of the workhouse. All this suffering, from outlandish examples to the ordinary exertion of power, had a purpose, which was to transform the inmates, to give them work discipline by setting up a direct relationship between labour and the satisfaction of bodily needs. This was not an 'economy of grace' to redeem the workhouse masters or board of governors, but an 'economy of suffering' which aimed at transforming the inmates themselves.

Consider, for instance, Jeremy Bentham's *Outline of a Work Entitled Pauper Management Improved*. Perhaps most famous for his utilitarian philosophy – the idea that the morality of any act lies solely in its consequences – Bentham argued that choice was at the centre of human life, and that everyone chose rationally, avoiding pain and seeking pleasure, which thereby opened up human conduct to management and manipulation. Bentham is also a key figure in the history of government, most famously for his disciplinary architecture of the *panopticon* – an ideal prison where inmates were constantly under surveillance, a design which was first an attempt to efficiently oversee workers (Graeber, 2011).

Interestingly, Bentham adapted this architecture to the case of the poor, in his development of an outline of a perfected 'industry house' – a reformed poorhouse designed for redeeming the poor. In *Pauper Management* he specifies in minute detail his plan for a network of institutions for the management of the poor, orphans, widows, the sick, beggars and beyond. Through his disciple Edwin Chadwick, Bentham's ideas were the inspiration for the 1834 Poor Laws and are persistent in welfare policy – especially in the idea that humans will choose whatever is easiest. Bentham exemplifies governmentality, both in terms of Foucault's 'pastoral power' but also in the secondary providence of the state as described by Agamben – Bentham captures his approach deftly: "Sow *causes* and you will reap *effects*" (Bentham, 2010: 422, emphasis in original). The resonances of the phrase are as much religious as agricultural: you reap what you sow.

The goal of 'improving' the existing provision for the poor – a 'reformation of welfare' is clear in *Pauper Management*. Replacing the ad-hoc parish provision for the poor by rates and charity, Bentham envisages a private company, run on profitable lines, aided by legislation and franchised across England. 'Bentham's plan amounted to no less than the levelling out of the business cycle through the commercialization of unemployment on a gigantic scale' (Polanyi, 2001: 112–3) As an enterprise, it will be efficient because of the 'self-liberation principle, whether a man works more or less, makes no difference to the Company; the better he works, the sooner he is out: the less he works, the longer he stays' (Bentham, 2010: 383). Effectively, the poor enter debt slavery within the workhouse, paying for their own subsistence through submission to labour (Graeber, 2011).

A standard building plan is outlined, involving the separation of paupers into different categories and their easy surveillance; exact accounts of food, firewood and every material are projected, a vigilant staff impose discipline: 'The direct and constant exercise of plastic power' – a line from Bentham which anticipates Foucault's 'analytics of power'. Those without means of support will be placed in the industry-house, and only released to secure work; those without visible employment can be coerced into submitting to the workhouse; men can place children and apprentices there, and even their wives with the assent of magistrates. Thus, Bentham is not only concerned with the inmates of his institution, but governing the entire society, the population as a whole.

Initially, the 'industry-house' appears akin to a prison or asylum, but Bentham distinguishes it on the basis that it reforms its inmates, giving them a work ethic, providing them with character references and a connection to the labour market. Craft skills and rudimentary education are offered, such that the author of the plan anticipates that the industry-house will be a popular alternative for the chronically poor who may place their children in it for their betterment. This reformatory, transformatory character is emphasized by Bentham: '*Fiat Lux,* were the words of the Almighty – *Fiat experimentum*, were the words of the brightest genius he ever made. O chemists! Much have your crucibles shown us of dead matter; but our industry-house is a crucible for men!' (Bentham, 2010: 437). While this is a footnote and Bentham rarely makes comparisons with the divine, the idea that the industry-house allows for the growth of knowledge and permits experiments is frequent in the text. In particular, knowledge of humans becomes possible: how they work under different circumstances like diet or temperature; their health, motivation and so forth – a whole range of psychological and sociological questions open up for investigation. Beyond promising knowledge, Bentham claims the potency of transubstantiation – turning paupers into workers as alchemists turned lead into gold.

Pauper Management also criticizes existing poor law as inefficient and counterproductive, not just supporting paupers inadequately but failing to motivate them into work, and thereby creating intergenerational poverty. This singles out charity: 'Every penny spent is the reward of industry: Every penny given, a bounty upon idleness' (Bentham, 2010: 401). The economy of grace in the form of alms for paupers and charity is accused of creating economic and moral problems. Furthermore, existing poorhouses are seen as lacking personalized provision for different cases with different needs:

> The existing poor-houses know of no such distinctions; they know of no such claims. Everything lies prostrate upon the same dead and dreary level: the virtuous and the vicious, the habitual beggar and the man of fallen fortunes, the healthy and the agonizing – all are confounded together, in the poor house as in the grave. (Bentham, 2010: 429)

Repeatedly, sometimes even in tables of comparison, Bentham distinguishes his new industry-house from prisons and other institutions. He emphasizes how individuals can make their transition back to ordinary society swift through hard work. The metaphor of death earlier is telling – there everyone is the same, in a hellish permanent residence – by contrast to the reformatory powers of the industry-house:

> Let it not be imagined that because the *place* is the same, the *treatment* given in it may not be infinitely diversified. There is nothing either in relief or in correction that should render them incapable of being administered – administered to the pinnacle of perfection – within the compass of the same walls. (Bentham, 2010: 420, emphasis in original)

The specificity of treatment is redemptive when fitted to each individual through the close application of discipline or 'plastic power'. Thus, Bentham's industry-house is not hell, but purgatory, a form of purifying suffering.

Perhaps ironically, he describes how the 'Pauper-Population Report' might be read by a minister, in a liturgy, with prayers and thanksgiving, as a gospel and good news. Within his industry-house, Bentham recommends

> a clear conscience, brightened by religious hopes: Seclusion from incentives to sin, and opportunities of sinning – the result of the sobriety of the regimen, the omnipresence of the rulers, and the aggregation and mixture of the guardian classes of the paupers themselves with the susceptible classes. Uninterrupted benefit of divine service. (Bentham, 2010: 481)

Here religion is part of the regimen, yet it is less the explicit content of religion which matters, whether it is preaching or the forbidding of sin; the central rationale of the industry-house is reformatory, transformative. Thus, not only the bodies of the workers but their 'souls' are to be managed and disciplined, by the provision of a purgatory on earth.

From his study of asylums, sociologist Erving Goffman developed the idea of 'total institutions', specially designed places where inmates spent their time in a structured fashion, where existing status and relations were replaced by the categorizations of the institution. Interestingly, most total institutions serve to transform inmates: schools for education, hospitals for healing, prisons for rehabilitation. The process whereby this happens is described by Foucault as 'disciplinary power', distinct from violence or obvious coercion; disciplinary power is exerted through the subtle guiding and governing of inmates, with threats and pressure for non-compliance, but mainly unobtrusively. Times for waking, requirements to walk in single file, standing for prayers, required hygiene, designated work practices and a plethora of other minute and specific regulations serve to 'discipline' the inmate. Partially this is done by exposing them to authority, making them constantly visible, so that any infraction of rules can be noticed and punished; power by surveillance. Over time, this surveillance and the demand for compliance become internalized, the inmate keeps to the required conduct when no one is looking and when they leave the workhouse. Although it is no defence against economic unemployment or structural poverty, the workhouse effectively imposes a work ethic on its inmates – or it pushes them into other total institutions, whether the prison or the asylum.

Echoes of the workhouse can be seen in contemporary welfare provision: for instance, consider Knatchbull's 'workhouse test', whereby the 'idleness' of applicants as demonstrated by their preference for the workhouse over the labour market is a justification for the harshness of the regime within the institution (Fraser, 1992: 40). As a parallel, consider the UK 'work-fitness test', whereby applicants for disability benefits are stringently tested to determine the severity and authenticity of their condition, which has lead to several deaths by heart attack, sometimes during the test, and sometimes induced by stress at being required to seek work or face sanctions after being declared 'fit to work'. These are outrageous practices, but our concern is to capture the intrinsic approach of contemporary welfare.

Historically, workhouses displaced 'outdoor relief', that is, parish and state support in the form of direct subsidies or relief-works for the poor outside any institution. Contemporary welfare does not incarcerate the poor, yet it has a strongly institutionalizing power, governing the unemployed through their 'labour market transition'. Rather than containing a population until they are transformed, the idea is to create an ideal subject – the jobseeker, who adopts the work ethic and stringent self-discipline beyond the welfare office or Jobcentre. Like those entering the workhouse, the unemployed must be categorized: beyond filling out forms, they are subjected to algorithmic sorting to determine their likelihood of finding work, and to psychometric testing to determine what sorts of activation should be dispensed to them. They must comply with mandated jobseeking activities, ranging from generating a new CV to registering with online job-matching services and looking for work. This involves exposing themselves to scrutiny, surveillance and moral judgement; an officer or work coach will examine their experience and skills, and assess their efforts to find work on a weekly or monthly basis – and direct them to education, training or workshops such as 'confidence training' or 'jobseeking skills', including staged interviews. Together, the unemployed are given training which exhorts them to be more active and responsible, akin to the moralizing sermons of old, and individual interviews scrutinize their attitudes and efforts, with their responses recorded on a file which defines them but to which they have limited access or appeal.

Like workhouse discipline, the perspective of the 'master' becomes internalized, perhaps gradually or incompletely, yet many jobseekers come to regard their own lives in terms of the requirement to seek work, to improve themselves and to never waste their time in idleness. Finally, the disciplinary power of the welfare office also relies on hunger: jobseekers who do not comply with directions, even being late for scheduled meetings or failing to provide evidence of their efforts to seek work, can be sanctioned – a reduction or suspension of their benefits or entitlements for a number of weeks, months or even years. This pushes the unemployed to rely on food banks, charity or family members, in some cases becoming homeless, involved in crime or prostitution, or even resorting to suicide. Despite such cases, these sanctions are considered by the institution as a good and necessary punishment, being 'cruel to be kind' or 'for your own good'; and implicitly, general compliance with the processes of activation and demands of jobseeking are guaranteed by the constant background threat of sanctions.

Our suggestion that purgatorial impulses connect workhouses and welfare is not simply a condemnation of cruelty. While the workhouse has many historical horror stories, it is worth remembering that some were run more humanely and that the working conditions within them were not necessarily worse than poverty or exploitation outside them. Our current moral feelings about the dispossession of peasants and the exploitation of early industrialism are not central to the problem of understanding why unemployment is so unpleasant. Clearly, contemporary jobseekers generally only spend around an hour a week or even a month at the unemployment office, far from the 'total institution' described by Goffman. However, the disciplinary power is internalized by the jobseeker, a constant self-scrutiny of jobseeking efforts and abhorrence of idleness, which is implicitly punishable. This is how free time is transmuted into a punishment, a purgatory to be endured.

In concluding the Protestant ethic thesis, Weber describes how Protestantism abolished the monastery but made it so that every man should now be akin to a monk. Our argument is that the logic of purgatory continues from the Poor Laws through to contemporary activation, so that every jobseeker carries the workhouse with them. This logic of a continuous test even infiltrates work in the new millennium; management gurus celebrate this: 'The truth is, no matter what we call it, we are on probation every day at work' (Moran, 2016: 24). Outside of the 'elect' who have secured lifelong contracts, the spectre of welfare purgatory haunts the steps of go-getting, job-changing careerists and precarious workers alike.

The economy of suffering

Seemingly, the guiding principle of contemporary welfare and workfare is 'Whatever does not kill them makes them stronger', to adapt Nietzsche's most quotable axiom. For Nietzsche, one of the greatest peculiarities of our civilization was the positive valuation given to suffering, particularly by Christianity – a religion which he often denounced but also diagnosed as animating modern society. Indeed, our whole approach draws from Weber as inspired by Nietzsche, who famously attempted to understand contemporary morality as a hangover from history. In particular, Nietzsche criticized the 'ascetic priests': those who used suffering and privations of food, sleep or sex as modes of purification or spiritual elevation. Theologies which position suffering as a positive mode of transforming the self, purging sinful habits, have clearly persisted into modernity.

Workhouses institute new forms of pastoral power, not simply admonishing sinners to confess their sins and remedy their behaviour but deliberately imposing certain forms of discipline and punishment upon the poor. Thus, the historical movement here is from an economy of grace to an 'economy of suffering': the target of redemption shifts from the souls of the rich to the souls of the poor. Rather than almsgiving prompting divine forgiveness for the rich, the focus is on governing the lives of the poor. The position of the rich here is more or less coterminous with the role of the governors, those who implement divine providence through the apparatus of the state.

Both of these 'economies' involve making exchanges based on equivalences: in charity, a gift to the less fortunate is somehow commensurate with forgiveness for a certain amount of sin, assuming divine intercession, which depends on genuinely charitable almsgiving. In the punitive economy of suffering, an equivalence is inferred between suffering and redemption. Punishment by imprisonment was relatively unknown in the medieval period, but now the maxim 'You do the crime, you do the time' and a view of incarceration as 'working off your debt to society' seem reasonable, straightforward propositions. Forcing the unemployed to complete certain tasks, threatening them and occasionally making them suffer is now conceived as a pragmatic mechanism of retraining and making people 'job ready'; the underlying idea of purification and redemption is unnoticed but powerful. The supposed sin of idleness can only be expiated by penance, whereby every moment of non-work robs life of its ordinary pleasures, turning time into a burden.

Our argument that the movement of charity to welfare means that the older economy of grace is supplanted by an economy of suffering is more clearly visible where the welfare state is more actively punitive and cruel, interfering with and directing people's lives. Yet, there is still something quite enigmatic about how welfare processes render life and time itself burdens. To understand this, we have to examine ideas about exchange and debt more closely.

A foundational theory in anthropology is 'gift exchange', most famously rendered in Marcel Mauss' book *The Gift*, which contains a strong thesis of how society is bound together by gift relationships because they create continuous loops of interdependency and respect (Mauss, 2000). Within society, people give each other things: food, water, shelter, care, time, attention and so forth, and usually receive something different in return, often reflecting differences in ability or social status; for instance, youths may give labour to elders and receive wisdom, knowledge or culture in return. Gift-relations are not simply a 'social contract', because the exchange is not rigidly determined, instead gifts are simultaneously voluntary and obligatory; they must be given, received and reciprocated, but with flexibility: giving involves customary expectations *and* individual discretion.

The political impact of *The Gift* was considerable; Mauss was a key inspiration for Richard Titmuss, one of the key post-war figures of the UK welfare state. Interestingly, Titmuss declares that 'the grant, or the gift or unilateral transfer...is the distinguishing mark of the social' (1970: 21–22). What is interesting here is the idealistic reading of the gift as given in a spirit of pure generosity; it is 'unilateral' like the grace of God. By contrast, there are more sceptical or even cynical readings of *The Gift*, for instance, the introduction by Mary Douglas (Mauss, 2000) insisting 'there is no such thing as a free lunch', and that all gifts demand a certain return in exchange. Indeed, this approach to welfare is commonplace; even the Fabians – Sidney and Beatrice Webb – intended to oblige the recipients of beneficence to certain forms of behaviour. Or consider Gide in the late nineteenth century, who set out a vision for state welfare in what was to become *L'etat Providence*: 'To modify man by firstly modifying his environment through action by the State understood as the visible expression of the invisible bond uniting living men in the same society' (Charles Gide, 1889, cited in Gane et al, 1993). Here, the idea of the transformability of the individual through governance sits alongside the idea of an invisible bond in society, that is, a providential order. So, two strongly religious ideas are joined together: the larger society will be charitable and thereby elevated, but the individual will be worked upon to become worthy of that support, and repay it in time.

While *The Gift* collates a vast amount of anthropological, historical and mythological material, it is by no means a neutral account, but reflects various religious conceptions of giving, debt, social cohesion and reciprocity. Indeed, Mauss drifts between an idealistic interpretation of the gift as a unilateral grace and an exchange oriented approach: 'There must be more good faith, more sensitivity, more generosity...However, the individual must work. He should be forced to rely upon himself rather than upon others' (Mauss, 2000: 88). Rather than adding to the voluminous debate between the idealistic and sceptical interpretations of gift-relations, it is crucial to recognize both as inspired by religion. On the one hand there is the Covenant, a deal and exchange made with God, a sort of contract where good behaviour is exchanged for liberation from Egypt – and subsequent political and military disasters are presented as punishments for transgression. Yet, on the other hand, there are unilateral gifts, the grace of deliverance from enemies, or forgiveness of transgressions, on promise of reform, and even the unilateral gift of the divine son in a sacrificial exchange, 'to take away the sins of the world'. Something of an exchange mechanism can be seen in the everyday life ethics of Christianity, whereby rituals of confession atone for sins, and good deeds must outweigh sins – likewise faith is measured against doubts.

Whatever the 'spirit' of gift relationships, within their own orbit they produce or construct forms of equivalence in order to facilitate the exchange, because very different things are given and received, for instance, when people 'sing for their supper'. The older economy of grace by charitable almsgiving resolved the asymmetrical nature of the exchange between the benefactor and the beggar by imagining a unilateral gift of grace from God. Within the modern economy of suffering, the gift of welfare benefits is implicitly a debt, repaid only when a new job is found. Accordingly, any form of training or education are also unreciprocated gifts, except insofar as they transform the individual into being 'more employable', which is only manifested properly when they secure a job. Interestingly, many of those we spoke to had become redundant after decades of paying taxes, and for a period this meant that their entitlement was *unconditional*, implicitly a repayment for their long-time contributions, and not subject to demands that they look for work. Attitudes to the unemployed here neatly replicate the logic of exchange.

The enigma of the burden of time experienced by the welfare recipients begins to make sense; every moment of survival without work appears as a sort of debt, a sin, and all pleasures within it are undeserved indulgences. That debt can only be paid off through suffering, which is imaginatively rendered as useful, as equivalent to redemption somehow. The timeline and horizon of unemployment is always uncertain, except for those who are close to retirement or have a contract with a future start date secured. Thus, each day of suffering through time is a contribution to an indefinite, almost limitless process of transformation: *what doesn't kill them will make them stronger*. Along the way, this life of debt creates persistent doubts about the future, making having faith in the labour market a huge challenge; debit and credit here mirror doubt and faith in important ways, and in our next chapter we will explore at greater length how this sets up an interminable pilgrimage through the labour market.

There are darker implications to this economy of suffering: suffering is made equivalent to unemployment benefits and becomes a means for transforming those on welfare. However, this 'economy' extends beyond the welfare office and the jobseeker, to express a larger, political economy. This refers to the peculiar relationship between the state and its citizens; in recent years the gift of tax is increasingly given begrudgingly, in bad spirit, with the suspicion that the state is dispensing it in arbitrary or unproductive ways (Keohane and Kuhling, 2015). To appease taxpayers, the state must demonstrate 'value for money' and that it compels the unemployed to be active jobseekers and will not tolerate slackers or spongers. Here, the darker logic of sacrifice emerges again, whereby the jobless function as scapegoats whose suffering is unifying for the larger polity – alongside many other hapless victims, particularly migrants and minorities in recent years (see Jones, 2012; Kotsko, 2018; Tyler, 2020).

Paradoxically, this moralizing pressure, which creates transformation through suffering, is both religious in inspiration and has a distinctive opposite within theology. While the imperative of purging the self of sin runs through our culture, it is balanced by the opposition to suffering, especially to making sacrifices or scapegoats of others – another form of exchange (Girard, 1987). Theologically, this is also linked to a demand not to judge, not to criticize, indeed to forgive. As an alternative to a purgatorial complex, we will return to this in our conclusion.

Conclusion

Following our analysis of Bentham, contemporary governmentalization of welfare once followed the process of the containment unto transformation of the poor; the unemployed are sequestered, categorized, gathered and secluded until that in itself will change them. This governmentality is partially inspired by the notion of purgatory, drawing on the probationary status of the novitiate into the monastery, the seeker joining the brethren. Thus, they are involved in a game of truth and power, subjected to suffering and surveillance, made to speak, to give voice to the processes occurring within them. Echoing the forms of confession and conversion, these are ways of telling the truth which transform the subject. Historically, these local processes are displaced by the subjectification and socialization of the institution – purgatory follows the jobseeker in their pilgrimage for work. This transformation relies on the providential conditions outside of the institution – job creation, not welfare activation, allows people to escape unemployment. Thus, the contained transformations within workhouses now become the life ethic of jobseeking.

6

Pilgrimage: The Interminable Ritual of Jobseeking

Among those we interviewed, people who moved into jobs occasionally used phrases such as 'It felt like fate' or 'I guess it was just meant to be' when narrating their success. The elation of securing a job tended to obscure the difficulties of previous weeks, months or even years of unemployment, as if everything was 'leading to this moment'. Perhaps these are just clichés which people resort to as shortcuts in storytelling, yet they are still used because an underlying conception of providential fortune animates our culture. Either way, the balance of anxiety and hope which attends jobseeking cannot be ignored; faith in the labour market persists and helps people persist, yet the words of Ecclesiastes might be wiser: 'All is vanity'.

Words and terminology do not correspond neutrally with the objects and things they seek to describe. For instance, people who used to be described as 'unemployed' are now termed 'jobseekers', particularly within social policy documents and in the internal processes of welfare offices. Newspaper reports and popular parlance still prefer the term unemployed, particularly when talking about a group; 'the unemployed' are imagined as a shadowy collection of the jobless, pitiable yet worrisome. The term 'jobseeker' is resolutely focused on the individual and deserves close scrutiny as a 'sign of our times': this change is not a mere name change but reflects a shift in contemporary ideas about work, individuality and unemployment.

Over history, those in need of welfare, whether in the form of parish charity or state subsistence, have been assigned different names; the term 'unemployed' emerges late in the nineteenth century as a new way of thinking about 'the poor' – who were not always treated sympathetically but often conceived of as vagabonds or idlers (Walters,

2000). Folk wisdom suggests that 'the poor will always be with us', and imagines individuals in their families and communities in terms of poverty. By contrast, 'the unemployed' means a fluctuating number, a group of individuals dispersed over a state, temporarily surplus to the requirements of industry. While somewhat cold and statistical, the term 'unemployed' reflected the emerging welfare state imperative for society to support workers who were made redundant.

The term 'jobseeker' focuses in on the individual, as an active person who is striving autonomously to gain employment. Implicitly, they participate in the labour market, locating openings and positions and 'selling themselves' through a burnished CV. They are mobile, socially and geographically, constantly hunting for new contracts and projects or ways to retrain or hone their skills. Any setbacks are a chance to gather feedback and return to seeking work again, undaunted, indefatigable. Jobseekers are not necessarily unemployed; they may well be job changers or upshifters or entrepreneurs (Lane, 2012).

Typically, academic and journalistic commentators either ignore this new category of 'jobseeker' as an insignificant neologism foisted on the unemployed by social-policymakers, or critique the word as 'capitalist ideology'. Obviously, the heroic image of the jobseeker is unrealistic, and for many it represents a myth generated by neoliberalism, of a totally autonomous agent who surfs the market seeking to sell themselves for a better wage, with better conditions. Such jobseekers can be described as 'entrepreneurs of the self', not just involved in enterprise but converting their whole life into a project of self-development; every aspect of identity can be monetized as a portfolio of skills and 'unique selling points'. Rather than settling, the imaginary enterprising jobseeker is constantly on the lookout for better opportunities.

This critique takes into account considerable changes in the world of work. For instance, Boltanski and Chiapello's *The New Spirit of Capitalism* (2005) traces a shift since the 1990s away from secure lifetime contracts towards short-term projects among networks of highly skilled and mobile professionals. Doubtlessly this change is lauded more in management textbooks than it is practiced across the workforce. Arguably, jobseeking is imposed rather than chosen, as employers now offer comparatively fewer secure long-term positions (Standing, 2011). Thus, not only is this image of the jobseeker a myth, it is a difficult economic predicament. Furthermore, the experience of jobseeking is often retold retrospectively, portrayed as worthwhile suffering, as a 'learning experience', a challenge overcome, even a transformation of the self.

Herein, our purpose is not to expose the idea of the 'jobseeker' as illusory, but to understand it as expressing a cultural ideal. There is no totally neutral way to describe the unemployed, even the phrase 'unemployment' emphasizes work as being crucial to personal identity. While the term 'jobseeker' may seem like a glib new description of the situation of the unemployed, it also has deeper historical connotations, and recognizing these is crucial if we are to understand why politicians, policymakers and the public are slowly adopting this new concept.

The term 'jobseeker' clearly emphasizes the active verb 'to seek', as do variants, like 'job hunter', 'career changer' and so forth. Whereas the unemployed are defined by their lack of a job, the jobseeker is defined by their activity of seeking work. Perhaps this seems a trivial difference. Historically, the 1919 ILO defined the unemployed as being 'without, available for, and seeking work', another attempt at a definition which changes over time, and in recent decades there is increased emphasis on 'seeking', as implemented within welfare offices in activation policies. Implicitly, jobseekers are 'active', and there are whole policies focusing on 'activeness'; for instance, Denmark's 1997 *aktiv arbejdsmarkedspolitik* ('active labour market policy act'), which has parallels across the OECD (Hansen, 2019). This activity of seeking is even idealized; phrases like 'job quest' and 'career hero' depict the practice of engaging with the labour market as an exciting journey, not a pleasure cruise but an adventure, where trials are endured bravely on an epic journey towards success and personal transformation.

Yet, this journey is not modelled on a romantic notion of an errant knighthood; rather it is modelled on the idea of pilgrimage. Like purgatory, this religious practice was dismissed by Protestantism and generally appears as a superannuated relic in modernity. If contemporary sociology pays any attention to pilgrimage, it is to explain contemporary mass tourism in its historical context, giving nigh-upon-identical explanations for trips to the Camino de Santiago, Glastonbury and Machu Pichu. By contrast, our argument is that jobseeking, from the early industrial revolution to contemporary welfare activation, is a sublimated version of pilgrimage, which gives a very particular meaning to the trials of jobseeking.

Pilgrim's persistence

The difference between medieval and reformed pilgrimage emerges clearly by contrasting two of the most famous examples in English literature: Chaucer's *The Canterbury Tales* (1387) and Bunyan's *The Pilgrim's Progress* (1678). Their authors had very different lives;

Chaucer was a court poet who composed his rambling tale over several decades, whereas Bunyan was a preacher who wrote his most famous work while imprisoned for his convictions. They use very different form and style: Chaucer roped together a series of adventure stories and bawdy tales, whereas Bunyan has a central protagonist undergoing a series of moral trials. Some of Chaucer's work is lost or incomplete, but in any case the work is an assemblage of tales, each one unique and peculiar, a series which could be added to indefinitely. Bunyan's work has a definitive narrative arc, a progress from the start of pilgrimage to salvation; when he repeats the narrative to include the pilgrim's wife, the story is essentially the same.

In Chaucer's time, pilgrimage was a popular religious ritual, an onerous journey to a distant sacred location. Mainly it was a means to purify the soul for past sins; purgatory in the form of walking, though not always, as it could also be an act of thanksgiving for recovery from illness or undertaken to be released from a vow. Chaucer's tales already express scepticism about the selling of alms, in the rather cynical presentation of the 'pardoner' who effectively sold time off purgatory by papal dispensation. The pardoner is a charlatan and hypocrite: 'I preche nothyng but for coveitise' (l 433, p 471); 'And telle a hundred false japes moore' (l 394, p 470). Through this figure Chaucer criticizes the abuses of pilgrimage: "All my prechyng, is for to make them free [generous] / To give their pennies, and namely unto me. / For my intent is naught but for to wynne, / And nothyng for correction of synne" (l 401–4, p 470, text modernized).

Yet, this is not a critique of the principle of salvation through ritual or almsgiving but of the duplicity of this particular pardoner, whose 'tale' is only a pretext to invite payments. Indeed, the host of the tales threatens to disembowel him, but they eventually 'kiss and make up', and continue on their pilgrimage happily.

Clearly, *The Canterbury Tales* describes individuals joined in religious ritual, rather than integrated and organized communal worship. The ensuing tales are full of idiosyncratic characters, from self-important knights to ebullient housewives. Occasionally authority is mocked or the tables are turned on the powerful, yet for all these glimmers of modern autonomous individuality which might resist power, these tales express a sense of unshakeable 'social order'. While anyone can tell a tale, or even interrupt a speaker, the different 'estates' remain fixed: monks, merchants and millers retain their place and profession.

This is typical of pilgrimages; a sense of communal togetherness animates the group while they are in transit, but this is only temporary (Coleman, 2004; Turner and Turner, 2011). During the journey – a word which covers a vast number of experiences today – people can question the social order, speak freely, ponder the unknown, but arriving home generally means a return to a predictable social structure. However, in the modern world, in the resurgence of pilgrimage on older religious routes and in new forms of travel, pilgrimage is very often oriented towards self-transformation.

Transformation from sinner into saved is central to Bunyan's *The Pilgrim's Progress*, where a 'progress' might mean a walk but with connotations of advance rather than mere rambling. The narrative concerns a long journey undertaken by 'Christian', but there is really no terrestrial destination which he seeks. Rather, the impetus to start walking comes from his realization that his sins are like a burden on his back and that he must change his life or face damnation. From there he passes through a number of trials and tribulations; for instance, the 'slough of despond' where he is tempted to despair, or when he is lured towards the consumptive 'vanity fair' of the marketplace. Whether by his own wise choices or by divine intervention Christian avoids or escapes each of these stumbling blocks. Gradually, his journey purifies him, reducing the burden on his back, incrementally cleansing him of the sins which lead him into trouble; for instance, his pride gets him into a tangle with a giant, but by the end of the narrative he seems able to decipher danger or temptation in advance.

Although fictional, *The Pilgrim's Progress* is also a work of popular theology, which explicitly offers an interpretation of trials and tribulations as a means by which God tests his subjects: 'His forbearing at present to deliver them is on purpose to try their love; whether they will cleave to him to the end' (Bunyan, [1678] 1965: 53). Life is not a series of random events, nor is society a loose assemblage of individuals, nor is the natural world itself indifferent; rather, all of these things are recognized as 'creation', a testing ground for the individual soul. Accidents, misfortune, challenges, inequality and all sorts of economic woes are not just inconvenient facts but the source of trials and tribulations which hold out the possibility of self-transformation.

First, life as pilgrimage entails continuous tests and tribulations. These may be varied or repetitive, but they are certainly recursive, and the trial is never decisively complete: 'The trials that those men do meet withal / That are obedient to the heavenly call, / Are manifold and suited to the flesh / And come, and come, and come again afresh' (Bunyan, [1678] 1965: 66). Thus, the pilgrimage does not end decisively at a destination, but is always 'until further notice'; death itself is just another step in the divine testing and judging of the soul.

Second, this form of trial is purgative, purifying the soul of previous sins or misdemeanours, a series of 'salutary life lessons' in modern parlance, yet noting the religious sense of 'salutary' as 'salvation'. Thus, a pilgrimage is a penitential transformation, not a metamorphosis but a salvation or redemption which assumes there is a core to the self from which sins are shriven or sloughed off. The cultural distinction between the true or core self and inessential habits or tendencies has a long history in the West, within theology and beyond. Modern philosophers and contemporary neuroscientists have sought to debunk this distinction, but our aim is to understand it. Narrating one's life as a trial means distinguishing between the core self and mere appearance, but most especially it involves retrospective narration, describing the past as error, as per the hymn: 'I once was lost, but now am found, once blind, but now I see'. Difficulty, danger and even disaster appear as opportunities to test oneself, to 'become a better person', as the slogan goes.

Thirdly, this pilgrimage involves an interpretative effort, alongside his 'progress', Christian continuously has to decipher the world around him, detecting temptations and dangers, and recognizing the will and intervention of God. As a literary fable, the reader is drawn into this effort to understand, and although Bunyan is often didactic, there are also many symbolic incidents, akin to parables which provoke insight. Once life is considered a pilgrimage, banal or random events can be taken as evidence of providential intervention: if one gets a new job it was 'meant to be' – and even redundancy is an event to be deciphered in terms of its personal meaning; 'A world in which it was necessary to decipher hidden truths that showed themselves by hiding and hid by showing themselves, that is to say it was a world that was filled with ciphers to be decoded' (Foucault, 2007: 236) Thus, personal choice and actions become fundamental; no matter what structural changes are happening in the labour market, the narrative of the individual pilgrim prevails.

Absent from Bunyan's narrative is Chaucer's depiction of collective camaraderie, whereby everyone appears to be on the road together, and as the contemporary road-trip movie has it: 'What goes on the road stays on the road'. Solidarity and transformation through friendship play little role in personal salvation – although Bunyan's pilgrim does make friends, these usually fall by the wayside, and he abandons wife and children at the outset of the narrative – they are rejoined in the sequel, but without criticizing Christian, rather the failure of his wife to follow him is the problem! What matters here is that the institution of jobseeking takes on the individualistic spirit of pilgrimage, where personal journey and transformation overshadow communal concerns. Conceiving life as a pilgrimage, like purgatory, is an individualizing aspect of Christian religion: 'The self basically appeared as the aim, the end of an uncertain and possibly circular journey – the dangerous journey of life' (Foucault, 2005: 250). Just as Weber saw monastic work ethics spread through capitalism, or purgatory became incarnated in reformatory institutions, pilgrimage is no longer a self-contained ritual but permeates life itself.

Herein, our aim is to understand how pilgrimage, among other factors, shapes how jobseeking and careers are understood in the contemporary labour market. In our interviews we came across individuals whose tenacity and commitment to seeking work was extraordinary; there were single parents enduring cycles of precarious work and welfare, or men nearing retirement who were willing to retrain in new industries.

One woman who had left school and been constantly unemployed for over two decades had good results in a series of training courses, but because she had no experience, she never succeeded in job interviews: "I have never actually got away from the system, I would give anything to get away from the system". Nevertheless, she continued to pursue her career, even though it seemed like "chasing the carrot" with dwindling prospects, as employers tended to focus on her lack of experience. Yet she carried on, enduring the difficulties of unemployment and poverty, still hopeful. Partly, her actions can be explained by the threat of sanctions, and she was cut off for twelve weeks without support on one occasion, but she was clearly doing more than just "going through the motions". To understand her life and choices and motivation, we need to understand the ethos which gives meaning to jobseeking: pilgrimage. First, we must examine how pilgrimage moved from being an occasional ritual into a model for life itself.

Life and pilgrimage

The origins of pilgrimage are ancient and widespread, pre-existing the world religions, found in tribal societies across the globe and possibly even among prehistoric peoples. Archaic sites such as Stonehenge or Gobekli Tepe were not necessarily permanent settlements but probably the centres of annual festivities, where the assembly of ever larger numbers of hunter-gatherer tribes may have spurred on the development of agriculture (Horvath and Szakolczai, 2019). Sites of cave paintings, Lascaux and Chauvet may have been the sites of periodic pilgrimage. The Camino de Santiago, where hordes of both Christians and non-Christians walk today, may have been a pilgrimage route several thousand years ago.

This vast history and geography straddles a swathe of cultural differences, so the term 'pilgrimage' needs to be specified, or else it might include any movement of any people. Inevitably, there are no neutral definitions; our theoretical frameworks are themselves inescapably informed by Christian models of pilgrimage, but these are also most appropriate to our topic. Following our earlier chapters on how historical models shape the present, it is also necessary to recognize that any religious model of pilgrimage has been transformed over the centuries, and that it shapes our supposedly secular times in very peculiar ways.

Within Christianity, pilgrimage is clearly a form of ritual. To go on pilgrimage involves stepping outside of ordinary life, from the profane into the sphere of the sacred. In Durkheim's classic *The Elementary Forms of Religious Life* (1995), this distinction between the sacred and the profane was central to defining religion. However, his account of ritual tends to describe mere ceremonies which always serve to create social cohesion and ensure collective belief. A much more dynamic account of ritual is found in the work of the anthropologist Victor Turner (1969). Tellingly, he views rituals as transformative, from tribal societies through to the modern world.

Frequently a ritual confirms a change which is already underway, giving cultural meaning to the passing of the seasons, the birth or death of humans and so forth. Such rituals typically involve the whole of the community, and occur locally, sometimes at designated sacred spaces. Occasionally rituals give shape to changes which are less definitively marked; for instance, confirming a relationship through marriage, or a ritual of initiation for those who are 'coming of age'. Thus, rituals do not simply reflect changes, they make them happen through a persuasive social performance (Alexander, 2004). Beyond the glib phrase 'social construction', rituals effectively 'socially construct' *something*. This is especially visible in rituals within politics; for instance, declaring war, elevating a chief or royal coronations.

How exactly do rituals work? For Turner, rituals are 'liminal', a phrase which literally refers to a threshold, boundary or limit. Ordinarily society is structured, that is, composed of groups and individuals with well-defined statuses and relations, with regular processes and routines, predictable institutions and so forth. However, society never runs like clockwork, like an abstract system, but it is periodically challenged and renewed by change, even from within itself. Thus, a liminal ritual is one where structures are transformed.

There are three relatively distinct phases of any ritual: first, some structures must be suspended, and ordinary life temporarily is interrupted, as either the whole community or those undergoing the ritual begin to behave differently. Second, in the properly 'liminal' period, some sort of performance is enacted, usually something transformative; a couple are wedded, a baby is named, youths undergo a test and come of age, someone passes into the 'next life' or perhaps an individual becomes a leader. Only in this threshold, when structured, ordinary life is suspended, are such transformations possible. Finally, the whole community finishes the ritual by acknowledging the change, often by feasting and celebrating, but certainly reflecting the new status or reality which was created through the ritual.

To modern sensibilities rituals often seem decidedly alien or irrational. Changing social arrangements hardly seems to require these elaborate, colourful, emotionally charged events of symbolic performance. For instance, Boltanski (2011: 83) describes rituals as formulaic or wooden ceremonies. Of course, this antipathy itself is not outside cultural history but is informed by our inheritance of both Puritan rejection of 'pomp and ceremony' and the prophetic critique of 'idolatry'. However, the strangeness of rituals, the feeling that they are merely empty ceremonies, and the absence of meaningful rites of passage in our society today is also part of the broader history which this book is concerned with. Rituals of leaving school, gaining work, apprenticeship, promotion, redundancy or retirement are absent or weak in modern society.

Turner's conception of liminal rituals is immensely influential and quite simple and flexible: a rite must have a beginning, middle and end, and something must be changed by it. Additionally, this is a welcome antidote to overly 'structural' accounts of society which give the impression that individuals are created and constrained by a 'system' (Thomassen, 2013).

Yet, within this persuasive account of ritual, there are complex implications: any ritual starts with the suspension of structure, but this is not necessarily as simple as taking a holiday from routine. To suspend structure is to separate people from their status and relationships, so that identity and being appear flexible or even arbitrary. Such an experience is perhaps initially thrilling, a burst of freedom from rigid society, but also full of existential uncertainty and danger. When structure is suspended, individuals necessarily must reflect, question and even doubt their own culture and society – the 'dark night of the soul' or 'fear and trembling'. Balancing this, Turner emphasizes the camaraderie of rituals, which he terms *communitas*, that is, a community without structure, as people share in the collective experience. Strikingly, the experience of a ritual is approximately equivalent to 'liberty, equality, fraternity', the slogan of the French Revolution, a clearly liminal transformation (Sewell, 1996). Basically, being on the road together in pilgrimage generates solidarity.

The central phase of a liminal ritual is peculiar: most obviously there are symbolic performances; for instance, an exchange of rings, immersion in water or a crowning. Many rituals also involve a sort of a test or a trial, particularly those for 'coming of age'; in order to become adults, the youth must prove themselves worthy. In tribal societies this might have been through heroic athleticism, whereas in the modern world it is through educational attainments. A ritual gives meaning to suffering and difficulty, often incurred deliberately; Turner highlights the Indo-European root *per* within 'suffer', meaning to undergo something, to pass through. Giving meaning to experience is precisely what happens in a 'symbolic performance' – objects, acts and words take on a special and transformative character. Saying 'I do' only involves a self-transforming and lifelong commitment if it is said in special ritual circumstances. Generally, such ceremonial performances are predictable and meaningful, but the urge to interpret, to find meaning in events, even small details, incidents or accidents, emerges from rituals.

Finally, a ritual returns to ordinary life, through celebration, which seems relatively straightforward. Usually structure is renewed, rejuvenated through ritual, yet, perhaps, if the performance is not convincing, or the suspension of structures prolonged, the experience of liminality may begin to pervade ordinary life, the feeling that everything is 'socially constructed'. The *perigrinatio* – Latin for pilgrimage – may become permanent. Of course, the successful conclusion and meaningful character of a ritual is generally assured by tradition and by the 'masters of ceremony', the shamans or priests who oversee its various stages and supervise the symbolic performance.

Christian pilgrimage

Christian pilgrimage corresponds to this three-phase model, with a beginning, middle and end. First there is the departure, usually announced in advance and prepared for through confession and prayer. Second, there is the journey itself, a long and arduous test and trial, punctuated by waymarks and roadside shrines, with succour and shelter provided by a network of monasteries, culminating in the arrival at the destination or shrine, where devout or even ecstatic worship takes place. Finally, there is the return home, to resume ordinary life, but implicitly the returning pilgrim is transformed. Of course, there is a vast variety over centuries of Christianity, influenced by Jewish practices and Graeco-Roman precedents. Different geographies and changing institutions also alter the character of pilgrimage, yet there are also continuities. Initially, pilgrimage was mainly to Jerusalem, to witness the scenes of the biblical narrative, even if they were in disrepair, rebuilt or mere artifice. Another variety of early pilgrimage was to seek out anchorites, monks who had travelled into the wilderness to escape the temptations and distractions of the world, who ironically found themselves surrounded by devotees.

Popular penitential Christian pilgrimage has medieval roots, emerging slowly but distinctly from the Dark Ages, but was strongly enough established by the turn of the first millennium to form part of the preaching of the First Crusade and the main basis of the ill-fated 'Children's Crusade'. Going on pilgrimage was genuinely risky – a pilgrim was often presumed dead if they did not return within a year and a day. As roads became more secure in the more stable late Middle Ages, pilgrimages became commonplace, and Pope Boniface proclaimed a jubilee for 1300: a special remittance of sins for pilgrims to Rome. This jubilee, where sins, like debts, are forgiven, is repeated in 1350, 1390, 1423, 1450, and then regularized to occur every twenty-five years. Pilgrim routes and destinations become more varied over the centuries, as the birthplaces of saints gave way to more popular urban centres where holy relics were preserved.

What distinguishes a pilgrimage from a mere journey is that it is supposed to be a transformative ritual. Travelling the long road to the sacred shrine implicitly purges the individual of their sins or repays the grace of God in alleviating illness. Of course, such an abacus of purification, walking in exchange for holiness, was occasionally criticized by church figures, such as Gregory of Nyssa or at the Council of Nicea in 432, but eventually pilgrimage was institutionalized as a form of penance required after confession, as a technique of redemption. The *peregrinatio*, or the journey, by foot or by sail, always through danger, serves as a sort of trial of physical fortitude and spiritual faith. Rather than simply travelling through space, the pilgrim undergoes a symbolic journey, detecting providential intervention in the passing scene, the weather or chance encounters; setbacks can appear as a further test, good luck as a surety of divine favour. Arriving at the destination, seeing the shrine and the holy places is an experience of the presence of the divine – in the sense that pilgrims attribute special symbolic qualities to buildings, places or objects. Often pilgrims walk in circles around particular holy places, partake of divine waters or go through special passages, to participate in the sacred place. After some days of worship the pilgrim will return home, perhaps along the same route, but now having been transformed. Pilgrims are purified, even sanctified, surrounded with the air of the holy place they have visited. Often they bring home a souvenir or memento, which symbolizes their transformation, and thereafter, the narrative of life is punctuated by the pilgrimage; it becomes the watershed date of 'before and after', which gives meaning to life.

Much contemporary scholarship attempts to compare medieval pilgrimage with modern tourism, and certainly the parallels are obvious. Indeed, the word 'holiday' derives from the religious 'holy day'. However, we do not aim to identify approximations of pilgrimage in contemporary society, and clearly economic journeys such as migrant labour, internships and 'gap years' are very different cases. Rather, the question is how the model of pilgrimage informs how jobseekers interpret the labour market.

Despite the persistence of Christian pilgrimages, clearly the practice declined after the Reformation. This is partially due the hostility of Luther, Calvin and many other Puritans to rituals, especially those which involved the corruption of faith through alms. There was vague scriptural precedent for forms of pilgrimage in Deuteronomy, and some Protestants maintained forms of pilgrimage while theologically eschewing any worship of saints or icons. Famously, the Puritans arriving in America are called the 'Pilgrim fathers', and many colonial journeys are understood through biblical metaphors; for instance, John Gray in *Goode Speede to Virginia* (cited in Linebaugh and Rediker, 2000: 29) compares the English venture to the conquest of Canaan.

Interestingly, England is strongly culturally Protestant after the ravages of the Civil War, if less theologically so (Voegelin, 1969). Ideas of pilgrimage are popular and commonplace, as per Bunyan's book. Between then and 1830, agricultural lands were comprehensively enclosed, dispossessing peasants and making them into the proletariat of the Industrial Revolution. How the jobseekers of this great labour market understood their experience is largely unrecorded, but the idea of a great trial and going 'off to seek your fortune' clearly combine together here.

Among Christian rituals, pilgrimage is idiosyncratic: while most rituals take place within local communal bounds, the pilgrim goes from one Christian church to a distant holy shrine, departing from their community as an individual. Of course, most pilgrimages involve groups of travellers, banded together for safety and mutual support, but generally they are strangers to one another, creating the possibility for 'communitas' (Turner, 1969). Yet, these groups were not composed of neighbours or parishioners, and pilgrimage is not like the duty to go to Mecca, indeed, most medieval peasants probably never undertook a journey longer than a local one-day 'pattern' for a saint's day. Thus, pilgrimage is already individualizing, setting the pilgrim apart from their parish; by necessity they depart from their local priest and only briefly meet other masters of ceremony along the way in monasteries or at the destination.

Despite the popular historical picture of medieval Europe as a 'collectivist' culture, Christianity has distinctly individualizing tendencies; while there are some communal rites, salvation is an individual matter. This old debate of communal versus individual, structure versus freedom, does not concern us here. What really matters is how pilgrimage as an idea becomes decoupled from its ritual boundaries. This happens in obvious ways, such as the proliferation of travel for trade, war, colonialism and even pure curiosity. More important here is how the three stages of the ritual of pilgrimage become diffused as models for life in general, becoming repetitive and chronic; a sort of permanent pilgrimage.

The idea of life as a journey through this world has precedent in the Church fathers and in the Old Testament, where wandering, exile and journeys are prominent. For instance, Augustine describes life as a constant pilgrimage away from God: 'As long as I am away from you, during my pilgrimage I am more aware of myself than of you' (1961 10: 5, p 208). Thus the subject is forced to reflect on themselves. Furthermore, this is a period of testing: 'Is not our life on earth a period of trial. For who would wish for hardship and difficulties?' (Augustine, 1961: 10:28, p 232). This influential conception of life as alternating between sinning and confessing exhorts an ethos of constant self-reflection and atonement, in acts of charity as discussed earlier, and interminable efforts in the labour market.

Protestantism revived this idea of life as a trial. Quite distinctively, Protestant conceptions of salvation through 'faith alone' mirror the first stage of pilgrimage. As detailed in Chapter 4, Calvinists must look anxiously for signs of salvation, as only the elect are predestined for heaven, and they must decipher God's blessings and tests of faith. While 'good deeds' play a prominent role in Protestantism, 'faith alone' comes to eclipse rituals like prayer, fasting, charity or pilgrimage as the means of salvation.

What is faith? Beyond the vast theological debate there are numerous subjective meanings of 'faith', and broadly, the experience of faith means a hopeful disposition towards or even certitude about God. 'Now faith is the substance of things hoped for, the evidence of things not seen' (Hebrews 11.1). Certainly, a positive attitude for jobseekers! More importantly, faith provides a sort of interpretation of events: things become symbols, signs of a transcendent power – even setbacks and adversity can represent the will of God in the form of a test. To go on pilgrimage involves an imaginative leap, seeing physical things like roads or the wilderness as purifying trials, interpreting certain buildings or objects on arrival as spiritually sanctified. Crucially, *you must see it for yourself*. Like Protestant Bible reading, salvation is personal; even if there are charismatic pastors, ultimately the individual is responsible for themselves.

Rituals have a climactic symbolic performance, and similarly a pilgrimage culminates in the arrival at a destination. Yet, if life is a continuous pilgrimage, then there is no ultimate destination, except mortality. As the modern quip has it: 'It's not the destination, it's the journey'. Thus no single event is decisive or central, whether falling in love, landing a dream job, a career highlight or a personal victory, none of these are conclusions, only peak experiences – there are always further challenges. After jubilation, the afterglow fades, and the journey resumes anew in search of another goal. Rather than the ritual moving towards a conclusion, it is short-circuited quickly back to the first phase: another test, another trial, another transformation of the self.

Weber's Protestant ethic thesis concludes with the image of the 'iron cage', a metaphor for how the ideal of work in a vocation becomes twisted into a cold, rational, joyless pursuit of profit. Weber analyses the paradox whereby 'the care for external goods should only lie on the shoulders of the "saint like a light cloak, which can be thrown aside at any moment". But fate decreed that the cloak should become an iron cage' (1992: 181). While it is easiest to see the iron cage in the form of bureaucracies or large corporate organizations, the metaphor also points towards pilgrimage. A pilgrim visits a saint or their relics, but is also themselves 'sanctified'; the source of the earlier quote within the quote is the Puritan Richard Baxter who distinguished between the 'saints' and 'worldlings', that is, the reformed faithful and the corrupt followers of worldly powers. Strikingly, the 'light cloak' is the characteristic garb of the pilgrim. Thus, the iron cage is not just an external set of rules and regulations but an internalized discipline, whereby the career-oriented modern worker cannot rest but is compelled to constantly seek achievements.

Perhaps our focus on jobseekers constantly seeking for career attainment seems unbalanced, considering that many people attain settled and stable careers, sometimes within quite fixed professions. Nonetheless, more workers than ever before are involved in more career changes than ever before across the world, due to recessions, restructuring and career complexity (Standing, 2011; Gershon, 2017). So, while the ritual of job-hunting may appear to be over once employment is secured, what matters is the character of the transformation – a test which reshapes the malleable subject. Pilgrimage is a penitential ritual, wherein the self is purified of sins through the difficulties of the journey. Indeed, the transformation which interests us here is not the attainment of a new status, like being given a new job title and responsibilities; rather it is the purging of the old self, how the individual must jettison their existing identity, with all its assumptions and expectations, to be *remade*, stepping out into the void of the labour market. This is clearly evident in both career-change guidebooks and the manner in which jobseeking is managed by unemployment offices.

Job pilgrimages: penance, waymarks and the Promised Land

A spatial journey is abundantly clear in certain forms of work: historically, some European apprentices travelled with few possessions from master to master to hone their craft and test themselves – a practice which persists as an exception to the rule of jobseeking in the labour market. Contemporary instances include a 'gap year' working away from home, or managers of franchises travelling to headquarters for training or team building through 'away days'. Yet what matters here is the individualized and internalized model of pilgrimage, a career of intermittent jobseeking at the behest of welfare offices or Jobcentres. There are three elements here: first, life is envisaged as a journey of self-transformation; whether a career is continuous or fractured, it is a mode of 'self-actualization' in Maslow's terminology, rather than simply a means of making ends meet. Second, on this journey, individuals employ interpretative categories, hoping to find meaning in their experiences, detecting symbols and waymarks along their path. Third, suffering and setbacks encountered along the way are broadly interpreted as trials and tribulations to be overcome, ways of improving the self, perhaps clues about the need for redoubled efforts, but never as cause for despair. Negatives are turned into positives. Thus, even when a job pilgrimage is undertaken at the behest of a welfare office which forces claimants to search for and accept any job, this activity is given meaning as a penitential and transformative process.

Herein we examine how the idea of pilgrimage persists in a variety of sources, from policy documents about jobseekers through to their own words. This is not to claim that jobseekers are actually thinking of pilgrimage or know anything about its long history, but rather that the model of pilgrimage, as outlined earlier, is reflected in their words. Indeed, seeking work need not be a pilgrimage, for instance, if it consisted simply in being available and making applications within a limited economic sector (Sharone, 2013), but within post-Christian cultures, these resonances are unmistakeable. Importantly, when examining how individuals interpret and describe seeking work, there are many other ideas at play; our contribution is to recognize pilgrimage as a pattern which helps people make sense of their experiences *and* how social policy governs the lives of others.

Penitential pilgrims: first steps

The logic of pilgrimage is visible even within the most impersonal documents of welfare; for instance, the UK Jobseeker's Allowance: Back to Work Scheme guide (JSABWS1, 2018). Functionally, this document explains the various options which unemployed people may consider while seeking to return to work, in conjunction with their 'work coach', a more entrepreneurial term which has replaced 'case officer', another change of emphasis from the administration of support to the pursuit of a job through coaching – work upon the self which is now ubiquitous in modern culture (Marquis, 2016).

Before examining these various schemes, it is worth noting that the work coach does not just give access to various schemes but holds the power of recommending a sanction, a cut or suspension of welfare payments for a period of varying severity. Just as pilgrimage was prescribed as a penance, jobseeking is required on threat of suffering. The obligation to comply with the instructions of the work coach or face sanctions is set out in detail after each scheme is outlined, and the mechanisms of sanctions are set out in detail over several pages (JSABWS1, 2018). Differences in the levels of possible sanctions are outlined but what is most striking is the very high minimum threshold required of all jobseekers: repeatedly, the document demands that a jobseeker must 'do all you can to find work'. The 'contract' between the Jobcentre and the jobseeker is described as one in which supports are offered, because 'most people do all they can. If you don't your benefit payment could be temporarily stopped'. So the effort required is implicitly limitless, extending to every waking moment, each action, all possible resources a person may have. Thus, while a pilgrimage sets out a stern test of individual fortitude, the contemporary pilgrimage of jobseeking potentially demands even more: an unlimited duty to an indefinite process. In reality, few jobseekers do absolutely 'all they can', but engage in reasonable efforts to find suitable work; there are limits to what efforts might actually be useful. Yet, in our interviews with jobseekers, the possibility of being sanctioned for any moment of idleness clearly weighs upon them as a constant anxiety.

By setting out a variety of Back to Work Schemes – all the while requiring claimants do 'all they can' to seek work – the Jobcentre indicates a pathway for jobseekers. Indeed, the metaphors of pathways, routes, 'taking the first steps' or 'starting a journey' suffuse the documents which the state uses to govern the labour market. Through these schemes, the Jobcentre provides a model for jobseeking as a process of self-transformation. The most elementary among these are training in 'skills', specifically literacy, numeracy and customer service, a sort of remedial intervention which is primarily aimed at ensuring 'work readiness' by 'building confidence'. Such a course is prescribed after the work coach has assessed the jobseeker, by examining their experience, qualifications and personal characteristics – sometimes using algorithms. Here the jobseeker does not even encounter the labour market, but must engage in reflection on their inner potential – implicitly unfulfilled – and their implied failings and need for self-improvement. Working on skills is not simply adding competencies or building human capital but a sort of remedial intervention, akin to penance to redeem the unworthy.

Beyond enrolment in skills training, a work coach can recommend a traineeship or sector-based work academy programme. Each of these connects the jobseeker directly to the labour market, because they are working for an employer, though possibly without proper remuneration. Clearly, these schemes do not constitute a guaranteed stepping stone to an actual job; there *may* be an interview, but the jobseeker is only assured of 'experience' or 'confidence building'. Rather than a state-sponsored apprenticeship scheme with a predictable outcome, these schemes deliver cheap labour to employers, through interns who serve their time but are merely candidates at interviews to whom the employer owes nothing more than 'feedback'. Despite coercive governmentality, the liberal principle holds in the labour market; the jobseeker sells their labour in competition against others. The state presumes this will 'unlock the great potential of young people', implicitly an attempt to transform them. More importantly, the whole process is akin to setting off on pilgrimage: an initial trial by work, testing one's mettle, giving a chance of success but a guarantee of feedback – signals to be interpreted. And in the background, there is always the possibility of sanction.

Waymarks: the path to self-transformation

Internet job websites are unabashedly positive, presenting enticing images of possibility, a new horizon, a perfect fit or a bright future. Within these formats there are also various advice forums which deserve close scrutiny; these are generally quite standardized, with formulaic advice on CV preparation, making applications, cover letters and personal statements and tips for interviews (Gershon, 2017). This involves shaping the self, but also scrutinizing opportunities: 'The trick to a winning personal statement is to tailor it to the job role you're applying for.'[1] Such brief advice columns are distillations of book-length jobseeking advice tomes, and occasionally make reference to psychological or marketing research, lending them a mild 'scientific authority'. Quite who reads such articles is hard to know, but they are a standard part of most websites and have to cater not only to those who have just uploaded their CV or applied for their first job but also those who have been repeatedly rejected and are browsing with greatly diminished hopes.

While mainly upbeat and pragmatic, these columns do acknowledge the difficulties of jobseeking: 'Job-hunting is a frustrating and stressful time for anyone',[2] or 'Fact: nobody enjoys job hunting'.[3] Having recognized the difficulties of jobseeking, the trials of pilgrimage, these articles always recommend redoubled efforts or new tactics. Often they prescribe self-scrutiny, to discover the faults within the jobseeker themselves, or a change of direction, finding new avenues for job searching, pursuing a job in a different sector or for less money. The jobseeker is expected to put on a brave face, managing the experience of constant disappointment and a lengthening bout of unemployment, and always put their best foot forward, take on a positive attitude and sell themselves, particularly in interviews – described as 'emotional labour' by Hochschild (2003). Thus, the jobseeker is repeatedly almost arriving at the shrine of their pilgrimage, the long-sought-after job, but nothing is certain; this may well be another dead end or false dawn, yet they must keep the faith.

Whether an individual jobseeker actually gets a job depends on the quality of the other candidates and the decision of hiring panels. Yet, how the outcomes of this complex and impersonal labour market are interpreted is curious: the highly contingent and even random process of getting a job is constantly interpreted as reflecting the jobseeker's individual character, actions and choices. Advice on these websites encourages readers to make sense of events in particular ways; for instance, '7 Warning Signs That a Job Is Not for You',[4] or advice about how to decipher what an interview board really wants and who really holds the power to hire or fire.

Most importantly, jobseekers are instructed to react to their failure to secure employment through an intense interpretative effort. They must decipher what went wrong:

> So, you didn't get the job – ask yourself, why not? Take some time to sit down and think over the interview, what were the strong points, and what were some of the questions you struggled with?[5]

> It's happened. You got home from an interview that you thought went well and you receive the phone call saying that unfortunately you were not successful this time. You've gone from a high to a low in a matter of seconds and your confidence has been knocked and you feel you are back to square one. However, this isn't necessarily the case. You should be asking yourself (and the interviewer if possible) why you were declined, and then working to improve those areas so you can be successful in your next interview. This process of learning from your mistakes is incredibly powerful and will be the key to progressing your career.[6]

Here, the labour market is not a simple market transaction wherein levels of supply and demand create prices. Nor is it simply matching skills and experiences to opportunities. For the unemployed, jobseeking is not just a relentless flurry of filling in applications or even of tailoring CVs; it is an indefinite effort of self-reflection requiring persistent hope. Readers are instructed to scrutinize their memories and evaluate the course of the interview as an encounter. Rejection is instructive: in the earlier longer quote, the old religious idea that suffering is edifying and improving emerges.

Explicitly in this advice, even dead ends and disappointments are part of the journey of jobseeking. Beyond simply securing employment, the whole process of finding a job is imagined as a personal transformation: 'Sometimes unlearning the things we've come to believe about ourselves can make the biggest difference' (O'Callaghan, 2009). Many career guides describe jobseeking as a form of personal growth, not just change, but self-overcoming, so a jobseeker can escape from the 'box' or 'rut' which previously limited their horizons (Boland

and Griffin, 2015). This is also reflected in the contemporary idea of 'networking', wherein all family, friends and even chance encounters are taken as an opportunity to find clues, follow leads, make connections and thereby gain employment. Thus, the whole of society becomes a landscape of jobseeking, a wilderness of life wherein the signs and waymarks on the personal pilgrimage trail can be detected – either as guides to future tactics or in retrospect to explain how one gained a job.

Perhaps these comparisons between pilgrimage and jobseeking occasionally seem a little strained; conversely, the logic is sometimes made absolutely explicit, for instance in jobseeking advice books which position redundancy as a 'gift' or opportunity for self-transformation, or cryptically suggest that 'everything happens for a reason' or even that the unfortunate *jobless* reader has been chosen to undergo this trial because they are stronger than their peers. Indeed, the international bestselling *What Colour Is Your Parachute?* was written by Richard Bolles, an evangelist who explicitly endorsed a religious interpretation of work and unemployment – and this text has been reprinted and updated annually since 1970. Not only did he endorse the Protestant ethic of hard work in a vocation as an expression of God's will, but he declared that unemployment was a trial sent to test our faith and finding a job a mixture of hard graft and the intervention of the invisible hand. 'Make something beautiful out of our suffering', he suggests as a prayer in one of his last articles. Of course, most jobseeking advice texts are shorn of any religious echoes, but the advice they give is identical, and the meaning they give to unemployment and jobseeking is wholly compatible with such providential interpretations.

Beyond practical guides to the distinct task of jobseeking, some texts reconsider the career itself as an enterprise; for instance, Hakim's *We Are All Self-Employed* (1994). Drawing from management gurus such as Tom Peters, Charles Handy, Peter Drucker and others, Hakim is a career coach who recommends that all workers should refuse to become 'trapped' in dependency by a formal employment contract which narrowly defines their role. This involves challenges, struggles, disappointments and eventual triumphs: 'Conscious loneliness is part of the journey' – and what sort of a journey is this? One of constant self transformation: 'The closer you are to who you are, the more responsibility and empowerment you have' (Hakim, 1994: 170). Here the Protestant work ethic becomes a dedicated lifelong pilgrimage. Interestingly, Hakim also describes the work of jobseeking and self-transformation as heavily interpretative, a matter of introspection and 'reframing' one's situation, constantly learning from failures, taking risks and finding meaning, even in suffering through unemployment and other setbacks.

What goes on the road ...

Contemporary research into the lives of the unemployed or precarious workers often emphasizes resistance or critique; it foregrounds how individuals question the categories they are placed into as stigmatizing or unjust, how they negotiate the various hoops they are forced to jump through by Jobcentres. Several people we spoke to objected to systems of activation; for instance, one said, "I cannot describe my fury when I saw that job was re-advertised as an internship". Some indicated that there were jobs they would be unwilling to take, even if pressured by the threat of sanction, for instance, 'sweeping the streets', and perhaps jokingly, prostitution. Others described a continuous, indefinite job search, chasing work all the time, not receiving a reply, imagining their carefully prepared CVs being put straight into the bin. One person described their daily struggle: "Frantically looking for jobs online for two hours every morning, and then crying into your Coco Pops because you can't find anything, that has been, that is the routine". This experience of jobseeking is far from the heroic quest of overcoming challenges and becoming a better person but involves continuous suffering and disappointment.

To counterbalance this sense of jobseeking as a struggle bordering on despair there are elements of hope – the dynamic of economic activity identified by Pecchenino's (2011, 2015). For instance, 'Bob', made redundant during the great financial crash from a mechanical job, became long-term unemployed and was approaching his sixties. He was encouraged when several employers wrote back to him stating that they would keep his details on file and by the fact that a letter of refusal from a local employer was signed by hand and made reference to his experience as valuable. He had not gained work but a clue as to what might secure work for him, a sign of future possibilities which might get him off the "scrapheap". In another interview he discovered that a particular job was effectively a 'zero-hours' contract with no long-term security, and withdrew his application immediately, provoking an apology. Exerting some degree of choice and agency was important to how he described his job search, although he resisted the imposition of the category of 'jobseeker':

> 'Like, a jobseeker, is like a label that's put on you, that you are now officially a jobseeker, like, from here on until you receive a job, like your raison d'être is a job, when you get a job, you have advanced on from being a jobseeker to a job holder.'

He was aware of our work criticizing activation and sanctioning policies in Ireland and in the UK context, for instance, newspaper coverage of Universal Credit and the film *I, Daniel Blake*. However, he insisted that some unemployed people were 'slackers', unwilling to work, in sharp contrast to his own dedication.

Subsequently he found part-time work as a gardener and groundskeeper under a local community employment scheme. Although far from ideal, he held the position with pride, attributing his success to his strong work ethic and the volunteering activities he had pursued over years of unemployment. While unemployed he had acquired more experience as a carpenter and handyman, and even in administration in a local voluntary association. It seemed to him that his willingness to work had paid off, that his volunteering had led to his subsequent employment. Yet, looking back over his experience, he did recall that there were times when he felt like giving up or only found comfort in a bottle of spirits. His years of unemployment and poverty were perhaps lightened by the model of pilgrimage, and his resolve to 'keep on keeping on'. His current role was likely to run out in a few months, but he remained hopeful that his work and dedication would be rewarded.

Another particularly revealing example was 'Rachel', a qualified art teacher. She had come to teaching later in life and never secured a permanent contract, but had covered maternity and sick leave for years at a time. When we first spoke to her she was working as a substitute teacher, which effectively meant being available every morning from 7 am, waiting for a phone call from a local school, hoping against hope until 8:45 to be called in for a day's work. She described her situation as "treading water" and found her current experience of more or less total unemployment depressing and demoralizing. She attempted to fill her time with activities and ad hoc continuous professional development. Clearly, she held out hope for a permanent job, and felt that she compared favourably to other teachers in various schools who seemed lazy and complacent to her. Despite being "qualified to the hilt" in her own words, as she was approaching fifty, she felt that her age worked against her.

In a follow-up interview four years later, Rachel was coming to the end of a six-month contract as a substitute teacher in a different subject – she knew the school principal and described how she "got through a crack in the door". She was certainly more comfortable financially and seemed happier having had steady work. However, she had been called to interview for a permanent job as an art teacher in another nearby school, but had been unsuccessful. Although she knew the woman who got the job, she explained the outcome of the interview in terms of her own actions: that she had "wobbled" or "faltered" on certain questions, particularly around continuous professional development, and had failed to mention her experience of volunteering. She also thought that ageism had played a part in the employer's decision.

Soon Rachel would be returning to the Sisyphean task of waiting for work and being constantly available every morning. Again, she was considering the possibility of doing a master's of some kind to improve her prospects, or perhaps going abroad, as she liked the idea of new opportunities and had had good experiences in the past. Indubitably, Rachel found unemployment depressing, and she repeatedly mentioned the insecurity and the maddening boredom of it. However, she kept going relentlessly, seeking to improve herself, trying to decipher the demands of employers, always distinguishing herself from the 'real unemployed'. Day by day, year by year, she was a pilgrim in search of the promised land of secure work.

Conclusion

Pilgrimage gives meaning to jobseeking, helping the unemployed to maintain their hopes despite continuous rejection. Redundancy, recession and other economic disruptions can appear as tribulations, challenges rather than pointless suffering. Disappointments are transformed into occasions for deciphering the labour market and learning. Career changes can be considered 'personal growth' rather than difficult readjustments. Even long-term unemployment and precarity can be a sort of purifying road of self-invention. Nevertheless, this transpires in the shadow of sanctions – the threat of punishment – which implies that seeking for work is a remedial quest for self-transformation.

Of course, the cultural model of pilgrimage exists alongside a plethora of other ideas; for instance, selling yourself involves a sort of theatrical logic: jobseekers are told to make a good impression and project confidence in interviews, having burnished a personal 'brand' via CVs, and having already 'processed' the difficult experience of being unemployed. Unpredictable and unfixed arenas of life, such as a career, are always given a meaning somehow or other; there is no neutral way of describing these defining events in our lives. Alternative stories might help; rather than a pilgrimage wherein one is tested, perhaps the Buddhist idea of 'equanimity' might be more helpful!

This archaic anthropology of contemporary pilgrimage not only illuminates how jobseeking is interpreted as a penitential purification, seeking the intervention of providence in the form of a job, it also highlights the intersection of theory and theology: Turner's influential idea of 'liminality' may be less a discovery of an anthropological universal or a part of human nature than a recasting of a cultural model of transformation in theoretical terminology. Anthropology itself echoes pilgrimage (Dubisch, 1996). Thus, matching liminality theory with theology and historical pilgrimage with contemporary jobseeking is less a matter of imposing a model than recognizing the threads of cultural history.

As we saw earlier in Chapter 5, the purgatorial interpretation of unemployment means that jobseeking pilgrims are already subject to a sort of penance. This penance is made manifest in the directions of work coaches and the threat of sanctions. Until one arrives at the destination of a job, the pilgrimage seemingly must go on. Perhaps a more forgiving conception of jobseeking would be more humane and more realistic about the contemporary labour market. We will address that possibility in our concluding chapter.

7

Curriculum Vitae: Confessions of Faith in the Labour Market

The CV is the central document of the labour market, the crucial communication between would-be workers and employers. There are variants; job application forms, both online and off, cover letters and personal statements. Sometimes called a 'résumé', the snappy abbreviation 'CV' stands for curriculum vitae, a cumbersome Latin phrase meaning the 'course of life', positioning human existence as a series of formative experiences and training. Over recent decades, this document has become not only essential but is used more frequently, as 'jobs for life' have become rare and shorter contracts and projects become the norm – amid the shocks of recession and redundancy (Standing, 2011). Becoming unemployed is the main reason people 'refresh' their CV, making it a strange document, a self-definition under constant revision, showcasing achievements and ambitions, written under pressure to find work, including demands from welfare offices.

Seemingly, the CV is an innocuous document, a mere pragmatic list of personal details and a record of education and employment history. CVs are a common target of criticism because they serve to 'sell' labour and are thereby inauthentic, prone to being 'massaged' and exaggerated, replete with jargon and cliché. Moreover, they serve to commodify the individual, making them complicit in the capitalist process of competitive labour markets. There is some validity to these critiques, both the puritan or romantic critique of fakery and theatrical posing and the socialist critique of how the individual is drawn into the processes which exploit them (see Boltanski and Chiapello, 2005).

Herein we go further, reading the contemporary CV as a form which translates religious practices into the economic sphere. Effectively, the CV is a form of confession, especially when it is produced under pressure from welfare offices to explain gaps, position

141

present unemployment as temporary and articulate a determination to find work. Historically, confession involves 'telling the truth about yourself', alone or to a spiritual advisor, which serves to purify and redeem the soul. Furthermore, it was a 'profession' of faith, a declaration of personal hope for salvation, just as a CV is a 'personal statement' of experiences and ambitions. Indeed, the CV is also a 'prayer', an expression of humility as required by authorities and institutions, which expresses faith that the labour market will produce opportunities which might save the petitioner from their current state of unemployment, or guide the careerist through the maze of possibilities so that they find their destiny. A CV reasserts adherence to the creed of the labour market.

Of course, individuals do not think in quasi-religious terms while they create their CVs, but these unrecognized cultural models inform the experience of writing and submitting and rewriting a CV, often a highly repetitive process. These religious models exist in a broad cultural mix, so by drawing attention to confessional prayers in CV writing we may seem to exaggerate their importance. Yet, even the most commonplace critiques confirm this reading; the idea that misrepresenting the self in a personal advertisement is not simply strategic but inauthentic implies that 'telling the truth' about the self is a moral duty. Obviously, 'putting your best foot forward' is permissible, but this is simultaneously a desire to be redeemed, saved by the labour market from unemployment, hoping to 'make a good confession'.

Herein we will examine a diversity of sources: advice books which give instructions and templates for CVs and advice about cover letters, interviews and jobseeking in general replace pastors or preachers, exhorting sinners to redeem themselves. Much of this long-form advice has been replaced by online versions: shorter, constantly updated advice, hosted on websites which offer CV templates and digital interfaces for creating online profiles – these are the confession boxes of the modern jobseeker, who hits 'send' and hopes that the labour market answers their prayers. Strikingly, the jobseekers who we spoke with often described CV-writing as a mixture of self-doubt and hope, wherein they had to examine their lives, their consciences, and try to represent themselves as good workers to unseen judges. Beyond analyzing the persistence of confession in CV writing, our thesis develops one of Foucault's crucial insights: that there is a particular mode of 'telling the truth about the self' derived from Christianity which shapes modern selfhood thereafter. As the economy becomes the greatest 'trial of the soul', we find this truth-telling has migrated into CV writing.

Curriculum vitae

In Paul Willis's 1979 classic *Learning to Labour*, the role of career guidance teachers was just becoming institutionalized within 'comprehensive schools', even for working-class youths whose future careers often rested on their rejection of formal education. Then, the role was new, alternately interesting and irrelevant to students; today the idea of career suffuses education and even primary school children knowingly deploy the phrase 'It'll look good on my CV'. Where the idea of 'career-guidance' once implied identifying skills and traits to ensure a good fit between work and person for a lifelong career, today, the CV is a patchwork of projects and experiences, key qualifications, constantly updated, less a career than an enterprise of the self (Rose, 1996). The clichéd question 'What do you want to be when you grow up?' still exists, but nowadays the singular choice of profession has been displaced by the need to 'develop your CV'. Indeed, the advantage of the middle classes today is partly that their CVs are always in development; even when they are not excelling in education or in gainful employment, their lives cultivate forms of 'cultural capital' which 'look good on a CV' (Friedman and Laurison, 2019).

'What do you want to be when you grow up?' is a question that deserves careful scrutiny; it is not a neutral enquiry about already existing things, but implies motivation and aspiration. Here the idea of 'interpellation' is useful (Althusser, 1971). Beyond the standard Marxist critique of ideology, interpellation concerns how capitalism shapes its workers as individuals. An interpellation hails or calls us and models a certain type of selfhood; by responding, we recognize ourselves as a certain kind of being. Education, welfare offices, HR companies, online job-search facilities and social-media networks serve to interpellate individuals, from the cradle to retirement and beyond. From family members asking about career ambitions to pop-psychology quizzes about aptitudes, we are enticed to scrutinize our education, employment and our selves – our talents, potentials, desires – until gradually we become careerists. Thus, for Althusser, interpellation is not just a tempting illusion but a practice which forms individuals.

Careers are presented as enticing futures to children, inviting them to imagine and shape themselves as future workers. The cliché 'What do you want be when you grow up?' *interpellates* a child by addressing them as a certain sort of being, drawing them into thinking about themselves, their inner desires, their plans and future opportunities. Althusser considered this as 'ideology', described as 'the imaginary relationship of individuals to their real conditions of existence'

(1971: 109). Children are told they can fulfil their ambitions with sufficient hard work and ambition, but in reality, the economy is not a meritocracy, social mobility is limited and rigged in favour of those with money behind them (Friedman and Laurison, 2019).

Children quickly learn that questions about what they want to be are not invitations to philosophical rumination; they learn to designate their future as some career or another. It matters little which career or whether the child persists with it, whether it is realistic, like 'precarious service worker', or fantastical, like 'pop star'. In answering appropriately, children construct themselves in a number of ways: first, they claim inner desires for specific things. Second, they acknowledge they are growing up and therefore malleable. Third, they claim capabilities of self-transformation, of becoming something through their own choices and actions. Effectively, it is through 'doing' that the individual finds their 'being' – they study and become qualified, work and achieve things, rather than being defined in terms of kith and kin, place and belonging.

Throughout childhood, individuals are encouraged to pursue a career and build their CV, until they eventually encounter the labour market and either must find work or face welfare activation programmes which demand they work on their CV. Except for criminals and the independently wealthy (not always the same people), creating and developing a CV is compulsory in the modern economy. Yet, composing a CV is also quite an odd activity: it is not a natural expression of the self or a simple matter of filling in a form. The necessity of providing career advice at every stage of life and in every institution indicates the uncertainty and difficulty of writing a CV – and this advice frequently changes and is never unequivocal; it always depends on the context and its validity is only assured by success.

CVs, résumés and job applications require a peculiar mode of writing about the self. It is not just a letter to an employer, expressing a desire to work for them – even if accompanied by a cover letter. Such letters are balancing acts; authors supposedly write about themselves *objectively*, reporting on their skills and willingness to labour, despite being *subjectively* deeply concerned with the result. Thus, the CV requires that an individual write about themselves as though from the outside, adopting an external point of view, that of the employer, or in contemporary parlance, presenting themselves as a 'business solution'. What they are to others, from the perspective of others, is produced by the CV; the self becomes an object of scrutiny. Not only must the tone of the document appear neutral, offering a factual reportage of life, but the grammatical tense of the CV is the present continuous, speaking about the self not just as the accumulation of experiences and skills or future desires or ambitions but in a temporal current of the continuous now. Phrases like 'dedicated worker', or 'good timekeeper' or the dreaded cliché 'works well independently or in a team' are so generic they escape our attention, but what is really curious is how they present an individual as a resource offering key qualities. Moreover, the CV marks that individual as the product of their education and employment, shaped by life experiences and implicitly capable of change.

A further curiosity of CV writing is that each version is presented as 'true', a statement which corresponds to the author, yet most are unsuccessful, swiftly discarded or 'kept on file'. At the time of its writing, the author must examine their life and character in order to present them successfully, but also be ready to rewrite their CV and tweak it flexibly, becoming something of a chameleon. Yet whenever they are successful, the 'self' represented on the CV is validated, verified as a worthy worker; that self-representation has its truth and value affirmed by the market – the only test that matters in the economy. Here, the vital elements of hope and belief are expressed: despite the toil of repeatedly sending CVs, modifying them for different jobs and enduring rejection, each is sent 'in good faith'. No matter how the CV is strategically massaged, it represents a version of the self; it tells 'the truth' about a life, and if that self is employed, it is enshrined on the CV thereafter.

Clearly, the CV is a complex document, full of strange practices and contradictions. To understand this, a historical detour is necessary, initially into the use of letters and documents in the labour market, but more importantly into the genealogy of how the truth about the self is generated in the Western world, where distinctly modern practices have theological precursors.

Curriculum vitae of the CV

The labour market is relatively recent; for centuries, peasants simply farmed the land, while their lords appropriated surpluses and the church took a tithe. Economics was organized by custom, which restricted liberty, but interestingly medieval people had more holidays – holy days – than most contemporary workers. The fairytale figure of the young lad 'off to seek his fortune' is relatively modern, and was mainly limited to England, where agriculture moved earlier from feudal subsistence to profit-driven enterprise (Macfarlane, 1988). Indeed, the Industrial Revolution relied enormously on the Agricultural

Revolution, not just on new technologies for increased food production but the expropriation of the peasantry, moving agricultural workers en masse from the countryside to the towns as a source of labour power (Woods, 1999). Becoming involved in the labour market was less an opportunity than a compulsion, as nigh-upon destitute crowds gathered around factories looking for work (Polanyi, 2001). Indeed, this supposedly 'free' labour market was even created by government intervention, as liberal politicians moved to 'enclose' lands in the 1830s, ending collective ownership in favour of private enterprise.

Initially, CVs were absent from jobseeking. Specialized medieval trades were controlled by guilds, which regulated local numbers of masters and apprentices, which ensured quality, price and a future living for apprentices (Graeber, 2018). Seasonal work in agriculture involved hiring fairs, vast gatherings of workers hoping to be taken on based on their physical appearance or social connections, without supporting documentation. Tradespeople occasionally produced advertisements for their wares, but these were more brochures of services for hire than CVs. Perhaps the earliest precursors of the CV are 'references' provided for domestic servants who were moving to new employers.

By the late nineteenth century, letters applying for employment became more commonplace across different sectors, including professions. Increasingly, individuals addressed letters to unfamiliar employers, introducing themselves, making declarative statements about their own abilities (Popken, 1999). Strikingly, clergymen were listed as 'character references', as moral watchdogs who would warrant the honesty and integrity of individuals. In America being a member of 'good standing' in a church congregation was crucial to acceptance in a business community (Weber, 1991). Early letters seeking employment are notably stilted, as the writer has no familiarity with the recipient, leading to a halting style. Indeed, these letters even resemble CVs in listing personal characteristics as bullet points, yet include details like height, marital status, whether the applicant was a smoker and other moral indicators alongside educational attainments and employment history. In the early twentieth century, third level educational institutions, particularly business schools, started to give advice on writing these letters of application, résumés or CVs, and their texts notably explain the whole concept to readers who are presumably unfamiliar with them (Gershon, 2019).

Since then, instruction manuals in CV writing have become a familiar dimension of jobseeking advice: occasionally CVs are called résumés, less frequently identified with job-application letters, and traditionally separate 'cover letters' are recommended, but now the 'personal statement' and even 'self-branding' are increasingly incorporated into the CV. The very existence of such guides demonstrates the peculiarity of this mode of self-presentation, with extensive advice on simple matters, such as what to include and exclude. Herein we draw from book-length treatments from the 1970s to the present and from web pages; incrementally paperback instruction manuals have come to resemble web pages, with scarcely a page of paragraphed text amid the plethora of bullet points, tables, inspirational quotes and self-assessment quizzes. Various emphases come and go; for instance, presenting the self as a flexible, creative teamworker oriented towards projects was central during the 1990s (Boltanski and Chiapello, 2005), but this has become routine and been displaced by a new emphasis on the worker as 'business solution' (Sharone, 2017). Initially, these texts may seem banal, even hackneyed, yet for jobseekers anxiously creating a CV and fervently hoping to get work or even just an interview, they are crucial. Creating a curriculum vitae is an exercise in introspection and self-examination, a recurrent struggle to define oneself as a good worker and declare your worth to employers. Yet, these employers remain anonymous, addressed both by the 'objective' description of the self in the CV and the personal cover letter, expressing hopes, sincerely.

However, the emergence of the CV in the twentieth century should not lead to a truncated history. It does not emerge from nothing, but adopts and adapts time-hallowed modes of talking about the self which are central to Western Judeo-Christian culture. Indeed, there is something particular and peculiar about our labour market practice of CV writing, because an individual is at least partially valued on the basis of their capacity to produce an account of themselves. Writing about the self, telling the 'truth about the self', is what the CV demands, and this is a practice with a long theological provenance.

Indubitably, the CV involves professing the work ethic, declaring the author's resolve to labour and even climb the complex career ladder, seeking for success. Evidently, 'job-changers' wish for better things. For jobseekers who attempt to overcome redundancy or escape unemployment, the CV is implicitly a confession of faults; all guides instruct their readers to conceal or explain gaps, giving contrite excuses for economically unproductive periods of life – and welfare offices treat unemployment as though it were an individual pathology to be cured. Implicitly, the Protestant ethic is unlimited, requiring continuous work and success, following rational plans for vocational labour or enterprise, yet creating a CV also implies the requirement to scrutinize life as lived and forge it into a career trajectory. Strikingly, jobseeking advice and CV-writing guides repeatedly reference Maslow's idea of self-actualization: the idea that work will transform the self, an open-ended form of continuous self-development. Interpretive efforts are inescapable here, for while faith may be concerned with 'things unseen', both religious and economic 'believers actively seek concrete proofs of the presence of God' (Coleman, 1996: 109). Signs and symbols, manifestations, demonstrations of the truth are deciphered in the world, and particularly in the labour market.

Rather than claiming there is an essential, unchanging 'true self' to be discovered within each individual, contemporary thinkers from Althusser to Foucault insist that even our internal experience of conscience or individual identity are socially formed. Such ideas about the self have a rich cultural history; for instance, the legacy of Graeco-Roman thought about the self, and 'spiritual exercises', which are then taken over by Christian practices of confession (Foucault, 2005, 2014). While confession is a contemporary religious practice, it has a complex history expressing a very distinctive selfhood, whereby individuals are required to purify themselves by telling the truth about themselves. Confession was initially close to conversion, the declaration of the self as a Christian, then subsequently a baptismal rite or sometimes 'canonical penance', then became public demonstration of guilt for penitents who wished to be reconciled to the church community – the *ecclesia*. These elements eventually become subsumed into monastic versions of confession, which combine classical philosophical exercises and early Christian rites of purification and provide the model for lay confession from the thirteenth century.

Distinct from classical philosophical reflection, the 'truth' examined in confession was the past behaviour and internal thoughts of the subject; the 'soul' examined was actually personal conduct. For institutionalized Christianity – in stark contrast to Gnostics and other sects – the soul could be saved, but never rendered perfect, and thus, the work of redemption became chronic, interminable. 'This conversion, this establishing a relationship of subjectivity to truth requires probation, the test, bringing the truth of oneself into play' (Foucault, 2014a: 160). The acceptance of mysteries or dogma and the ascetic exercises of penance alone were insufficient; instead, Christianity insists upon the individual putting themselves into discourse, telling the truth about themselves. Conversion is less a single and decisive transformation that saves the soul than a continuous process: 'This movement by which one turns around must be maintained' (Foucault, 2014a: 177). No subject is entirely safe from relapse or backsliding; to presume otherwise would be pride, another sin.

Christian subjects are enticed into continuous attention to themselves – 'Monitoring the flux of our thoughts' (Foucault, 2014a: 298) – not just through private prayer but in confession, usually to a spiritual director: an abbot in a monastery, a priest in a parish. Theologically, the self is presumed to be constantly assailed by sinful urges and devilish deceptions. Speaking about these is an expulsion, a cleansing act, simply by rejecting concealment – the ruse of the devil. In contrast to ritualistic models of purification, confession requires 'verbalization', telling the truth about the self, putting the self into discourse, repeatedly, perpetually and always to an auditor. Crucially, confession is connected to self-transformation; 'the revelation of the truth about oneself cannot be dissociated from the obligation to renounce oneself' (Foucault, 1993: 221). Thus, confession is not merely about developing self-knowledge or control in an incremental effort, but shrives elements of the past self to create the new, purified subject. Personal transformation in Judeo-Christian thought is not simply a matter of metamorphosis but occurs through conversion, which excises and jettisons part of the self; this is dramatically expressed as a death of the old self and a birth into new life, even expressed by the Crucifixion: 'For we know that our old self was crucified with him so that the body ruled by sin might be done away with that we should no longer be slaves to sin – because anyone who has died has been set free from sin' (Romans, 6:6–7). However, singular conversion experiences are routinized or institutionalized in the continuous work of confession, constantly purifying the self, for instance, of sloth, pride, avarice and any other sin which impedes the constant pursuit of work.

Importantly, the Christian production of the truth of self through verbalization also implies power relationships as a guarantor of the truth of confessions. The novice in the monastery or the layperson in confession takes on a relationship of obedience to their auditor, sometimes reflecting status hierarchies, but not necessarily, the crucial element being obedience: 'To obey in everything and to hide nothing' (Foucault, 1993: 266). These commands go together; to obey and tell the truth. Visible compliance with orders and directions demonstrates the authentic character of the revelation of self. While the theological precepts around this relationship are no longer explicit, this relationship appears between therapists and patients, teachers and students, coaches and athletes and elsewhere. Furthermore, this obedient truth-telling about the self is expressed in the relationship of jobseekers to welfare officers, work coaches and CV advisors.

Thus, in Christianity, the self is constituted through truth-telling within power-relations, which continues into modernity, albeit with

Protestantism making this relationship of confession more private, an internal dialogue or supplication to the absent presence of the deity.

> It involves establishing a relationship of obedience to the other's will and at the same time establishing, in correlation with, as condition of this obedience, what I would call not a jurisdiction but a veridiction; this obligation constantly to tell the truth about oneself with regard to oneself in the form of confession. (Foucault, 2014a: 308)

Confession was a central theme in Foucault's later work, expressed with rhetorical flourish: 'Western man has become a confessing animal' (1976: 59). Foucault repeatedly claims that the 'conduct of conduct' which emerges in confession is of central significance for modernity – though not as a fixed practice but one which is adopted and adapted over history: 'The Christian pastorate is also absolutely innovative in establishing a structure, a technique of, at once, power, investigation, self-examination, and the examination of others, by which a certain secret inner truth of the hidden soul, becomes the element through which the pastor's power is exercised' (2007: 183). For Foucault, pastoral power and especially confession are central to modern governmentality, and thus, the genealogy of confession can illuminate how CV writing forms contemporary subjects.

Frequently, Foucault identifies confession as a mode of telling the truth about the self which transforms the subject (1976, 1993, 2014a, 2014b). Importantly, this 'truth of self' can be about acts, but also about thoughts or the minutiae of experiences: 'All, or almost all, of an individual's life, thought and actions must pass through the filter of confessions' (2003: 177). Obviously, CVs list education and employment history but also contain 'personal statements', and composing these involves a thorough self-examination of attitudes and 'inner' thoughts, dispositions, ambitions and so forth. Confessional culture encourages subjects to speak about themselves and thereby define and transform themselves, an imperative experienced variously, from the pleasures of self discovery to disciplinary coercion (Taylor, 2008).

Confession comprises disparate elements, most prominently the profession of faith, a declaration of belief in scripture and the avowal of faults and sins. This tension between the truth of dogma and the truth of self is productive, allowing for scripture to give moral direction to conduct and for confessions about personal conduct to reshape and transform individuals; 'Avowal had to begin with an act of faith' (Foucault, 2014b: 188) While Foucault tends to focus on the avowal of faults, professions of faith are also important (Taylor, 2008), and while every CV involves an avowal of past experiences, they also require a profession of hope for a further career trajectory, imploring the 'invisible hand' of the labour market to bestow success upon an applicant – or even a supplicant.

Interestingly, medieval confession operated to efface sin through avowal – once revealed, a sin could be forgiven – whereas contemporary confessions tend to record the truth of self as a reflection of identity. Confession once meant 'to tell everything in order to efface everything', but in modernity these avowals are now 'deposited in an enormous documentary mass' (2000: 166). Of course, modern confessions reflect different forms of normalization, and can discover 'positive' personality traits as well as faults and sins. Here Foucault's focus on avowal could be complemented by Butler's (1997) discussion of disavowal as a mode of forming the self by rejecting internal thoughts or disowning past acts. Indeed, the avowal of sins and disavowal of parts of the self are close parallels or inversions of each other; the self is formed by excising elements of past conduct, admitting them and rejecting them to purify the self – with purgative confession as ritual penance (Boland, 2019).

Strikingly, confession emerged from public rituals of purgation, but through monasticism and the institutional church they became a repetitive and interminable practice. For Augustinian inspired Catholicism, sinners cannot be perfected or purified without the risk of relapse (Taylor, 2008). Thus, confession creates 'a permanent court' (Foucault, 1976: 20). Once-in-a-lifetime rituals are replaced by regular practices, and this imperative for confession is spread across society, and then becomes insidious and ubiquitous throughout modernity, becoming

> a ritual that unfolds within a power relationship, for one does not confess without the presence (or *virtual* presence) of a partner who is not simply the interlocutor but the authority who requires the confession, prescribes and appreciates it, and intervenes in order to judge, punish, forgive, console and reconcile. (Foucault, 1976: 62, emphasis added)

While obedience might be paid to an individual pastor – a priest, psychiatrist or welfare officer – importantly for the CV, it can also be a 'virtual' auditor; the normalizing expectations of career or the anonymous labour market. Telling the 'truth' is authenticated by the difficulty of the revelation, admitting to faults or distancing oneself from prior conduct as somehow 'other' – attributed to madness, delinquency, idleness or weakness. Salvation through governmentality is less a spiritual projection to the afterlife than a mundane transformation of the self into a good citizen and productive worker. Interestingly, the authenticity of the truth about the self is guaranteed by obedience to interpersonal directions and compliance with institutional normalization, but also by difficulty: 'The transformation into good takes place at the heart of the very suffering caused, insofar as this suffering is actually a test that is recognized, lived and practiced as such by the subject' (Foucault, 2005: 443). Salvation through suffering, truth established by testing, indefinite forms of obedience: these are the marks of pastoral power and contemporary governmentality. Beyond simple disciplinary control, the process is linked to market outcomes as tests of worth – or the market serves as a 'mode of veridiction', to borrow the terminology of Foucault's analysis of ordo–liberalism (2008).

There are obvious differences between the confession and the CV – the former has an other-worldly orientation, whereas the worth of the latter is apparent only through economic outcomes – yet even this encodes the idea of a providential order (Agamben, 2011). Indeed, there are many subtle similarities: putting the self into discourse is crucial, even if CV confession is a private prayer to a virtual auditor or is sent into the void of an anonymous market. Strikingly, jobseeking advice describes self-work and CV drafting as a difficult process of self-transformation, with the relatively easy tasks of listing education and employment history positioned as mere preliminaries to the difficult and repetitive task of presenting the self through a personal statement. Thus, while religious confession is an interminable process of purifying oneself for an after-world, CV writing is a repetitive process of transforming oneself to achieve market success.

Faith in the labour market

Beyond claiming welfare, unemployed individuals often described their efforts at jobseeking, composing and rewriting CVs, scouring the internet and real world for jobs, filling out applications, creating digital profiles, all under the threat of sanction. Insufficient or unproven efforts to 'genuinely seek work' could result in the reduction or suspension of welfare benefits for up to nine weeks in Ireland.

While we sought out people who were short-term unemployed to get their perspective, at the start of our study the average length of time spent unemployed was around two years – our fieldwork focused on the long aftermath of the 2008 great financial crash. Still seeking work, but enduring constant rejection, these individuals persisted in hoping:

Interviewer:	You'd hope there was something, you really would but you have to keep optimistic, like, if you're being pessimistic about it and that the whole time, I mean ...
Interviewee:	It only brings you down.
Interviewer:	Exactly! So you always have to think, yeah, so fingers crossed.

Here hope appears as a tool, a means to ward off despondency; this woman felt that without deliberately maintaining a positive attitude she might lose any chance of gaining work. Metaphorically she thinks with her fingers crossed, hoping that luck will come her way, that the market will bestow a job on her.

Maintaining a positive attitude was partially a tactic of self-preservation, but equally formed a strategy to convince prospective employers. A young man described how he used volunteering experience to fill out the 'gaps' in his CV so that prospective employers would not think he had been doing nothing or suspect that he had moved into the "pub or the bookies". The imaginary descent from real work to the netherworld of unemployment – where supposedly sloth, avarice and lust have free rein – is often invoked. Potentially, hopefully, volunteering work as a form of experience in lieu of a job might serve to redeem his career trajectory. This was a common theme, the attempt to transform oneself through interminable assorted jobseeking activity to maintain hopes of gaining employment, avoiding becoming one of the 'real unemployed' – an imaginary category stigmatized beyond redemption.

The difficulty of adapting to digital platforms for CVs was considered an obstacle by some older interviewees. More often, individuals objected to the condescending attitude they encountered in the welfare office, where CV-writing classes were considered to be for the 'brain-dead'. Either way, the demand for CV writing was backed with sanctions, whereby new CVs for the recently unemployed and tailored CVs for different jobs were compulsory. Moreover, where an individual was unsuccessful in jobseeking, the discourse around CVs – finding one's talents, presenting them persuasively – set the individual the task of rewriting their CV despite constant rejection. For instance, a young man in an urban area who had been more or less consistently unemployed since leaving school said:

'You have to be genuinely looking for work as well. Recently I got a letter from them asking for an update on places I'd been looking for work or handed in CVs and I had to update them and tell them the places that I'd been looking for. And so I told them that I'd basically been in town looking for, handing out CVs a lot and my CVs was just getting put on file; I wasn't getting anything. They asked me about if I would look for anything, anything in work and I said I would.'

Interestingly, he mirrors the official phrase 'genuinely seeking work', identifying himself as a good jobseeker – yet nonetheless he is consistently under threat of sanction. Beyond enduring unemployment, he has to document his repeated failures to gain work. At intervals a case officer would work with him on his CV, as though individual efforts would solve the macroeconomic problem of supply and demand.

Over time, maintaining this fruitless routine became increasingly personally difficult, due to the lack of results and a creeping feeling of shame; being visible, in town, giving his CV again and again to front-counter workers to give to managers, sometimes repeatedly in the same shops:

> 'I would hand in CVs and I'd try to have a positive mindset but they'd just keep telling me "oh we'll put it on file; we'll put it on file", and I'd rather them to be up and honest with me and tell me that they're not looking for anyone because when someone says they're putting it on file they're pretty much throwing it in the bin and I don't want, you know, I don't want people giving me false hope because I'm kind of here, I'm looking, desperate here, I need to do something, you know, I need some sort of work and you giving me false hope isn't going to help. It's going to make it worse.'

Achieving a positive mindset – remaining hopeful, having faith – is described as a necessity, an effort. However, this jobseeking routine increasingly appeared to him like a Sisyphean effort, a constant toil for no reward. The vague possibility of a job becomes a painful form of false hope as he begins to drift towards despair.

Not only is this a difficulty of an individualized response to an economic problem, but it reflects the challenge of making sense of bad fortune – the luck of others and the vagaries of chance are a source of frustration for another young man:

'But when I see some of my friends and they get jobs straight away and I'm here, you know, dying for a job, you know, dying to work and I just don't think it's fair really. I'd like to think that I've a good chance ... I think everyone should think that they have a good chance really because there's no point if you think you don't have a good chance; what's the point in applying for the job then? So only time will tell really but I still try to stay positive though.'

Perhaps the biggest challenge of his account is the requirement to retain hope – to believe in one's chances, by 'trying to stay positive'. This mental strategy is not only a psychologized response to the economy but a culturally specific way of thinking about the economy: enduring the sufferings of Job. No matter what misfortunes or trials befall him, no matter how unjust the world appears, faith is the only route towards redemption.

Unprompted, many individuals declared that they would never fabricate anything or even massage their CV, but also mentioned the difficulty of composing this document. Presenting themselves to unseen employers was awkward, and boasting of their skills and abilities seemed, frankly, boastful, particularly after repeated rejection. Beyond this, a peculiar combination of tenses had to be negotiated, so that future plans, for instance to 'increase sales' or 'complete a course' became conditional, prefaced by the aspirational 'I hope to' rather than the definitive 'I will'. The future was uncertain for these individuals, many of whom had experienced redundancy and harboured doubts of ever gaining employment again. While composing cover letters or other communications with employers, many highlighted their uncertainty: 'If taken on I will ...', rather than simply 'I will ...'. Repeatedly, humility in self-presentation prevailed, perhaps more pronounced for women, yet expressions of willingness to work, hopes of being taken on, persisted nonetheless.

Curiously, writing a CV draws individuals into expressing themselves in an aspirational mood, evoking ambitions and transformations. CV guides advise that the conditional 'If employed I hope to' should be rewritten in the definitive 'I will', so desire and volition are united in imagination, making the individual identical to their career trajectory. The subjunctive feeling of doubt and possibility actually felt by the jobseeker – 'If I were to have a job then I would be ...' – is occluded by the personal statement, which represents them as an accomplished career worker in the present-tense 'I am'. These modes of talking about the self could be fruitfully understood as prayer; prayer is socially learned, but individually spoken or thought, yet addressed to the sacred, the beyond: *'prayer is a religious rite which is oral and bears directly on the sacred'* (Mauss, 2003: 57, emphasis in original). Without making metaphysical assumptions, it is important to recognize that the act of prayer is effective for the praying individual, under whatever social circumstances and with whatever power-relations are involved; it brings comfort or produces a desired subjective feeling – purity for the believer, work readiness for the jobseeker.

Prayer, ritual and worship render their objects sacred, making things into idols, ideas into ideals – an economic form of the glorification which confers legitimacy on political power (Agamben, 2011: 223). As professions of desire for work, confessions of obedience to the institutions of education and employment, CVs are sent hopefully to employers; as prayers or even acclamations of faith (Dean, 2017). Drawing from Agamben (2011), Dean argues that political power sanctifies itself through rituals of acclamation, from medieval coronations to democratic elections, which serve to confer legitimacy and even glory through popular acclaim. Extending this beyond the realm of politics to the economic, each CV is an acclamation that implicitly conveys glory upon the labour market, implying that work – on the market and on the self – serves as salvation. Implicitly, these socially transmitted forms of prayer connect the individual who wills and hopes to an imaginary beyond – the market now, rather than God – but in such a way as to transform the individual, converting them into a good jobseeker through repetitive confession of the self via the CV.

Governing the curriculum vitae

Few individuals do not have a CV, and though the vaunting careers of professionals and entrepreneurs are more commonly associated with this document, it is compulsory for welfare claimants. For unemployed jobseekers, the CV is required by the Jobcentre or welfare office as a step towards finding work, as an exercise in becoming 'work ready' – a requirement that is backed up by the threat of sanction for non-fulfillment of this task. More importantly, the personal CV is reviewed by a case officer or work coach, and directions for revision or 'tailoring' for specific roles can be required. The individual is instructed to examine their own life in detail and report this to someone who has power over them, who in turn scrutinizes them and often directs them towards further exercises – these may be skills-development or even remedial training, but the parallel to confession is unmistakable. Beyond this explicit power relationship, the 'truth' of any CV is also guarranteed by clear compliance with broader institutional norms: the judgements of educational institutions must be revealed, personal employment history must be relayed truthfully, and references must be relied upon – today, the older moral appraisal of workers' characters by the clergy is taken on by previous employers. Evidently, the CV is not a freestyle 'story of your life' but a report made according to the norms of the labour market – and these are governmentalizing norms, forming the individual in certain ways, giving them particular capacities and qualities.

While compulsory, the exercize of writing a CV is presented as an opportunity, a series of choices wherein the author can represent themselves freely. For instance, the website JobcentreNearMe.com condenses the advice that fills whole books elsewhere into a dozen bullet points and a link to an online CV service. Broadly, this advice is to be brief – 'Usually, normal CVs are only one A4 page' – and only include things which matter to employers: 'It is completely up to you how you arrange this information and where you put it in your CV. The most important thing is that it is all there to help the employer learn more about you.'[1] Here, the CV is described as a simple, pragmatic document with information about the self, arranged tactically by its author to communicate clearly with prospective employers. Yet, our interviews with the unemployed reveal that the process of actually composing a CV is full of toil and uncertainty. Indeed, even the earlier purportedly neutral and sensible statement expresses a peculiar power relation: whoever composes their CV is obliged to reveal a certain amount of information about themselves, and this is to be gathered by self-reflection and examination. While they can 'arrange' the information as they please, their goal is to communicate with the employer, not about the job but about themselves: even if they are writing strategically, they must consider the perspective of the employer, scrutinizing themselves as though from the outside, adopting the gaze of another, becoming an object of assessment for themselves.

Like many others, this site recommends a 'personal statement' in addition to the factual information on the formal CV – a replacement or reduction of the older form of the cover letter with a very brief summation of the self. Again, this is described by the JobCentre website as a simple statement: 'This is a sentence or two where you sell your skills, experiences and personal qualities. It should be original and it should sum up your background and character in a positive way.'[2] The website recommends using buzzwords, active verbs and positive adjectives. The tension between the factual character of the remainder of the CV and this 'sales pitch' for the self is notable. Most interestingly, this 'truth' about the self can be revised to match whatever job the CV is written for, yet it is never supposed to be false or even misleading.

The realm of jobseeking is often criticized as being full of pretence and simulation, where interviews are theatrical performances and CVs are works of fiction, so that the seller of labour appears a marketeer (Agnew, 1986). Indubitably, individuals are trained to sell themselves, akin to actors, which provides an obvious target for criticism: 'A certain bureaucratization of the spirit is expected so that we can be relied upon to give a perfectly homogeneous performance at every appointed time' (Goffman, 1990: 32). Yet, rather than examining the 'end result', where the CV is a sales pitch for the worker as a saleable commodity – a self-advertisement – what matters is the underlying process of self-scrutiny. Each CV is written and sent with the faint hope of not being instantly discarded or merely 'kept on file'; the CV is composed in 'good faith' and sent 'in hope of success'. Rather than criticizing the CV as charlatanism, we might attempt to understand it as a contemporary mode of 'telling the truth about the self'.

While the contemporary 'cutting edge' may be CV-creation software and sites such as LinkedIn which provide a digital interface for personal profiles in a virtual labour market, these tend to give very brief advice, and so our analysis includes older, book-length guides to CV writing. These include practical titles such as *The CV Writing Guide* (Johnson, 1993) or those with more audacious promises such as *Brilliant CV* (Bright and Earl, 2000) – many of which have been rewritten, newly titled and reprinted without substantial change. Such advice books have remained relatively stable over the last fifty years, despite changing fashions for jargon or different combinations of résumé and personal letter and so forth. As texts, these books have become increasingly brief, with more recent iterations resembling the format of a web page, with text boxes, indents, bullet points and a paucity of continuous text – a whole page is rarely filled by paragraphed text.

As such, these guides are less texts than apparatuses, a discontinuous series of injunctions and instructions which describe and demand self-work, rather than meditative wisdom regarding jobseeking. Increasingly, authors are described as experts with professional practice in career guidance, business school credentials or authorship of psy-science research into CV creation and jobseeking. Reading these guides neutrally is scarcely possible, as they continuously address or interpellate their audience (Althusser, 1971). Furthermore, the texts are delicate textual performances, as the range of possible readers is immense – sample CVs range from manual trades to managerial positions. Yet, the mode of discourse addresses the reader simply, as an essential, universal subject – a worker out of work, a jobseeker, a career changer hoping for social mobility; a self-interested economic actor.

Advice books replace individual advisors; they model and direct the self-examination and production of truth about the self for almost any reader. Beyond gathering information about themselves, the reader is required to examine themselves, their character and their decisions from the point of view of the labour market. While the overarching aim of these advice books is a 'killer CV', the actual process begins with self-reflection. For instance, multiple quizzes and exercises aimed at self-assessment are provided, even accompanying workbooks for jobseekers. Many books provide templates for CVs, directing their reader to fill out various versions, and there are often a plethora of sample CVs included, which the reader is invited to assess and criticize, thereby modeling self-scrutiny. Once the reader has gathered their information and presented it on a template, they must revise and rewrite it tactically, orienting it towards different jobs: 'Every role has unique requirements, so sending out a one-size-fits-all CV just won't work. With each application, review your experience ... tweak your work history to prove you're the perfect fit'.[3] Implicitly, every attempt is hopeful, yet rejection and repetition is taken for granted, and therefore the whole process is recursive and continuous. Thus the texts address both the first-time and returning reader, potentially the same person, perhaps within the same spell of unemployment. Regardless, the reader is unstintingly directed to revise their CV, to return to scrutinizing their life and to rewrite their personal statement.

Through various exercises of self-scrutiny, the reader is incited and cajoled into rethinking their life as a 'career' that has a 'trajectory': education appears as formation of skills, employment as a series of professional accomplishments – so the current jobseeker is a transitional subject, offering themselves to employers as a resource, yet capable of transformation. Obedience to the institutions and cultural values of the workplace are assumed and required, and moreover this warrants that any given CV will actually 'tell the truth about the self' – despite the widespread popular critiques of massaging CVs or the vapid language which emerges from them. Indeed, the circulation of this generalized suspicion of self-aggrandisement both acts to dissuade job-seekers from excessive claims about themselves, and normalizes the process of self-scrutiny involved in composing the CV. Most guides suggest that readers are too modest or brief in describing themselves, that they need to scrutinize themselves to identify their skills and qualities or even their 'unique selling point'. Furthermore, these efforts are implicitly limitless: 'Your CV is a living, breathing document and

the primary CV you so carefully developed is never really finished'
(Yates, 2015: 78). Like confession, CV writing is recursive and
implicitly interminable.

Repeatedly, CV-writing guides exhort their readers to take on the
point of view of employers and even consider the busy work routines of
recruiters. Not only must skills be sold, but these should be evidenced
by past successes, quantified in numbers and data, and beyond that the
jobseeker should present themselves as a 'business solution'.

> Employers don't just buy skills, they buy solutions, so show
> how can you make the company money and how can you
> resolve the problems that they have.
> Put yourself in the shoes of your clients or colleagues ...
> Make it clear that whatever it is they want, you're able
> to fulfil their needs.[4]

Despite the CV being a personal document, wherein an individual
reports upon themselves, perhaps conveying private information,
usually as an attempt to escape personal unemployment, the individual
is enticed to view themselves from the outside. This ranges from
suggesting that employers are 'customers' to suggesting that hobbies
imply skills or that society is a network. Effectively these discourses
propound an economic ethos which transforms all conduct into
potential: 'Do a lot with your life so there is good interesting material to
include in a well presented CV' (Bright and Earls, 2002: 50). Taking on
the perspective of employers is posited as a canny tactic, but also requires
that Jobseekers self-scrutinize speculatively, imagining in advance how
they can conform to the requirements of unseen market gatekeepers.
Partially, this is the logic of self-commodification, yet equally, this is
a petition to anonymous judges, a prayer to the powers of the labour
market, that the providential invisible hand might bless the supplicant.

While these guides are generally upbeat, even adopting a casual
or sympathetic tone, they attribute personal responsibility for
unemployment: 'Many jobseekers send out dozens of application
without getting a single interview. They complain bitterly about their
lack of success but the fault often lies in their own hands' (Johnson,
1993: xi). Thus, the structural condition of unemployment and the
competition for scarce jobs is rendered as an individual struggle of
self-scrutiny and self-presentation. Often the work ethic is invoked,
promising that effort, strategy and relentless competition are guarantors
of success. Perhaps unemployment is acknowledged as bad luck, but
these guides imply that writing a good CV is the key to securing new

work, and therefore within the compass of any reader. Strikingly, discussions of unemployment and redundancy are almost absent from many of these guides, yet CV gaps are often mentioned: 'If you have long gaps in your employment history or you are re-entering the job market or changing the focus of your career, a cover letter can explain these circumstances in a positive way' (Hansen and Hansen, 1990: 2). Here, life events appear as interruptions to a career, which need to be explained to employers. Similarly, Fish4.co.uk recommends that employment history 'should read as a chronological flow with gaps accounted for'.[5] Implicitly, gaps are failings by the applicant, which must be accounted for, akin to a confession of faults or sins, an entreaty for forgiveness by employers, almost a supplication for the indulgence of a 'second chance'.

Despite the upbeat tone of most of these manuals, the difficulty of translating a life into a CV is noted: 'No one wants to write a CV. On the list of things we "want" to do, it comes just above hitting yourself on the head with a hammer, and in part that is because of the self-analysis involved' (Yates, 2015: 1). Unemployment is invisible here – poverty, anxiety and pressure from welfare offices are not mentioned – instead the difficulty is self-analysis, the hard work of subjectification or soul-searching. Yet, the implicit assumption of such guides is that jobseeking is a long process – not only because of serial rejection by employers but because of the chronic self-analysis, the repeated restatement of personal capacities, the repetitive process of CV writing 'in hope of success'.

A peculiar style of writing about the self is often described briefly, or simply modelled in sample CVs. Beyond the list of factual information, there is the 'personal statement', summing the individual up 'in a nutshell', yet which is revised and tailored for each job application. Therein, the applicant is directed to write about themselves and their skills like a reporter gathering observations: 'Key project manager in sales force' or 'Responsible for liaising with suppliers'. This clipped prose facilitates brevity, yet there is something curious about these pronouncements – often they use subjectless verbs, avoiding claims that start with 'I'; seemingly objective rather than subjective. Indeed, even in personal statements where 'I' is allowed or even encouraged, the recommended tone and style is peculiarly flat. Partly this may be because of the anonymity of the process – the CV necessarily addresses strangers, and attempts to give a credible picture of the applicant. Effectively, the CV attempts to produce a transparent picture of the applicant, a life seen at a glance, assessed by remote judges. Aside from the pressures of welfare activation described in prior chapters, this competition brings its own demands, requiring self-scrutiny, telling the truth transparently, usually repeatedly, until the mysterious market finally chooses the applicant. Getting a job not only alters the CV – with new employment history, skills and career trajectory – it serves to validate a particular CV as being effectively the 'truth' about the individual.

Templates for transformation

Paperback CV-writing guides often provide CV templates, usually with a variety of formats, which serve as examples and illustrations to their readers. Of course, as a hybrid, constantly updated form, nothing is 'set in stone', and every individual is told to adapt the recipe to their own purposes. These templates are even more prominent on digital CV-writing platforms, and many jobseeking websites now provide both sample files and access to CV-writing software. Indeed, MS Word is now directly linked to LinkedIn, the largest network of professional profiles on the web, a sort of permanent labour market, so the platform is now just a click away; indeed, beginning to write something that resembles a CV triggers the software to proffer its services. Again, the provision of templates, digital interfaces and 'helpful hints' for CV writing may seem merely pragmatic, yet it is worth ruminating on at greater length.

Users are afforded either templates in word-processor format or digital forms which collate personal information into printable or online CVs. Before or after the process of filling out the template, different styles can be chosen, as befit the job in question or personal preferences. The user then gives information about themselves: details, contacts, education and employment history, references, skills, qualifications and a personal statement. These range from the simply factual to larger claims about accomplishments or 'potential' – and while these templates are described as quick and user-friendly, they may actually take hours to fill in, in a repetitive process of revision and procrastination, repeated at intervals after short contracts. Jobseekers are advised to constantly update and refine their personal statement and keep different CVs on file.

Often these templates are advertised with exaggerated claims about their capacity to help people find a job. Occasionally, they are also linked to additional software behind a paywall, or connected to experts in CV writing, career guidance and so forth. That there are now a host of individuals whose job is to help others find a job is remarkable in itself, the new hustlers of the labour market. Yet, what matters here is the peculiar process envisaged by the CV template, regardless of the outlandish claims made for its efficacy. Most advice, online and offline, recommends a clear, uncluttered CV, and these templates guarantee just that – particularly those created through digital interfaces: jobseekers are invited to fill out a series of boxes with personal information, education and employment history and so on, and the software composes this neatly onto a single page – if it fits. A complicated life and muddled work history is translated by a series of sterile boxes into a preformatted image of a career – although it is still up to the user to discover their 'skills' and 'accomplishments' through self-scrutiny, and to create their own personal statement. Effectively, what these templates offer is a process whereby the user will give information about themselves, which will be presented in an optimal manner for busy employers or HR departments – who reportedly spend thirty seconds on average looking at any CV – the real beneficiaries of the site (Sharone, 2017).

CV templates claim to offer users a better chance of securing employment. While they are usually free – few jobseekers can afford to pay for CV advice and it is provided or even imposed by welfare offices – the CV template offers a peculiar exchange: the user must scrutinize themselves, not just collecting and collating information but discovering their skills, appraising their career, creating a personal statement and so forth. Effectively, they must 'tell the truth' about themselves as a potential worker in an era of 'surveillance capitalism' (Zuboff, 2019). Templates offer to render this 'truth' into the most effective document possible, partly because the worker is encouraged to present themselves in the best light possible, but also because the template makes this individual life clear and transparent via the CV format. The self becomes visible, legible, transparent – viewed through the gaze of the labour market.

Beyond scrutinizing a complex life and producing a transparent single-page text, there is a further exchange involved here: the user tells the truth about themselves, which implicitly transforms them from an ordinary individual – perhaps with a muddled biography or chaotic life – into a careerist, an ambitious entrepreneur of the self, ready for new opportunities, projects and collaborations. After self-scrutiny, the individual can speak about themselves, tell the truth about themselves, and thus, transformation brings forth the 'truth'. Simultaneously, it is telling the truth about the self via the CV that will allow the individual to become employed, which thereby transforms the individual from a jobseeker into a worker – the modern economic form of salvation. Again, here it is worth noting that this process is repetitive, as most applicants are not chosen, and even when employment is secured, it is often a short contract, so the process will begin again, just with another notch on the CV.

At risk of simplification, the CV template is partially the inheritor of the penitential confession box – the formatting of individual data serves to shape personhood (Koopman, 2019). In Foucault's formulation, these are 'spiritual exercises', not in assuming metaphysical spirit or soul but by denoting things that a subject does to themselves in order to know the self: 'It postulates that for the subject to have right of access to the truth he must be changed, transformed, shifted and become somehow other than himself' (Foucault, 2005: 15). There is a peculiar and long-standing relationship in the West between telling the truth and transforming the self; within theology or religion the ultimate arbiter of this is God, whereas within economics it is market outcomes. If one tells the 'truth' about one's career aspirations or simply one's willingness to work, then this is the truth of the self *if and only if* that transformation occurs.

Largely unremarked upon is that applying for welfare payments and applying for jobs both require that the individual sign a document, endorsing the truth of the statement about the self. Within welfare, the individual must declare that they meet the ILO definition of unemployment, being without work, available for work and genuinely seeking work. Regarding CVs or application letters, the jobseeker signs, 'yours sincerely', warranting that the details they present are true and accurate. These innocuous signatures have a genealogy that stretches back to archaic oaths, declarations of will, fidelity to one's word, a binding moral contract expressed negatively by the damning phrase 'oath breaker' (Agamben, 2018). Very clearly, there are negative sanctions for failure to keep one's word – refusal of welfare and even recovery of previous payments, or being fired for misleading employers.

Yet, the oaths of the labour market also have a Christian thread in their genealogy. The declaration that one is unemployed is a penitential confession of failure in the labour market, an admission of guilt and of faults as yet unidentified, elements of character which will need to be reformed. Submission to judgement and resignation to the trials of welfare activation are implied in this oath. Each signed job application or CV is a profession of the self, an oath that asserts past deeds, present dispositions and future willingness. This is a submission to the market test, and swearing the truth of one's self is a necessary prerequisite. Yet, contemporary activation entails continuous and frequent applications, continuous professions of faith in oneself and the labour market. This dynamic of repeatedly confessing unemployment, accepting the need for reformation, admitting faults and professing one's character as a worker is an incessant mechanism for reshaping individuals and testing their faith in the labour market.

Conclusion

Of the labour market experiences investigated within this book, self-scrutiny and self-presentation via the CV is probably shared by most or even all our readers. For those who are relentlessly successful, the trial of doubt and faith, self-questioning and hope, may seem negligible, but for those who repeatedly must try and fail, who are rejected far more frequently than accepted, the meaning and struggle of this process is familiar. Even those not coerced by welfare offices to rewrite their CVs and apply to any job whatsoever will recognize this constant testing of the self as corrosive. Yet, the theological ideas surrounding these experiences, rendering suffering as purifying or a 'learning experience', at least serve to give meaning and shape to these processes – perhaps rendering success more sweet by contrast to the bitterness of failure – even though such outcomes are really shaped by forces outside any jobseeker's control.

By adopting employer's perspectives in advance, the CV may appear a strategic document presenting the self as a commodity within the labour market or a certain portfolio of skills as a 'business solution' (Gershon, 2017). Yet discourse is never neutrally pragmatic, and the technique of viewing the self as if from outside is not straightforward and simple – disregarding the difficulty any jobseeker faces in imagining or anticipating the viewpoint of employers (Handley, 2018). Genealogically, the discourse of professing one's past achievements and confessing one's need of work through a CV amounts to becoming an abbot or spiritual director to oneself, generating the truth of self in obedience to an another, in hope of redemption or salvation, repeatedly: 'For the price of pardon is as infinite as the pardon itself' (Foucault, 2014a: 133) – repeated confessions, relentless CV work, limitless dedication to career and ambitions are required, even of the successful.

Where the religious speak in hope of being accepted by a spiritual director or by an omniscient God, the jobseeker reports to a welfare officer or sends their CV in hope of the invisible hand of the market saving them. For those who have been through redundancy and unemployment and had their CV rewritten in the 'workshops' of the welfare office, the CV is a form of confession, an admission of past suffering, but also an account of 'conversion', how the individual has transformed themselves and regained their faith in the labour market

(Purser and Hennigan, 2018). That doubts assail those who are more frequently turned down is obvious; every new CV is sent 'in hope of success'; indeed, 'faith is the substance of things hoped for, the evidence of things not seen' (Hebrews, 1:11). Strikingly, despair is condemned by Christianity as unforgiveable (Pecchenino, 2015), and jobseekers are required to persist indefinitely, hopefully, actively and genuinely seeking work, the ILO definition of unemployment.

After the penitential work of self-examination and discipline, the CV is also an expression of faith in the labour market, unto which the self professes themselves as a worker. To 'give an account of oneself' is never a neutral narrative (Butler, 2001), rather the self is constituted through a 'game of truth' which involves 'power and knowledge'. The transformative power of accounting for the self is not pregiven or natural, but occurs through historically specific discourses and games of truth – whether CV or confession. While sociologists tend to discuss socialization and social construction as generalized, it may be concentrated through specific moments and practices; prayers which ready the self and confessions which transform are prime examples of 'performative speech acts' – that is, utterances which produce the things they describe. Partially, the formatting and assumptions of the CV formula constitute what can be said, yet the individual is inextricably involved in this process of self-accounting: the self is under trial, being tested in these truth games. Confession involves avowal, revealing sins and faults, which are shriven from the jobseeker – a disavowal of any part of the self which falls short of the work ethic or the jobseeking careerist (Butler, 1997).

While the disciplinary power of welfare offices provides the most clearly punitive penitential element here, every CV is a prayer composed in hope of being redeemed, composed under the injunction of advisors, yet directed to the market. Thus, the outcomes of jobseeking activity and all the attendant efforts of CV writing are interpreted as verifying the 'true' worth of the individual, and by extension, the 'truth' of their self-presentation; the worth of the confession or prayer is judged by the godlike market (Cox, 2016). Like a daily prayer, a repeated ritual, the CV is an expression of faith in the labour market, of willingness to undergo its tests and in the hope of being transformed into a worker – to be given a vocation or profession. Yet, as we suggested in Chapter 6, that can be a long and winding road, a continuous test of the self, a pilgrimage even.

8

Conclusion: Parables of Welfare

To conclude, we consider a new parable of Job, from our own historical experience of welfare reform. Like a series of Russian nesting dolls, reform has many layers, from states to the individual. Here we return to the Financial Crisis of 2008 – a potent intimation that Fukuyama's 'end of history' was a false dawn.

After two years of deep economic decline across the West, in the summer of 2010 the European project almost collapsed; particularly because the bottomless pit of the Greek economic crisis became an existential threat for the ECB. The slow metabolism of European politics had crystallized the problem: the PIIGS countries – Portugal, Italy, Ireland, Greece and Spain – were the weakest economies in the eurozone and those most likely to default on their debts. The Achilles heel of the European project is that it is forged through compromised solutions between countries with a deep enmity towards each other; each solution is the basis for the next crisis.

The practical meaning of a 'vulnerable economy' is that speculators bet against the economy in a test of strength. In the summer of 2010, the inflation-averse ECB, led by Jean-Claude Trichet, entered cycle after cycle of extending loans and imposing reforms on Greece. Greece entered a cascade of reforming intervention and escalation, twelve cycles in all; governments fell under the strain, and protest and poverty spilled onto the streets of Athens. In European meetings, old grudges were recalled, and ultimatums came and went. The argument coalesced around the disapproving and moralizing German Lutheran-ordoliberal tradition and the supposed irresponsibility of Catholic and Orthodox Greece.

Ireland fell next. This perennially poor country walked into the global financial crisis in unusually rude health, buoyed not least by a private building boom. Once this bubble burst, a cascade of bank rescues and a declining tax take led to large government deficits. As private capital evaporated in 2010, the ECB stepped in as lender to the Irish sovereign, which in turn held up the Irish banks as lender of last resort and guaranteed repayment of bank losses. Uncomfortable with rolling over the ever-increasing loans, the ECB foresaw threats to the sovereign's solvency. Having pushed Ireland into saving its banks at all costs, in a series of secret letters, Jean-Claude Trichet, bounced the country into an IMF-EU-ECB-funded bailout.

Was this trial imbued with a hidden theological significance? In Irish soul-searching, everything was picked over, from the famine to the complex tangle of Anglo-Irish relations, which circled back to Catholic fecklessness and German austerity. The resulting national economic strategy directly addressed that need. A viral photo of Irish football fans with a cheeky flag emblazoned 'Angela Merkel thinks we're at work' spoke of the paternalistic moralizing that was reforming Ireland. Having faced down and seen off Greek's socialist-economist finance minister Yanis Varoufakis, the flinty German finance minister Wolfgang Schäuble asserted against considerable evidence: 'It is undisputed among economists worldwide that one of the main causes – if not the main cause – of the turbulence – not just now, but already in 2008 – was excessive public debt everywhere in the world' (Hien, 2019). Schäuble insisted that Ireland should not receive more funding after the bailout as it would undermine confidence in its economy – the market would judge Ireland.

This snippet of economic history has the character of a parable (Hien, 2019), with reforms being imposed upon a country; yet the real transformation was a reformation of welfare aimed at the unemployed.

Ireland's bailout was not simply a case of the IMF, EU and ECB applying the 'shock-doctrine' remedy of neoliberal austerity. To justify the maintenance of the level of cash transfers and protect the welfare state generally, the Irish policy machinery understood the symbolic value of introducing 'labour market reforms' (Hick, 2018), a gesture aimed at regaining access to the international debt market. The 'troika' (the IMF, EC, and ECB) were mainly concerned with macro-level finances, and some amongst them felt the measures went too far, too quickly. The Irish strategy was to self-discipline, be the 'model pupil' in the PIIGS classroom and regain the trust of the ECB, the EU and international markets (Allen, 2012). Thus the conditions of the 'Bailout Memorandum of Understanding' also agreed to the implementation of activation policies and the reform of welfare. Unemployment was to be 'tackled' by removing poverty traps, rationalizing benefits, integrating services, profiling jobseekers and monitoring their efforts, enhancing conditionality and the institutionalization of sanctions for non-compliance. These welfare reforms were to be reported to the troika at intervals.

In line with the OECD criticisms of 'passive welfare policies', Irish policymakers, experts and politicians had been calling for these reforms for decades, not just 'balancing the books' but turning towards welfare activation, even during massive economic growth from 1992 to 2006. Protests at new taxes turned into mass movements which reversed some government decisions, but there was little public awareness, still less resistance, to welfare reforms. The national frame dominated, as Ireland seemed to take the fall for Europe and Irish taxpayers picked up the bill for a crisis created by banks, developers and policymakers. Yet what this crisis routinized was welfare reforms. What if anything these welfare reforms contributed to the economic recovery is debatable; many arrived after the unemployment crisis abated. Nonetheless, over the last decade welfare sanctions have become normalized, activation services have been privatized and precarious work has grown. The subsequent COVID-19 labour market crisis hit just as full employment was reached, and calls for new, better reforms persist.

Rather than a parable of neoliberalism being imposed by external powers on individuals, what emerges here is that the urge to reform is deeply embedded within our culture. Today, the Catholic/Protestant distinction between 'worlds of welfare' is being eroded as Ireland and various Mediterranean countries attempt to replicate UK- or German-style reforms. The market is accepted as the only valid test of worth, and those who stumble on the pilgrimage of their careers are consigned to a purgatory wherein they must submit to judgement and trials until they are redeemed by work.

Know your history

Criticism of the ineffectiveness and cruelty of welfare reform is widespread within academic circles, and even acknowledged by policymakers. Activation has some effects, but it is not the panacea envisaged by its advocates. Beyond this, welfare reform is increasingly part of larger political and geopolitical tensions – rising concerns over inequality and anger around issues such as migration, race relations and geopolitical cohesion in the face of climate change and pandemics. In the context of instability or even revolutionary threats, the pendulum may swing towards more generous welfare provision to stabilize the polity. Yet this may be wishful thinking or a temporary reprieve;

international policy horizons are fixed on further activation, the refinement of methods, better nudges, an unshakeable faith in reform.

History bequeaths us ways of thinking, being and living, oftentimes with forgotten lineages. Sometimes these are sources of strength, resources to face future challenges; occasionally they are absurdities. The 'Charge of the Light Brigade' against the cannons is idealized but futile, as was French cavalry mobilized for World War One in mass formations of brightly visible uniforms. Equally futile, even self-damaging, is labour market activation as a remedy for mass unemployment after the huge economic dislocations of the COVID-19 pandemic and crises yet to come, those recognized as imminent such as climate change and those not yet visible to us. Yet, modern faith in the labour market ensures that states and international organizations will try them anyway, because, as politicians endlessly repeat, 'Something has to be done'. Yet there are other possibilities.

This book provides an alternative reading of the impetus for welfare reform. Obviously we dispute the account of the authors of these policies, whose perseverance is inspired less by the 'evidence base' for the effect of active labour market policies than by a faith in welfare activation as a salve to national and individual ills. Of course, this is not to say that such policies do nothing; they sometimes have an effect, pushing people from welfare into work more swiftly, sometimes with retraining, and thereby increasing 'labour market participation rates' or even creating 'social mobility'.

Yet, these occasional successes come at the cost of making welfare conditional and thereby precarious and less supportive, exposing all individuals to existential insecurity. This can mean pushing people into precarious work they would not otherwise accept (Dwyer, 2019; Watts and Fitzpatrick, 2018). Welfare sanctions can have a scarring effect on individual lives. Indeed, welfare reforms are predicated on the plan to prevent the 'subjective deterioration' of long-term unemployment, but they may have even worse effects on mental and physical well-being. Absurdly, the main consequence of activation is the proliferation of jobseeking, not the creation of jobs.

However, while critical of welfare reforms as policy, this is not an exposé of the ideology or irrationality of politicians, policymakers or welfare officers. These policies are not a conspiracy to ensure a cheap supply of labour or to deliberately worsen working conditions or a covert project of punishing the poor; they are announced, debated and justified publically, with democratic assent (Hansen, 2019). Even where welfare reform involves sanctions, it is designed to impose reform – as the phrase goes, 'cruel to be kind', even though these policies are based on a misdiagnosis of the cause of unemployment as personal failure to be remedied by personal transformation.

The interminable battle between welfare reformers and revolutionary critics reflects a longer history, with a distinctly religious inheritance. Faith in governmental intervention as the pathway towards personal redemption stands in tension with impulses towards revolution and the ideal of egalitarian socialism – heaven on earth. Yet, distinct from both of these is the urge to alleviate suffering by providing support. Common to both of them is the idea of the possibility of reform and transformation – of individuals, of states. Today, many leftist critics seek to redesign activation policies to support individuals back to work, to give them liberty and independence to make their own decisions, find their own career. It is not just capitalists who have faith in the labour market.

Finding theology hidden in plain sight

While Nietzsche suggested that every philosophy was a veiled autobiography, an expression of how an individual felt and experienced the world, we suggest that every policy is a veiled theology. Government does not simply proceed according to technical or scientific logics, even though it calls upon these instruments to implement and evaluate itself. Rather, governmentality is driven by visions of the world that are significantly tinged by religion: ideas about human life as a series of continuous choices, how individuals might be saved or damned, about life as a test and redemption through suffering, and a vision of this world as a providential order. Yet within our policy dogmas there are tensions and variations, most obviously between those who think that struggle will lead to utopia and those who attempt to constitute their society as the earthly city of God, the chosen people of the invisible hand. Perhaps more importantly, there is the tension between the imperative to alleviate suffering and the urge to reform people.

Curiously, the modern model of religiosity is neither a priest nor a member of the flock but a hybrid of a pilgrim and a monk. Indeed, Weber hinted at this: 'For when asceticism was carried out of monastic cells into everyday life, and began to dominate worldly morality, it did its part in building the tremendous cosmos of the modern economic order' (1992: 181). Thus, modern *homo economicus* is not the simple stereotype of a calculating individual critiqued for decades but a self widely shared, both a dedicatedly self-disciplined worker and a seeker of self-transformation. Strikingly, both the monk and the pilgrim deliberately seek out privations and even suffering as a means of redemption. Implicitly, both are penitential, living in an order or travelling the road in order to purify themselves of sins. Yet, concurrently, their ethic is charitable, helping others along the road, giving succour to the needy.

Foucault's formulation of governmentality draws our attention both to how people are governed but also to the mentality of governors. Clearly, those governing the conduct of the unemployed are not exclusively charitable or cruel, but deliberately seek to prevent civil unrest and manage the labour market (Offe, 1984). Yet, this is not a purely pragmatic position outside history, but depends on the assumption of the malleability of people – that they are like clay – and therefore on the godlike capacity of the state to reform them. Thus, welfare reform as a genealogical inheritor of pastoral power imputes an extraordinary capacity to know and transform others. Of course, this power and knowledge is parcelled out over a plethora of agencies and institutions, from policy think tanks to the street level; today, the welfare state exercises a judicial function, less a 'stigma machine' than a judgement machine, making moral pronouncements on the conduct of the unemployed and demanding reform.

Yet, the limits and test of governmentality are located firmly within the market, the crucial test of the worth of people and the efficacy of policies (Foucault, 2008). For neoliberals like Hayek (2001), only economic outcomes signal the truth unequivocally. Ironically, this makes the market equivalent to divine will, whereas state governing can only react as a form of secondary providence, offering an infinitude of second chances for redemption (Agamben, 2011). Clearly, this idea of the economy is derived from religious thinking, and the dominance of economics over politics has obscured the relations of power now exercised through ever more extensive and intrusive governmentality. Welfare conditionality emerges as a new form of extrajudicial power, extracting compliance without proper contracts or oversight; a peculiar return of sovereign power, wherein street-level bureaucrats decide whom they afford the promise of 'social protection' implied by the welfare state (see Agamben, 1998).

Competing imperatives in welfare – providing supports, cultivating a mobile workforce, activating groups 'distant from the labour market', avoiding 'poverty traps' and so forth – are not merely contemporary concerns of social policy. Rather, these are a reoccurring inheritance of intertwined genealogies, full of tensions, contradictions and conflicts. The signatures of history are echoed in the multiple intractable skirmishes such as the Reformation or the EU's search for economic stability in the eurozone crisis. By our archaic anthropology, we recover the historical roots of the urge to welfare and the impulse to reform. The Lutheran and later Calvinist Reformation's cultural program to establish a more austere society reflected a pre-existing impulse already present in the Judaeo-Christian tradition, presented in the medieval 'reformatio', back to the 'city of God' formulation of Augustine, and beyond. Recognizing these tensions rather than forcing a rapprochement between these deep-seated models is our aim here.

Recovering an understanding of the economy from before the Enlightenment is politically relevant. Before Christianity, in ancient Greece, the economic concern of the household was to satisfy life's necessities and generate a surplus of time and means that could be spent on the higher activities of philosophy and politics (Lesham, 2016). Thus, the economy addressed prudent management and the desire for surplus and the idea that politics and philosophy were built upon the economy, and were effectively the ultimate accomplishments of the economy. Today, the tension between governmental providence and the market test has become increasingly unbalanced. The welfare state is a remarkable creation amid the twentieth century of wars, yet contemporary decades have seen the economy asserted over every aspect of politics. Obsession with welfare rates and reform are present-centric, yet the result of a longer history, one which is unstable and prone to generate its own conflicts. By subjecting political, social or moral questions to economic criteria of market efficiency or affordability, contemporary states risk losing their legitimacy (Dean, 2013). Exceptional times, events and calamities require both symbolic, political gestures and cautious policymaking, yet the pursuit of economic success and full employment are not the only ideals.

A provocation

We have consistently approached data as *things given* from the natural world, gifts that entangle us in cycles of generosity and reciprocity. We cannot simply pass through the field of welfare reform demanding that others should revisit history, find theology hidden in plain sight and pay attention to the deeper theological code, all pleas for richer understanding in theory and method. Inevitably, we share the concerns of reform and welfare.

To administer work, both as an economic goal but also culturally as a fulfilment of the divine plan, welfare states have set up institutions to exercise judgement over individuals, assessing their lives, their conduct, their souls even, and directing them in purifying and purgatorial exercises of redemption. Yet judgement in the *ecclesia* is reserved for

God: 'Who are you to judge? Do not criticize your brother' (James, 4:11). Of course, courts as institutions for administering justice are a central part of modernity and Christianity – where the rule of conscience is central. However, contemporary welfare activation sets up individuals as judges over other people, unleashing a cascade of judgements through the trials of life. The vagaries of providence are also anticipated in this culture: 'Every man's work shall be made manifest: for the day shall declare it, because it shall be revealed by fire; and the fire shall try every man's work' (1 Corinthians 3:13). Modernity has adapted Christian theology to set up incessant tests and trials.

Provocatively, this book claims that theology underpins the welfare state and its incessant attempts to reform its people and itself, as well as the mundane practices of jobseeking, all in the service of the economy. This flies in the face of the widespread belief of economists, sociologists and political reformers of the welfare state that the Enlightenment and secularization have made theological ideas irrelevant. Ironically, a glib misinterpretation of Nietzsche's famous aphorism 'God is dead' is often used to separate theology from contemporary concerns:

> God is dead. God remains dead. And we have killed him. How shall we comfort ourselves, the murderers of all murderers? What was holiest and mightiest of all that the world has yet owned has bled to death under our knives: Who will wipe this blood off us? What water is there for us to clean ourselves? What festivals of atonement, what sacred games shall we have to invent? (Nietzsche, [1882] 2001: 125)

Nietzsche envisaged our 'secular' times, our evidence-based research and policy studies, as new sacred games and festivals of atonement, as displacements of a longer history. Even the word 'secular' is a religious inheritance (Holland, 2019). Nietzsche asserted that modernity is inextricably Christian, with its liberal commitment to equality, freedom, empathy with suffering and ideals of progress – or sometimes revolution. Rather than accept that contemporary morality – ideas about good and evil – are simply matters of basic human feeling and natural reason, Nietzsche insists they derive from religion and permeated modern culture all the more thoroughly because they go unrecognized.

Ironically, just as our social policies increasingly implement the pastoral power of reform upon others, our recognition of ourselves as part of this longer history slips away. Nineteenth-century reformers recognized themselves as religious – the 'gospel of work' was common parlance, and welfare providers were aware they built upon parish networks. Today, this legacy is dismissed with a trite anachronistic history which separates church and state, where religion appears as a vestigial element displaced by modern social policy. Recognizing the longer history of contemporary impulses in welfare reform does not mean escaping them – we are part of this scene, not separate from it. If there are alternatives within society, they too have a history. Rather than offer revolutionary proclamations of the end of the world and the Second Coming, this book implies the need to recover the value of alleviating suffering, not reforming individuals but simply supporting them.

The tension between supporting people and transforming them clearly has religious roots, expressing the ideals of charity and reformation respectively. Clearly, the balance between these two in contemporary policy has shifted strongly towards the 'reforming zeal', and today 'charity' has a poor reputation as being patronizing or strategic (Dean, J. 2020). The rationale for charity, the old medieval economy of grace, has been eclipsed by welfare activation. Thinking of the poor as a means for the salvation of charitable donors makes no sense today, nor does the idea of the 'holy beggar' or the pauper as image of Christ. Now, the poor are considered a burden on society who must be reformed.

Yet, our current welfare activation policies are also premised on conditions which are changing and soon to be eclipsed. Automation, technology and roboticization have threatened the 'end of work' as we know it for decades (Rifklin, 1985). The goal of full employment is no longer even desirable, as our ecology will not sustain continuous growth but requires massive reduction in economic activity: work needs to be slowed down. Many critics suggest a universal basic income to replace the requirement to work (Standing, 2015), others advocate for a shorter working week (Coote et al, 2013) – both of which seek to create not just a more equal society but an ecologically sustainable economy (Koch, 2017). Yet, such revolutionary transformations are difficult and disruptive, so a first step might simply be to renew the impulse to alleviate suffering by making welfare entitlements unconditional: to end the most pernicious forms of activation, to demand another form of reform.

What kind of welfare policy does this mean? An unconditional welfare policy means more than just giving support, it means refraining from judgement. Those who need support have their reasons, and who is fit to judge them? Another gospel citation, 'Judge not, lest you be judged' (Matthew 7:1), chimes perfectly with contemporary parlance – 'Don't judge! Who do you think you are?' Rather than being part of an apparatus of reformation, welfare payments should be unconditional, given as a right and an entitlement. Offering training and education, the human-capital side of activation should continue, but always as a matter of choice – no one should be coerced into transformation, and freedom of choice is a central theological and modern cultural value. From the perspective of a paternalist welfare state or 'liberal authoritarianism', this is problematic, as individuals can drift into idleness or worse, yet pressuring many for the dubious purposes of redeeming a few is not just governmentally inefficient but morally dubious. Frugal government as idealized by liberals is better served by dismantling systems of conditionality, which would reduce the push towards precarious work.

Thus, the existing welfare state can be renewed by returning to its roots in charity. Here, it is worth recalling that the Greek *caritas* does not simply mean giving to the destitute but also love; the most famous passage of St. Paul, 1 Corinthians 13: 'Now abideth faith, hope, charity, these three; but the greatest of these is charity' (13:13) – often read at weddings with the term 'charity' changed to 'love'. Indeed, what is meant by charity here is clearly more than giving alms: 'If I give all I possess to the poor and give over my body to hardship that I may boast, but do not have love, I gain nothing' (Corinthians 13:3). Accordingly, it is not enough simply to give – it cannot be merely an instrumental policy, but must be done in the right spirit. Long forgotten in the history of the critique of alms by reformers is the expression of love towards the sufferers through the act of giving – an actual gift relationship (Mauss, 2000); and implicitly, giving is good for those who give.

Our prescription of unconditional welfare is not a utopian policy; it is not even expensive, but makes all systems of coercive reformation redundant. It simply requires that states cease to require anything from the unemployed – not even active jobseeking. The economic consequences of this policy would be minimal, so entrenched is the work cult of modernity that the vast majority of people will pursue work and training without compulsion. Indeed, the most famous spinner of parables suggested that there is no point in destroying the harvest by ripping up the weeds which grow amongst the crop (Matthew 13: 24–29). Furthermore, in the longer term they might well make better decisions about their careers without the pressure to find work as quickly as possible or the compulsion to accept any job whatsoever.

Finally, unconditional generosity might even reform those who give instead of those who receive, just as envisaged by the medieval alms. Giving generously, unconditionally, is not a mere conservative salve to unrest to forestall revolution but a means of restoring collective solidarity, and quite practically, slowing down the economy to prevent ecological apocalypse. In these times of crisis and massive economic disruption, it is a crucial, yet simple policy. Indeed, it might reform the spirit of the reformers.

Afterword

While this book reflects around a decade of sustained thought and discussion, and was written and revised over several years, one intense period of writing was spring 2020, when the COVID-19 virus spread across the world, leading to national lockdowns, rolling restrictions and unprecedented economic shutdowns. Even as we write, much of Europe is entering a 'second wave'; we are living through history, not looking back afterwards. Like in other recent epochal moments, from the oil crisis to the fall of communism in Central and Eastern Europe, the Asian financial crisis to the Global Financial Crisis, the carnival of the economy is volatile; the wheel of fortune will spin. Despite this state of emergency, this book addresses perennial elements of welfare and unemployment through an archaic anthropology rather than producing a hasty verdict on the current crisis. In this more relaxed form of an afterword, we consider what, if anything, the pandemic might reveal about unemployment and the labour market – or what reformations it portends.

The initial wave of infections prompted an extraordinary pause of economic activity, from Asia to Europe and beyond, so that only essential production continued – although America is another story. Such a suspension of economic activity was effectively required by the state, showing clearly that markets are not natural or automatic but partly constituted by state regulations of sites of exchange and competition. Millions lost their jobs overnight, yet curiously, they were not technically 'unemployed' as they did not meet the precise ILO definition used by EuroStat and other national statisticians. As the pandemic swept the world, states with established public health and welfare systems were in a position to protect their population and by extension their economies, society and politics. Indeed, the automatic and unconditional provision of support to those who found themselves jobless due to the pandemic was a striking example of welfare payments without the demand for personal reform; the careful and complex scrutiny exercised upon pre-COVID-19 unemployment applications – from means tests to the requirement to seek work – were notably absent, at least for those who lost their jobs because of the pandemic – another inscrutable accident of providence.

The welfare state combines two main impulses: the urge to conserve the status quo by alleviating the extremes of economic suffering, and the demand that individuals reform themselves, escape dependency by participating in the labour market and find work. The pandemic led to an extraordinary reversion to the former principle, as Asian and European states wisely supported their populations through uncertain times, preventing poverty and propping up consumer demand. Indeed, the language of social solidarity –'We're all in this together' – prevailed for the early months of the crisis. The scale, speed and firmness of state support belied the assertion that 'there is no alternative' or the end of history in free markets. This was particularly true in the return of European solidarity, so notably absent in the Global Financial Crisis, with the re-emergence of Keynesian economics, and a reassertion of the welfare state, public medicine and stimulus spending on capital projects, particularly greener infrastructure and renewable energies.

Yet, with the looming uncertainty of further waves of infection and further economic shutdowns, tensions resurface: support for those without work is diminishing, especially in harsher welfare regimes, as payments are recalibrated, tapered down to minimal supports, and individuals are expected to seek work or retrain or start new businesses, despite the risks of contagion and constantly changing regulations. With unprecedented numbers unemployed around the globe, the remedy of activation policies still appears as not just the 'silver bullet' but the *only* bullet in the armoury of social policy. While promoters of a universal basic income, a three-day working week or lower labour market participation have been vocal, these ideas have found little serious political traction, despite the sharpness of the economic crisis. So, if and when the pandemic subsides, the reformation of welfare will be reprised: the state will produce new schemes to 'activate' the unemployed, advised by experts in social policy and behavioural economics. Activation programmes will be implemented by the 'pastoral care' of street-level bureaucrats, who will impose self-scrutiny, CV writing, jobseeking, retraining and even workfare on jobseekers as a test or trial designed to transform them. This is less an ideological project, whether delusional or exploitative, than it is a deeply embedded cultural model which will only be evaluated by its own yardsticks – the measures of activation and reform – and which is furthermore shared by those who are governed as much as those who govern.

Already the pandemic has demonstrated that the work cult of modernity – the demand that everyone find a productive job within a fulfilling career – and the state-level pursuit of full employment are both misplaced. Despite the sudden shutdown and the continued mothballing of entire sectors of the economy – tourism, entertainment, recreation, arts, hospitality – all basic goods and services are still provided. Generally, state income tax receipts have proven to be surprisingly resilient. It appears that the economy can readily absorb the contraction – fewer people are actually needed in work, or less work overall is necessary. Indeed, the centrality of work to human existence, assumed by psychologists since Maslow and before, is clearly questionable, given the non-collapse of civilization during this extraordinary interruption to work. A further consequence is the welcome reduction in emissions, most obviously from interruption to air travel but broadly from the reduced busyness of a non-stop market. Indeed, speaking of looming apocalypses, future ecological shocks are anticipated to far exceed the impact of COVID-19, and if history has lessons to be learnt, it is that the pandemic should provoke us to remodel our economies to be sustainable; there clearly is an alternative.

Yet despite the demonstrable lack of umbilical connection between the labour market and the broader economy, across the world, politicians, economists and social-policymakers are concerned about the economic recovery in terms of a return to work. As those made jobless by the pandemic move across the classificatory threshold that defines 'long-term unemployed', policymakers have become increasingly concerned about the potential scarring impacts. Rhetorically, they warn that the temporary is becoming chronic; 'de-skilling' looms, and people might grow 'detached from the labour market' or become 'discouraged workers'. New educational places, training programmes, apprenticeships and job-search workshops will be designed and provided, and, eventually, subtly, the threat of reduced or suspended payments for non-compliance will be implemented. Critics are once again primed to decry these as neoliberal, cruel and moralizing judgements that commodify labour, punish the poor and support capitalism. Inescapably, the policymakers and bureaucrats who create and enforce these reformations share our common culture; they are deeply invested in a theology of work and their mission to save individuals. For them, work is assumed to be redemptive, welfare should be a purgatorial suffering, individuals must confess the truth about themselves through their CVs and transform themselves, and finding a job is a noble pilgrimage. Life itself within the economy at large is a trial, and there is no other way to discover ourselves and our worth; individuals must be put to the test.

As a form of plague, the pandemic has apocalyptic resonances, and the word 'apocalypse' literally means 'revelation'; reflected in widespread ideas that crises reveal tensions and structures within society. Our book is about the persistence of ideas and how deep religious models shape the state. For this reason, we do not find ourselves at a historic crossroads with decisive choices to make. The urge to reform others and the impulse to alleviate economic suffering may be rebalanced in the aftermath of the pandemic, just as they were in previous crises, but both will persist and endure because they are endemic to our culture. The work ethic, the market as a test of work, the pursuit of self-transformation, will persist. Ironically, these demanding, oftentimes cruel or punitive dimensions of our culture also give life meaning in modernity.

These complex theological influences are elaborated in dedicated chapters, but even our shared experience of the pandemic serves to illustrate the persistence of religious ideas. Identified as a consequence of intensive farming and the exploitation of nature, spread swiftly by global interconnections, the virus appears as a nemesis of our own creation, one of the four horsemen of the apocalypse, arrived to chastise us for our sins. Restrictions on our liberty and suspension of our privileges and pleasures can appear like a reassertion of the purgatorial interpretation of life, a purifying punishment. As individuals and as a society, the pandemic tests us anew, our personal resilience, our social solidarity, and even our cultural resources for making sense of the disease and its alien qualities. From the state level of statistics and public health measures to the household-based implementation of precautions, we must reform our conduct; thus the economy once more becomes the *oikos nomos* of Greek philosophy, literally the law of the household, where life is moralized as a communal endeavour of mutual care.

While this book is not a conventional analysis of social policy, our archaic anthropology suggests that the endless quest for full employment fuelled by the constant reformation of welfare, needs to be rethought. If anything, the pandemic provides another opportunity to consider other ways of living and governing, which might be both more sustainable and more humane. Inevitably we will collectively continue to adapt elements of our culture, yet there are resources within that for a more generous and forgiving, less judgemental social policy.

This book was written over years, and draws upon sustained empirical research and interaction with social policy, but also draws from theoretical and historical readings, and especially from a fresh engagement with theology through archaic anthropology. It has also been a reflexive journey, and every element which we describe herein as reflecting Western Judeo-Christian culture we have recognized in ourselves; from the impulse to charitable generosity and refraining from judging, to the work cult, the interpretation of suffering as purgative, the perpetual pilgrimage and the deciphering of life as a series of tests and trials which tell us the truth about ourselves and transform us. All this must be avowed; this book is not just about others – work coaches or jobseekers, critics or reformers – it is also about ourselves, the traditions which constitute our thought and the tensions and possibilities for thinking differently within them.

While the faults and eccentricities of this book are ours alone, it has benefited from the insight of many others. Serendipitously, we were both inspired early in our careers by the wonderful Weberian scholar Paddy O'Carroll, whose spirit imbues this work, and to whom we dedicate this book. Our initially tentative venture into historicizing welfare as purgatorial received timely support from attending Stefan Schwarzkopf's Markets, Money and the Sacred – Workshop on Economic Theology at Copenhagen Business School in 2017. Stefan, together with Mitchell Dean, has led the establishment of the new paradigm of 'economic theology', and brought the conversation to the Economy and Society Summer School which we host annually. We are also indebted to a huge range of fellow researchers and thinkers on welfare and unemployment, particularly Didier Demazière, Peter Dwyer, Sharon Wright, Magnus Paulsen Hansen, Janine Leschke, Imogen Tyler, Mary Murphy, Fiona Dukelow, Joe Whelan, Michael McGann, Philip Finn, Kenny Doyle, Zach Roche, Stephen Gaffney, Michelle Millar, James Wickham, Alicia Bobek, Sinead Pembroke, Shana Cohen, Sean Healy and many more – our apologies for any oversights or omissions. Within and beyond our institutions we are lucky to have many conversational partners: Arpad Szakolczai, Maggie O'Neill, Kieran Keohane, Ger Mullally, Tríona Ní Shíocháin, James Fairhead, Carmen Kuhling, Tom Moylan, Tina Kinsella, Damian O'Doherty, Aisling Tuite, Paul Clogher, Niamh Maguire, John O'Brien, Collette Kirwan, Tom O'Toole, Joan McDonald, Zach Roche, Patrick Gallagher, Emma Maguire, Katie Scallon, Noel Connors, Anthony Burke, Ann Burke, Wendy O'Leary and all at the Postgrad Symposium and many more besides. Time out of teaching to write this book was supported through the WIT Research Connexions fund, and this project has received funding from the European Union's Horizon 2020 research and innovation programme under grant agreement No. 870702, and an Irish Research Council New Horizons award. Thanks to Gormfhlaith for timely proofing and feedback amid the pandemic. Alongside thanks, our apologies also to those who we have imposed upon with this work, from our students who unexpectedly found themselves studying religious roots of welfare states, to our families who were persistently imposed upon with this strange obsession; hopefully the final result will be worth all the suffering.

Written in hope
1 November 2020
Ardmore

Notes

Chapter 6

1   https://www.fish4.co.uk/career-advice/how-to-write-a-cv/, accessed: 16 April 2020.
2   www.fish4.co.uk/how-to-handle-a-job-rejection-career-advice-expert-guidance-fish4jobs/, accessed: 16 April 2020.
3   https://www.fish4.co.uk/career-advice/7-warning-signs-mean-reject-job-offer/, accessed: 16 April 2020.
4   https://www.fish4.co.uk/career-advice/7-warning-signs-mean-reject-job-offer/, accessed: 16 April 2020.
5   https://www.fish4.co.uk/career-advice/handle-job-rejection/, accessed: 16 April 2020.
6   https://www.monster.co.uk/, accessed: 16 April 2020.

Chapter 7

1   https://www.jobcentrenearme.com/how-to-write-a-cv/, accessed: 16 April 2020.
2   https://www.jobcentrenearme.com/how-to-write-a-cv/, accessed: 16 April 2020.
3   https://www.fish4.co.uk/career-advice/how-to-produce-an-interview-winning-cv/, accessed: 16 April 2020.
4   https://www.monster.ie/career-advice/article/top-5-cv-tips-ie, accessed: 16 April 2020.
5   https://www.fish4.co.uk/career-advice/mature-jobseeker-cv-template/, accessed: 16 April 2020.

References

Agamben, G. (1993) *The Coming Community*, Minnesota: University of Minnesota Press.

Agamben, G. (1998) *Homo Sacer*, Stanford: Stanford University Press.

Agamben, G. (2011) *The Kingdom and the Glory: For a Theological Genealogy of Economy and Government*, Stanford: Stanford University Press.

Agamben, G. (2018) *The Sacrament of Language*, Oxford: Wiley & Sons.

Agnew, J.C. (1986) *Worlds Apart: The Market and the Theatre in Anglo–American Thought, 1550–1750,* Cambridge: Cambridge University Press.

Alexander, J. (2004) 'Cultural Pragmatics: Social Performance between Ritual and Strategy', *Sociological Theory,* 22(4), 527–73.

Allen, A. (2017) *The End of Progress: Decolonising Critical Theory*, Columbia: Columbia University Press.

Allen, K. (2012) 'The model pupil who faked the test: social policy in the Irish crisis', *Critical Social Policy*, 32(3): 422–39.

Althusser, L. (1971) 'Ideology and ideological state apparatuses (notes towards an investigation)' in L. Althusser, *Lenin and Philosophy and other Essays*, London: NLG.

Anderson, E. (2019) *Private Government: How Employers Rule Our Lives (And Why We Don't Talk about It)*, Princeton: Princeton University Press.

Aquinas, T. (1998) *Selected Writings*, London: Penguin.

Arendt, H. (1989) *The Human Condition*, Chicago: Chicago University Press.

Augustine, S. (1961) *Confessions*, London: Penguin.

Bacchi, C. (2015) 'The turn to problematization: political implications of contrasting interpretive and poststructural adaptations', *Open Journal of Political Science*, 5: 1–12.

Baehr, P. and Gordon, D. (2012) 'Unmasking and disclosure as sociological practices: contrasting modes for understanding religious and other beliefs', *Journal of Sociology*, 48(4): 380–96.

Barbier, J. (2004) 'Activation policies: a comparative perspective', in A.S. Pascual (ed) *Are Activation Models Converging in Europe? The European Employment Strategy for Young People*, Brussels: ETUI, pp 17–83.

Bardwick, J. (1993) *Danger in the Comfort Zone: From Boardroom to Mailroom – How to Break the Entitlement Habit That's Killing American Business*, New York: Amacom Press.

Bataille, G. (1998) *Essential Writings*, London: Sage.

Batsleer, J.R. (2008) *Informal Learning in Youth Work*, Los Angeles: Sage.

Bauman, Z. (1989) *Modernity and the Holocaust*, Ithaca: Cornell University Press.

Bauman, Z. (2000) *Liquid Modernity,* Cambridge: Polity.

Baxandall, P. (2004) *Constructing Unemployment: The Politics of Joblessness in East and West*, Aldershot: Gower Publishing, Ltd.

Beatty, R. (1989) *The Perfect Cover Letter*, New York: Wiley.

Beder, S. (2000) *Selling the Work Ethic: From Puritan Pulpit to Corporate PR*, New York: Scribe Publications.

Beer, D. (2019) *The Quirks of Digital Culture*, London: Emerald Books.

Benjamin, W. [1921] (1996) *Selected Writings* (Vol. 1), Harvard: Belknap Press.

Bentham, J. (2010) *The Works of Jeremy Bentham, Vol. 8*, New York: Gale, Making of Modern Law.

Berlin, I. (1974) 'The divorce between the sciences and the humanities', *Salmagundi*, 27: 9–39.

Besamusca, J., Stănescu, I. and Vauhkonen, J. (2013) *The European Youth Guarantee: A Reality Check*, Brussels: FEPS.

Beveridge, W. (1909) *Unemployment: A Problem of Industry*, London: Longmans, Green & Co.

Bercovitch, S. (2012) *The American Jeremiad*, Wisconsin: University of Wisconsin Press.

Block, J. (2002) *101 Best Resumes to Sell Yourself*, New York: McGraw Hill.

Boer, R. (2013) 'Revolution in the event: the problem of Kairos', *Theory, Culture & Society*, 30(2): 116–34.

Boland, T. (2019) *The Spectacle of Critique: From Philosophy to Cacophony*, London: Routledge.

Boland, T. and Griffin, R. (eds) (2015) *The Sociology of Unemployment*, Manchester: Manchester University Press.

Boland, T. and Griffin, R. (2016) 'Making sacrifices: how the ungenerous gifts of social welfare constitute the unemployed as scapegoats', *Distinktion: Scandinavian Journal of Social Theory*, 17(2): 174–91.

Boland, T. and Griffin, R. (2018) 'The purgatorial ethic and the spirit of welfare', *Journal of Classical Sociology*, 18(2): 87–103.

Bolles, R. (1970) *What Color Is Your Parachute?*, New York: Ten Speed Press.

Boltanski, L. (2011) *On Critique: Towards a Sociology of Emancipation*, London: Polity Press.

Boltanski, L. and Chiapello, E. (2005) *The New Spirit of Capitalism*, London: Verso.

Boltanski, L. and Thévenot, L. (2006) *On Justification: Economies of Worth*, Princeton: Princeton University Press.

Bonoli, G. (2013) *The Origins of Active Social Policy: Labour Market and Childcare Policies in a Comparative Perspective*, Oxford: Oxford University Press.

Bourdieu, P. (1990) *The Logic of Practice*, Cambridge: Polity Press.

Bourdieu, P. and Wacquant, L. (1992) *An Invitation to Reflexive Sociology*, Chicago: University of Chicago Press.

Bright, J. and Earl, J. (2000) *Brilliant CV: What Employers Want to See and How to Say It*, London: Prentice Hall.

Brodkin, E. and Marston, G. (2013) *Work and the Welfare State: Street-Level Organizations and Workfare Politics*, Washington, DC: Georgetown University Press.

Bunyan, J. [1678] (1965) *The Pilgrim's Progress*, London: Penguin.

Burnett, J. (2002) *Idle Hands: The Experience of Unemployment 1790–1990*, London: Routledge.

Bussi, M. and Geyer, L. (2013) *Youth Guarantees and Recent Developments on Measures against Youth Unemployment: A Mapping Exercise*, Brussels: European Trade Union Institute.

Butler, J. (1997) *The Psychic Life of Power: Theories in Subjection*, Stanford: Stanford University Press.

Butler, J. (1999) *Gender Trouble*, London: Routledge.

Butler, J. (2001) 'Giving an account of oneself', *Diacritics*, 31(4): 22–40.

Butterworth, P., Leach, L.S., Strazdins, L., Olesen, S.C., Rodgers, B. and Broom, D.H. (2011) 'The psychosocial quality of work determines whether employment has benefits for mental health: results from a longitudinal national household panel survey', *Occupational and Environmental Medicine*, 68(11): 806–12.

Callon, M. (1998) 'Introduction: the embeddedness of economic markets in economics', *The Sociological Review*, 46(1): 1–57.

Campbell, C. (1988) *The Romantic Ethic and the Spirit of Consumerism*, Oxford: Blackwell.

Card, D., Kluve, J. and Weber, A. (2015) *What Works? A Meta-Analysis of Recent Active Labor Market Program Evaluations* (IZA Discussion Paper no. 9236), Bonn: IZA.

Carey, J. (1987) 'Time, space and the otherworld', *Proceedings of the Harvard Celtic Colloquium*, 7: 1–27.

Chaucer, G. [1387] (2002) *The Canterbury Tales* (ed. D. Coote), Hertfordshire: Wordsworth editions.

Cohn, N. (1971) *The Pursuit of the Millennium*, London: Paladin.

Cohn, N. (1993) *Cosmos, Chaos, and the World to Come: The Ancient Roots of Apocalyptic Faith*, London: Yale University Press.

Cole, M. (2007) 'Re-thinking unemployment: a challenge to the legacy of Jahoda et al', *Sociology*, 41(6): 1133–49.

Cole, M. (2008) 'Sociology contra government? The contest for the meaning of unemployment in UK policy debates', *Work, Employment and Society*, 22(1): 27–43.

Coleman, S. (1996) 'Words as things: language, aesthetics and the objectification of protestant evangelicalism', *Journal of Material Culture*, 1(1): 107–28.

Coleman, S. and Eade, J. (2004) *Reframing Pilgrimage: Cultures in Motion*, London: Routledge.

Coote, A. and Franklin, J. (eds) (2013) *Time on Our Side: Why We All Need a Shorter Working Week*, London: NEF.

Coulter, C. and Nagle, A. (eds) (2015) *Ireland Under Austerity: Neoliberal Crisis, Neoliberal Solutions*, Manchester: Manchester University Press.

Council of the European Union (2013) 'Council recommendation of 22 April 2013 on establishing a youth guarantee', *Official Journal of the European Union*, 56: 1.

Cox, H. (2016) *The Market as God*, Boston: Harvard University Press.

Daguerre, A. (2007) *Active Labour Market Policies and Welfare Reform: Europe and the US in Comparative Perspective*, New York: Springer.

Dante, A. [1320] (1969) *The Divine Comedy: II – Purgatory*, reprint, London: Penguin.

Davies, G. (2000) *Religion in Modern Europe: A Memory Mutates*, Oxford: Oxford University Press.

Dawkins, R. (1976) *The Selfish Gene*, Oxford: Oxford University Press.

Dean, J. (2020) *The Good Glow: Charity and the Symbolic Power of Doing Good*, Bristol: Policy Press.

Dean, M. (1995) 'Governing the unemployed self in an active society', *Economy and Society*, 24(4): 559–83.

Dean, M. (2010) *Governmentality: Power and Rule in Modern Society*, London: Sage.

Dean, M. (2012) 'Governmentality meets theology: "The king reigns, but he does not govern"', *Theory, Culture & Society*, 29(3): 145–58.

Dean, M. (2013) *The Signature of Power*, London: Routledge.

Dean M. (2017) 'Political acclamation, social media and the public mood', *European Journal of Social Theory*, 20(3): 417–34.

Dean, M. (2019) 'What is economic theology? A new governmental–political paradigm?', *Theory, Culture & Society*, 36(3): 3–26.

Deleuze, G. (1994) *Difference and Repetition*, New York: Columbia University Press.

Demazière, D. (2020) 'Job search success among the formerly-unemployed: paradoxically, a matter of self-discipline', *Critical Policy Studies*, DOI:10.1080/19460171.2020.1746372.

Desiere, S. and Struyven, L. (2021) 'Using artificial intelligence to classify jobseekers: the accuracy-equity trade-off', *Journal of Social Policy*, 50(2): 367–85.

DeSwaan, A. (1988) *In Care of the State: Health Care, Education and Welfare in Europe and the USA in the Modern Era*, New York: Oxford University Press.

Devereux, E. and Power. M. (2019) 'Fake news? A critical analysis of the "Welfare Cheats, Cheat Us All" campaign in Ireland', *Critical Discourse Studies*, 16(3): 347–62.

Dingeldey, I. (2007) 'Between workfare and enablement – the different paths to transformation of the welfare state: a comparative analysis of activating labour market policies', *European Journal of Political Research*, 46(6): 823–51.

DSP [Department of Social Protection] (2012) *Pathways to Work*, Dublin: DSP.

Dubisch, J. (1996) 'Anthropology as pilgrimage', *Etnofoor*, 9(2): 66–77.

Dunn, A. (2014) *Rethinking Unemployment and the Work Ethic: Beyond the 'Quasi-Titmuss' Paradigm*, London: Palgrave Macmillan.

Durkheim, E. (1995) *The Elementary Forms of the Religious Life*, New York: The Free Press.

DWP [Department for Work and Pensions] (2018) *Jobseeker's Allowance: Back to Work Scheme [JSABWS1] Guide*, Department of Work and Pensions: London.

Dwyer, P. (ed) (2019) *Dealing with Welfare Conditionality: Implementation and Effects*, Bristol: Policy Press.

Dwyer, P. and Wright, S. (2014) 'Universal credit, ubiquitous conditionality and its implications for social citizenship', *The Journal of Poverty and Social Justice*, 22(1): 27.

Edgell, S. (2012) *The Sociology of Work*, London: Sage.

Edling, N. (ed) (2019) *The Changing Meanings of the Welfare State: Histories of a Key Concept in the Nordic Countries*, New York: Berghahn Books.

Ehrler, F. (2012) 'New public governance and activation', *International Journal of Sociology and Social Policy*, 32(5/6): 327–39.

Eichhorst, W. and Rinne, U. (2017) *The European Youth Guarantee: A Preliminary Assessment and Broader Conceptual Implications,* (IZA Policy Paper, no. 128), Bonn: Institute of Labor Economics.

Escudero, V. and Mourelo, E.L. (2017) 'The European Youth Guarantee: a systematic review of its implementation across countries', (Working Paper, 21), International Labour Organization: Research Department, Geneva.

Esping-Andersen, G. (1990) *The Three Worlds of Welfare Capitalism,* Princeton: Princeton University Press.

Esping-Andersen, G. (2002) 'Towards the good society, once again?', in G. Esping-Andersen (ed) *Why We Need a New Welfare State,* Oxford: Oxford University Press, pp 1–25.

Ewald, F. (2020) *The Birth of Solidarity: The History of the French Welfare State,* Durham: Duke University Press.

Fenn, R. (1995) *The Persistence of Purgatory,* Cambridge: Cambridge University Press.

Fisher, M. (2009) *Capitalist Realism: Is There No Alternative?,* Alresford: Zer0 Books.

Fletcher, D.R. (2011) 'Welfare reform, Jobcentre Plus and the street-level bureaucracy: towards inconsistent and discriminatory welfare for severely disadvantaged groups?', *Social Policy and Society,* 10(4): 445–58.

Fletcher, D.R. (2015) 'Workfare – a blast from the past? Contemporary work conditionality for the unemployed in historical perspective', *Social Policy and Society,* 14(3): 329–39.

Fletcher, D.R. and Flint, J. (2018) 'Welfare conditionality and social marginality: the folly of the tutelary state?', *Critical Social Policy,* 38(4): 771–91.

Fletcher, D.R. and Wright, S. (2018) 'A hand up or a slap down? Criminalising benefit claimants in Britain via strategies of surveillance, sanctions and deterrence', *Critical Social Policy,* 38(2): 323–44.

Folkers, A. (2016) 'Daring the truth: Foucault, parrhesia and the Genealogy of Critique', *Theory, Culture & Society,* 33(1): 3–28.

Foucault, M. (1966) *Les mots et les choses,* Paris: Gallimard.

Foucault, M. (1972) *The Archaeology of Knowledge,* London: Routledge.

Foucault, M. (1976) *The History of Sexuality* (Vol. I), London: Random House LLC.

Foucault, M. (1977) *Discipline and Punish: The Birth of the Prison,* New York: Random House LLC.

Foucault, M (1980) *Power/Knowledge: Selected Interviews and Other Writings, 1972–1977,* New York: Vintage.

Foucault, M. (1981) 'Omnes et singulatim: towards a criticism of 'Political Reason', in S.M. McMurrin (ed) *The Tanner Lectures on Human Values*, Salt Lake City: The University of Utah Press, pp 223–54.

Foucault, M. (1984) 'The subject and power', *Critical Inquiry*, 8(4): 777–95.

Foucault, M. (1988) *Technologies of the Self: A Seminar with Michel Foucault*, Boston: University of Massachusetts Press.

Foucault, M. (1993) 'About the beginning of the hermeneutics of the self: two lectures at Dartmouth', *Political Theory*, 21(2): 198–227.

Foucault, M. (1997) 'What is critique?' in S. Lotringer and L. Hochroth (eds) *The Politics of Truth*, New York: Semiotext(e).

Foucault, M. (2000) 'Lives of infamous men', in: *Power, Truth, Strategy*. McArthur Press, pp 76–92.

Foucault, M. (2003) *Society Must Be Defended: Lectures at the Collège de France, 1975–1976* (Vol. 1), London: Palgrave Macmillan.

Foucault, M. (2005) *The Hermeneutics of the Subject: Lectures at the Collège de France, 1981–1982*, London: Palgrave Macmillan.

Foucault, M. (2006) *Psychiatric Power: Lectures at the Collège de France, 1973–1974*, London: Palgrave Macmillan.

Foucault, M. (2007) *Security, Territory, Population: Lectures at the Collège de France, 1978–1979*, New York: Picador.

Foucault, M. (2008) *The Birth of Bio-Politics: Lectures at the Collège de France, 1978–1979*, London: Palgrave Macmillan.

Foucault, M. (2011) *The Courage of Truth: Lectures at the Collège de France, 1983–1984*, New York: Palgrave Macmillan.

Foucault, M. (2014a) *The Government of the Living: Lectures at the Collège de France, 1979–1980*, London: Palgrave Macmillan.

Foucault, M. (2014b) *Wrong-Doing, Truth-Telling: The Function of Avowal in Justice*, Chicago: University of Chicago Press.

Frankl, V. (2006) *Man's Search for Meaning*, Boston: Beacon Press.

Fraser, D. (1992) *The Evolution of the British Welfare State: A History of Social Policy since the Industrial Revolution*, London: Macmillan International Higher Education.

Fraser, N. and Gordon, L. (1994) 'A genealogy of dependency: tracing a keyword of the US welfare state', *Signs: Journal of Women in Culture and Society*, 19(2): 309–36.

Frayne, D. (2019) *The Work Cure: Critical Essays on Work and Wellness*, London: PCCS Books.

Friedli, L. and Stearn, R. (2015) 'Positive affect as coercive strategy: conditionality, activation and the role of psychology in UK government workfare programmes', *Medical Humanities*, 41: 40–7.

Friedman, S. and Laurison, D. (2019) *The Class Ceiling: Why It Pays to Be Privileged*, Bristol: Policy Press.

Frisby, D. (2013) *Fragments of Modernity: Theories of Modernity in the Work of Simmel, Kracauer and Benjamin*, London: Routledge.

Fuentes, A. (2007) *Improving Employment Prospects in the Slovak Republic*, Paris: OECD.

Fukuyama, F. (1989) 'The end of history?', *The National Interest*, 16: 3–18.

Furlong, A. and Cartmel, F. (2007) *Young People and Social Change: New Perspectives* (2nd edn), Maidenhead: McGraw-Hill/ Open University Press.

Gaffney, S. and Millar, M. (2019) 'Rational skivers or desperate strivers? The problematisation of fraud in the Irish social protection system', *Critical Social Policy*, 40(1): 69–88.

Gallie, D. and Paugam, S. (eds) (2000) *Welfare Regimes and the Experience of Unemployment in Europe*, Oxford: Oxford University Press.

Gershon, I. (2017) *Down and Out in the New Economy*, Illinois: University of Chicago Press.

Gershon, I. (2019) 'Hailing the US job-seeker: origins and neoliberal uses of job applications', *Culture, Theory and Critique*, 60(1): 84–97.

Giddens, A. (2013) *The Third Way and Its Critics*, New Jersey: John Wiley & Sons.

Gide, C. [1889] cited in Donzelot, J. (1993) 'The promotion of the social' in Gane, M. and Johnson, T. (eds) *Foucault's New Domains*, London: Routledge, pp 106–38.

Gillies, V. (2016) *Pushed to the Edge: Inclusion and Behaviour Support in Schools*, Bristol: Policy Press.

Girard, R. (1977) *Violence and the Sacred*, Baltimore/London: Johns Hopkins University Press.

Girard, R. (1987) *Job, the Victim of his People*, Stanford: Stanford University Press.

Goffman, E. (1990) *The Presentation of Self in Everyday Life*, London: Penguin.

Graeber, D. (2011) *Debt: The First 5000 Years*, New York: Melville House.

Graeber, D. (2018) *Bullshit Jobs*, London: Verso.

Gragnolati, M. (2005) *Experiencing the Afterlife: Soul and Body in Dante and Medieval Culture*, Boston: University of Notre Dame Press.

Great Britain, Cabinet Office, Social Exclusion Unit (1999) *Bridging the Gap: New Opportunities for 16–18 Year Olds Not in Education, Employment or Training*, London: Stationery Office.

Greenwood, W. (1933) *Love on the Dole*, London: Cape.

Greer, I. (2016) 'Welfare reform, precarity and the re-commodification of labour', *Work, Employment and Society*, 30(1): 162–73.

Greer, I., Schulte, L. and Symon, G. (2018) 'Creaming and parking in marketized employment services: an Anglo-German comparison', *Human Relations*, 71(11): 1427–53.

Grey, C. (1997) 'Career as a project of the self and labour process discipline', *Sociology*, 28(2): 479–97.

Grover, C. (2012) '"Personalised conditionality": observations on active proletarianisation in late modern Britain', *Capital & Class*, 36(2): 283–301.

Grover, C. (2019) 'Violent proletarianisation: social murder, the reserve army of labour and social security "austerity" in Britain', *Critical Social Policy*, 39(3): 335–55.

Habermas, J. (2008) *Between Naturalism and Religion: Philosophical Essays*, Oxford: Polity Press.

Hadot, P. (1953) 'Epistrophè et metanoia dans l'histoire de la philosophie', in *Proceedings of the XIth International Congress of Philosophy* (Vol. 12), Amsterdam: North-Holland Publishing Company, pp 31–6.

Hakim, C. (1994) *We Are All Self-Employed: The New Social Contract for Working in a Changed World*, San Francisco: Berrett-Koehler Publishers.

Hall, S. (1988) *The Hard Road to Renewal: Thatcher and the Crisis of the Left*, London: Verso.

Handley, K. (2018) 'Anticipatory socialization and the construction of the employable graduate: a critical analysis of employers' graduate careers websites', *Work, Employment and Society*, 32(2): 239–56.

Hansen, K. and Hansen, R. (1990) *Dynamic Cover Letters*, Berkeley: Ten Speed Press.

Hansen, M.P. (2016) 'Non-normative critique: Foucault and pragmatic sociology as tactical re-politicization', *European Journal of Social Theory*, 19(1): 127–45.

Hansen, M. (2019) *The Moral Economy of Activation: Ideas, Politics and Policies*, Bristol, Policy Press.

Harvey, D. (2010) *The Enigma of Capital*, Oxford: Oxford University Press.

Hayek, F. (2001) *The Road to Serfdom*, London: Penguin.

Heidenreich, M. and Rice, D. (2016) *Integrating Social and Employment Policies in Europe: Active Inclusion and Challenges for Local Welfare Governance*, Cheltenham: Edward Elgar Publishing.

Heron, N. (2018) *Liturgical Power: Between Economic and Political Theology*, New York: Fordham University Press.

Hick, R. (2017) 'Enter the Troika: the politics of social security during Ireland's bailout', *Journal of Social Policy*, 47(1): 1–20.

Hien, J. (2019) 'The religious foundations of the European crisis', *JCMS: Journal of Common Market Studies*, 57: 185–204.

Hochschild, A. (2003) *The Managed Heart*, London: University of California Press.

Holland, T. (2019) *Dominion: The Making of the Western Mind*, London: Hachette UK.

Horvath, A. (2013) *Modernism and Charisma*, Oxford: Palgrave Macmillan.

Horvath, A. and Szakolczai, A. (2019) *Walking into the Void: A Historic Sociological and Political Anthropology of Walking*, London: Routledge.

Humpage, L.V. (2015) *Policy Change, Public Attitudes and Social Citizenship: Does Neoliberalism Matter?*, Bristol: Policy Press.

Humpage, L. (2019) 'Innovation and improved social outcomes? "Payment for outcomes" in social services in New Zealand', *New Zealand Sociology*, 34(2): 149–74.

Ingham, C. (1994) *Life Without Work: A Time for Change, Growth and Personal Transformation*, London: Thorsons.

Ingold, T. (2011) *Being Alive: Essays on Movement, Knowledge and Description*, London: Taylor & Francis.

Istance, D., Rees, G. and Williamson, H. (1994) *Young People Not in Education, Training or Employment in South Glamorgan*, Cardiff: South Glamorgan Training and Enterprise Council.

Jahoda, M. (1982) *Employment and Unemployment: A Social–Psychological Analysis* (Vol. 1), Cambridge: Cambridge University Press.

Jahoda, M. and Zeisel, H. (2002) *Marienthal: The Sociography of an Unemployed Community*, New Jersey: Transaction Publishers.

Janoski, T. (1990) *The Political Economy of Unemployment: Active Labor Market Policy in West Germany and the United States*, Berkeley: University of California Press.

Jensen, T. and Tyler, I. (2015) '"Benefits broods": the cultural and political crafting of anti-welfare commonsense', *Critical Social Policy*, 35(4): 470–91.

Jessop, B. (2019) 'Ordoliberalism and neoliberalization: governing through order or disorder', *Critical Sociology*, 45(7–8): 967–81.

Jobcentre Plus (2010) *Find Your Way Back to Work: JobKit, Practical Advice and Help When Applying for Jobs*, London: Department of Work and Pensions.

Johnson, J. (1993) *The Job Application Handbook*, Oxford: How To Books.

Jones, O. (2012) *Chavs: The Demonization of the Working Class*, London: Verso.

Jordan, J.D. (2018) 'Welfare grunters and workfare monsters? An empirical review of the operation of two UK "Work Programme" centres', *Journal of Social Policy*, 47(3): 583–601.

Jung, C.G. [1952] (2010) *Answer to Job*, reprint, Princeton: Princeton University Press.

Juncker, J.C. (2016) *State of the Union Address 2016: Towards a Better Europe – A Europe that Protects, Empowers and Defends*, Strasborg.

Kagge, E. (2019) *Walking: One Step at a Time*, New York: KnopfDoubleday.

Kahl, S. (2005) 'The religious roots of modern poverty policy: Catholic, Lutheran and Reformed Protestant traditions compared', *European Journal of Sociology*, 46: 91–126.

Keohane, K. and Kuhling, C. (2015) *The Domestic, Moral and Political Economies of Post-Celtic Tiger Ireland: What Rough Beast?*, Manchester: Manchester University Press.

Koch, M. and Bucha, M. (2017) *Postgrowth and Wellbeing: Challenges to Sustainable Welfare*, Basingstoke: Palgrave Macmillan.

Koopman, C. (2013) *Genealogy as Critique: Foucault and the Problems of Modernity*, Indiana: Indiana University Press.

Koopman, C. (2019) *How We Became Our Data: A Genealogy of the Informational Person*, Chicago: Chicago University Press.

Kotsko, A. (2018) *Neoliberalism's Demons: On the Political Theology of Late Capital*, Standford: Stanford University Press.

Laanani, M., Ghosn, W., Jougla, E. and Rey, G. (2015) 'Impact of unemployment variations on suicide mortality in Western European countries (2000–2010)', *Journal of Epidemiology and Community Health*, 69(2): 103–9.

Lane, C. (2012) *A Company of One: Insecurity, Independence, and the New World of White-Collar Unemployment*, Cornell: Cornell University Press.

Lane, C. and Kwon, J. (2016) *The Anthropology of Unemployment: New Perspectives on Work and Its Absence*, Cornell: Cornell University Press.

Larsen, F. and Mailand, M. (2007) 'Danish activation policy: the role of the normative foundation, the institutional set-up and other drivers', *Reshaping Welfare States and Activation Regimes in Europe*, 54: 99–127.

Lassalle, F. (1862) 'On the essence of constitutions', speech delivered in Berlin, 25–31.

Latour, B. (1990) 'Technology is society made durable', *The Sociological Review*, 1: 103–31.

Latour, B. (1993) *We Have Never Been Modern*, London: Harvester.

Latour, B. (2009) *Reassembling the Social*, London: Polity Press.

Latour, B. and Woolgar, S. (1986) *Laboratory Life: The Construction of Scientific Facts*, Princeton: Princeton University Press.

Le Goff, J. (1984) *The Invention of Purgatory*, Chicago: University of Chicago Press.

Le Goff, J. (2009) *The Birth of Europe*, Oxford: Wiley.

Leschke, J., Russell, H., Smith, M. and Villa, P. (2019) 'Stressed economies, distressed policies, and distraught young people: European policies and outcomes from a youth perspective', in J. O'Reilly, J. Leschke, R. Ortlieb, M. Seeleib-Kaiser and P. Villa (eds) *Youth Labor in Transition: Inequalities, Mobility, and Policies in Europe*, New York: Oxford University Press, pp 104–31.

Leshem, D. (2016) *The Origins of Neoliberalism: Modeling the Economy from Jesus to Foucault*, New York: Columbia University Press.

Levitas, R. (2005) *The Inclusive Society? Social Exclusion and New Labour*, New York: Springer.

Lind, J. and Møller, I.H. (2006) 'Activation for what purpose? Lessons from Denmark', *International Journal of Sociology and Social Policy*, 26(1–2): 5–19.

Linebaugh, P. and Rediker, M. (2000) *The Many-Headed Hydra: The Hidden History of the Revolutionary Atlantic*, London: Verso.

Lødemel, I. and Trickey, H. (2001) *An Offer You Can't Refuse – Workfare in International Perspective*, Bristol: Policy Press.

Loewenberg, F.M. (1994) 'On the development of philanthropic institutions in ancient Judaism: provisions for poor travelers', *Nonprofit and Voluntary Sector Quarterly*, 23(3): 193–207.

Loewenberg, F.M. (1995) 'Financing philanthropic institutions in biblical and Talmudic times', *Nonprofit and Voluntary Sector Quarterly*, 24(4): 307–20.

Lynch, M. (2000) 'Against reflexivity as an academic virtue and source of privileged knowledge', *Theory, Culture & Society*, 17(3): 26–54.

Macdonald, R., Shildrick, T. and Furlong, A. (2014) 'In search of "intergenerational cultures of worklessness": hunting the Yeti and shooting zombies', *Critical Social Policy*, 34(2): 199–220.

Macfarlane, A. (1988) *The Origins of English Individualism*, Oxford: Wiley-Blackwell.

Marquis, N. (2016) 'Performance et authenticité, changement individuel et changement collectif: une perspective sociologique sur quelques paradoxes apparents du développement personnel', *Communication Management*, 13(1): 47–62.

Maslow, A. (1998) *Maslow on Management*, Oxford: Wiley-Blackwell.

Maslow, A. (2000) *The Maslow Business Reader*, Oxford: Wiley-Blackwell.

Mauss, M. (2000) *The Gift*, with an introduction by Mary Douglas, London: Routledge.

Mauss, M. (2003) *On Prayer: Text and Commentary*, Oxford: Berghahn Books.

McCloskey, D. (2004) 'Avarice, prudence, and the bourgeois virtues', in C.T. Mathewes and W. Schweiker (eds) *Having: Property and Possession in Religious and Social Life*, Michigan: William B. Eerdmans Publishing, pp 312–36.

McDonald, C. and Marston, G. (2005) 'Workfare as welfare: governing unemployment in the advanced liberal state', *Critical Social Policy*, 25(3): 374–401.

McGloin, C. and Georgeou, N. (2016) ' "Looks good on your CV": the sociology of voluntourism recruitment in higher education', *Journal of Sociology*, 52(2): 403–17.

McGuinness, S., Kelly, E. and Walsh, J.R. (2014) 'Predicting the probability of long-term unemployment in Ireland using administrative data', *Economic and Social Research Institute (ESRI) Research Series*, 51: 1–29, ESRI: Dublin.

McGuinness, S., O'Connell, P.J. and Kelly, E. (2011) *Carrots Without Sticks: The Impacts of Job Search Assistance in a Regime with Minimal Monitoring and Sanctions* (ESRI Working Paper No. 409), Dublin: ESRI.

Mead, L. (1986) *Beyond Entitlement: The Social Obligations of Citizenship*, New York: Free Press.

Mead, L. (1993) *The New Politics of Poverty: The Non-Working Poor in America*, New York: Basic Books.

Mead, L. (1997) *The New Paternalism: Supervisory Approaches to Poverty*, Washington, DC: Brookings Institute.

Michielse, H. and Van Krieken, R. (1990) 'Policing the poor: J.L. Vives and the sixteenth century origins of modern social administration', *Social Service Review*, 64(1): 1–21.

Miller, P. and Rose, N. (2013) 'Governing economic life', in M. Gane, and T. Johnson (eds) *Foucault's New Domains*, London: Routledge.

Minas, R., Wright, S. and Van Berkel, R. (2012) 'Decentralization and centralization governing the activation of social assistance recipients in Europe', *International Journal of Sociology and Social Policy*, 32(5–6): 286–98.

Mollat, M. (1986) *The Poor in the Middle Ages: An Essay in Social History*, New Haven: Yale University Press.

Moran, R. (2016) *The Thing About Work: Showing Up and Other Important Matters*, London: Routledge.

Murphy, M.P. (2016) 'Low road or high road? The post-crisis trajectory of Irish activation', *Critical Social Policy*, 36(3): 432–52.

Murray, C. (2006) *In Our Hands: A Plan to Replace the Welfare State*, Washington, DC: AEI Press.

Negri, A. (2009) *The Labor of Job: The Biblical Text as a Parable of Human Labor*, Durham: Duke University Press.

Nietzsche, F. [1887] (1998) *On the Genealogy of Morals: A Polemic*, Reprint, Cambridge: Cambridge University Press.

Nietzsche, F. [1882] (2001) *The Gay Science*, reprint, Cambridge: Cambridge University Press.

Nozick, R. (1974) *Anarchy, State, and Utopia*, New York: Basic Books.

O' Neill, M. and Roberts, J. (2019) *Walking Methods: Research on the Move*, London: Routledge.

O'Callaghan, C. (2009) *Surviving the Axe: The Irish Guide to Handling Redundancy and Finding a New Job*, Dublin: Liberty.

O'Carroll, J.P. (1987) 'Strokes, cute hoors and sneaking regarders: the influence of local culture on Irish political style', *Irish Political Studies*, 2(1): 77–92.

O'Connell, P. J., McGuinness, S., Kelly, E. and Walsh, J.R. (2009) *National Profiling of the Unemployed in Ireland*, Dublin: ESRI.

OECD (2019) *The Future of Work: OECD Employment Outlook 2019*, Paris: OECD.

Offe, C. (1984) *Contradictions of the Welfare State*, Massachusetts: Cambridge MIT.

Orwell, G. [1937] (2001) *The Road to Wigan Pier*, reprint, London: Penguin.

Papacharissi, Z. (2009) 'The virtual geographies of social networks: a comparative analysis of Facebook, LinkedIn and ASmallWorld', *New Media & Society*, 11(1–2): 199–220.

Pecchenino, R. (2011) 'Preferences, choice, goal attainment, satisfaction: that's life?', *Journal of Socio-Economics*, 40(3): 237–41.

Pecchenino, R. (2015) 'Have we cause for despair?', *Journal of Behavioural and Experimental Economics*, 58(3): 56–62.

Peck, J. and Theodore, N. (2016) *Fast Policy: Experimental Statecraft at the Thresholds of Neo-liberalism*, Minnesota: University of Minnesota Press.

Peck, J. (1996) *Workplace: The Social Regulation of Labour Markets*, New York: Guilford Press.

Petersen, A. (2011) 'Authentic self-realization and depression', *International Sociology*, 26(1): 5–24.

Piketty, T. (2020) *Capital and Ideology*, Cambridge: Harvard University Press.

Pleasants, N. (2019) 'Free will, determinism and the "problem" of structure and agency in the social sciences', *Philosophy of the Social Sciences*, 49(1): 3–30.

Polanyi, K. (2001) *The Great Transformation*, London: Beacon Press.

Popken, R. (1999) 'The pedagogical dissemination of a genre: the resume in American business discourse textbooks, 1914–1939', *Journal of Composition Theory*, 19(1): 91–116.

Purser, G. and Hennigan, P. (2018) 'Disciples and dreamers: job readiness and the making of the US working class', *Dialect Anthropology*, 42: 149–61.

Quinon, M. (1996) 'Welfare', *World Wide Words* [online], available from: http://www.worldwidewords.org/topicalwords/tw-wel1.htm, accessed: 23 May 2020.

Rifklin, J. (1985) *The End of Work*, New York: Putnam.

Roberts, K. (2004) 'School-to-work transitions: why the United Kingdom's educational ladders always fail to connect', *International Studies in Sociology of Education*, 14(3): 203–16.

Roberts, S. (2018) *Young Working-Class Men in Transition*, London: Routledge.

Robinson, J. (1964) *Economic Philosophy*, reprint, Harmondsworth: Penguin.

Rogers, R. (2004) 'Ethical techniques of the self and the "good jobseeker"', in H. Dean (ed) *The Ethics of Welfare: Human Rights, Dependency and Responsibility*, Bristol: Policy Press, pp 155–72.

Rosa, H. (2019) *Resonance: A Sociology of Our Relationship to the World*, New Jersey: John Wiley & Sons.

Rose, N. (1989) 'The enterprising self', in P. Heelas and P. Morris (eds) *The Values of the Enterprise Culture: The Moral Debate*, London: Routledge, pp 141–63.

Rose, N. (1996) *Inventing Our Selves*, Cambridge: Cambridge University Press.

Sahlins, M. (1972) *Stone Age Economics*, Chicago: Aldine-Atherton.

Scarpetta, S., Sonnet, A. and Manfredi, T. (2010) 'Rising youth unemployment during the crisis: how to prevent negative long-term consequences on a generation?', *OECD Social, Employment and Migration Papers*, 106: Paris: Organisation for Economic Cooperation and Development; Directorate for Employment, Labour and Social Affairs.

Schwarzkopf, S. (2011) 'The political theology of consumer sovereignty: towards an ontology of consumer society', *Theory, Culture & Society*, 28(3): 106–29.

Schwarzkopf, S. (2012) 'The market order as metaphysical loot: theology and the contested legitimacy of consumer capitalism', *Organization*, 19(3): 281–97.

Schwarzkopf, S. (ed) (2020) *The Routledge Handbook of Economic Theology*, London: Routledge.

Scott, J. (2017) *Against the Grain: A Deep History of the Earliest States*, New Haven: Yale University Press.

Serrano Pascual, A. and Magnusson, L. (eds) (2007) *Reshaping Welfare States and Activation Regimes in Europe*, Brussels: Peter Lang.

Sewell, W.H. (1992) 'A theory of structure: duality, agency and transformation', *American Journal of Sociology*, 98(1): 1–29.

Sewell, W.H. (1996) 'Historical events as transformations of structures: inventing revolution at the Bastille', *Theory and Society*, 25(6): 841–81.

Sharone, O. (2013) *Flawed System/Flawed Self: Job Searching and Unemployment Experiences*, Chicago: University of Chicago Press.

Sharone, O. (2017) 'LinkedIn or LinkedOut? How social networking sites are reshaping the labor market', in S.P. Vallas (ed) *Emerging Conceptions of Work, Management and the Labor Market* (Research in the Sociology of Work, Vol. 30), Bingley: Emerald Publishing Limited, pp 1–31.

Shildrick, T. and MacDonald, R. (2012) *Poverty and Insecurity: Life in Low-Pay, No-Pay Britain*, Bristol: Policy Press.

Shildrick, T. and MacDonald, R. (2013) 'Poverty talk: how people experiencing poverty deny their poverty and why they blame "the poor"', *The Sociological Review*, 61(2): 285–303.

Simmons, R., Thompson, R., Tabrizi, G. and Nartey, A. (2014) *Engaging Young People Not in Education, Employment or Training: The Case for a Youth Resolution*, London: University and College Union.

Singh, D. (2018) *Divine Currency: The Theological Power of Money in the West*, Stanford: Stanford University Press.

Skeggs, B. (2004) *Class, Self, Culture*, London: Sage.

Slok, C. (2020) 'Guilt' in S. Schwarzkopf (ed) *The Routledge Handbook of Economic Theology*, London: Routledge, pp 72–80.

Smith, A. (2003) *The Wealth of Nations*, London: Penguin.

Sørensen, B.M., Spoelstra, S., Höpfl, H. and Critchley, S. (2012) 'Theology and organization', *Organization*, 19(3): 267–79.

Spivack, B. (1958) *Shakespeare and the Allegory of Evil: The History of a Metaphor in Relation to His Major Villains*, New York: Oxford University Press.

Springer, S. (2016) *The Discourse of Neo-liberalism: An Anatomy of a Powerful Idea*, Lanham: Rowman & Littlefield.

Standing, G. (2011) *Precariat: The New Dangerous Class*, London: Bloomsbury.

Standing, G. (2015) *Basic Income, and How We Can Make It Happen*, London: Pelican.

Stark, R. (2006) *The Victory of Reason: How Christianity Led to Freedom, Capitalism, and Western Success*, London: Random House Incorporated.

Steinbeck, J. (1975) *The Grapes of Wrath*, London: Pan Books.

Stimilli, E. (2017) *The Debt of the Living: Ascesis and Capitalism*, New York: SUNY Press.

Stimilli, E. (2019) 'Debt economy and faith: philosophy in the Age of Terror', *Diacritics*, 47(2): 4–21.

Szakolczai, A. (2013) *Comedy and the Public Sphere: The Re-birth of Theatre as Comedy and the Genealogy of the Modern Public Arena*, London: Routledge.

Szakolczai, A. (2018) 'Neoclassical economics as a logic of subversion', in C.F. Roman, A. Horváth and G.G. Germain (eds) *Divinization and Technology*, London: Routledge, pp 165–86.

Szakolczai, A. and Thomassen, B. (2019) *From Anthropology to Social Theory*, Cambridge: Cambridge University Press.

Taylor, F.W. (1919) *Principles of Scientific Management*, London: Harper & Brothers.

Taylor, C. (1989) *Sources of the Self: The Making of the Modern Identity*, Cambridge: Harvard University Press.

Taylor, M.C. (2008) *Confidence Games: Money and Markets in a World without Redemption*, Chicago: University of Chicago Press.

Thomassen, B. (2013) *Liminality and the Modern*, London: Ashgate.

Thompson, E.P. (1967) 'Time-work discipline and Industrial Capitalism', *Past and Present*, 38: 56–97.

Throness, L. (2008) *A Protestant Purgatory: Theological Origins of the Penitentiary Act, 1779*, Aldershot: Ashgate.

Tilley, L. (2012) '"The bioarchaeology of care": The Archaeological Record (Special Issue)', *New Directions in Bioarchaeology*, 12(3): 39–41.

Titmuss, R. (1970) *The Gift Relationship: From Human Blood to Social Policy*, London: Allen & Unwin.

Turner, E. and Turner, V. (2011) *Image and Pilgrimage in Christian Culture*, New York: Columbia University Press.

Turner, V. (1969) *The Ritual Process: Structure and Anti-Structure*, London: Routledge.

Tyler, I. (2015) 'Classificatory struggles: class, culture and inequality in neoliberal times', *The Sociological Review*, 63(2): 493–511.

Tyler, I. (2020) *Stigma: The Machinery of Inequality*, London: Zed Books.

Tyler, I. and Slater, T. (2018) 'Rethinking the sociology of stigma', *The Sociological Review*, 66(4): 721–43.

Underberg, N.M. and Zorn, E. (2013) *Digital Ethnography: Anthropology, Narrative, and New Media*, Texas: University of Texas Press.

Urciuoli, B. (2008) 'Skills and selves in the new workplace', *American Ethnologist*, 35: 211–28.

Vallas, S. and Cummins, E. (2015) 'Personal branding and identity norms in the popular business press: enterprise culture in an age of precarity', *Organization Studies*, 36(3): 293–319.

Vallas, S. and Christin, A. (2018) 'Work and identity in an era of precarious employment: how workers respond to "personal branding" discourse', *Work and Occupations,* 45(1): 3–37.

van Berkel, R. and Møller, I.H. (eds) (2002) 'The concept of activation', in R. Van Berkel and I.H. Møller (eds) *Active Social Policies in the EU: Inclusion Through Participation?*, Bristol: Policy Press, pp 45–71.

van Berkel, R., de Graaf, W. and Sirovátka, T. (2011) *The Governance of Active Welfare States*, London: Palgrave Macmillan.

van Dijck, J. (2013) '"You have one identity": performing the self on Facebook and LinkedIn', *Media, Culture & Society*, 35(2): 199–215.

Van Maanen, J. (2006) 'Ethnography then and now', *Qualitative Research in Organizations and Management: An International Journal*, 1(1): 13–21.

Van Oort, M. (2015) 'Making the neoliberal precariat: two faces of job-searching in Minneapolis', *Ethnography*, 16(1): 74–94.

Varoufakis, Y. (2016) *And the Weak Suffer What They Must?: Europe, Austerity and the Threat to Global Stability*, New York: Random House.

Voegelin, E. (1969) *The New Science of Politics: An Introduction*, London: Aldwyn Press Ltd.

Voegelin, E. (1997) *Science, Politics and Gnosticism: Two Essays*, Washington, DC: Regnery Publishing.

Wacquant, L. (2009) *Punishing the Poor: The Neoliberal Government of Social Insecurity*, Durham: Duke University Press.

Walls, J. (2002) *Purgatory: The Logic of Total Transformation*, Oxford: Oxford University Press.

Walters, W. (2000) *Unemployment and Government: Genealogies of the Social*, New York: Cambridge University Press.

Warr, P. (1987) *Work, Unemployment and Mental Health*, London: Clarendon Press.

Watts, B. and Fitzpatrick, S. (2018) *Welfare Conditionality*, London: Routledge.

Webb, D. (2007) *Pilgrimage in Medieval England*, New York: Hambledon Continuum.

Weber, M. (1991) *From Max Weber: Essays in Sociology*, London: Routledge.

Weber, M. (1930) *The Protestant Ethic and the Spirit of Capitalism*, reprint, London: Routledge, 1992.

Wee, L. and Brooks, M. (2010) 'Personal branding and the commodification of reflexivity', *Cultural* Sociology, 4(1): 45–62.

Weeks, K. (2011) *The Problem with Work: Feminism, Marxism, Anti-Work Politics and Post-Work Imaginaries*, Durham: Duke University Press.

Weil, S. [1952] (2003) *The Need for Roots: Prelude to a Declaration of Duties Towards Mankind*, reprint, London: Routledge.

Weinrich, H. (2008) *On Borrowed Time: The Art and Economy of Living with Deadlines*, Chicago: University of Chicago Press.

Weishaupt, T. (2010) 'A silent revolution? New management ideas and the reinvention of European public employment services', *Socio-Economic Review*, 8(3): 461–86.

Whelan, J. (2020) 'We have our dignity, yeah? Scrutiny under suspicion: experiences of welfare conditionality in the Irish social protection system', *Social Policy & Administration*, 55(1): 34–50.

Wilkinson, R.G. and Pickett, K.E. (2009) 'Income inequality and social dysfunction', *Annual Review of Sociology*, 35: 493–511.

Willis, E. (2008) 'The invention of purgatory: contributions to abstract time in capitalism', *Sociology*, 44(3): 249–64.

Willis, P. (1977) *Learning to Labor: How Working Class Kids Get Working Class Jobs*, New York: Columbia University Press.

Winter, Y. (2012) 'Plebeian politics', *Political Theory*, 40 (6): 736–66.

Wood, E.M. (1999) *The Origin of Capitalism*, New York: Monthly Review Press.

Wright, S. (2016) 'Conceptualising the active welfare subject: welfare reform in discourse, policy and lived experience', *Policy & Politics*, 44(2): 235–52.

Wrigley, L. (2017) 'From "NEET" to "unknown": who is responsible for young people not in education, employment and training', *Youth and Policy: The Journal of Critical Analysis*, available from: https://www.youthandpolicy.org/articles/from-neet-to-unknown/, accessed: 13 January 2021

Wrong, D.H. (1961) 'The oversocialized conception of man in modern sociology', *American Sociological Review*, 26(2): 183–93.

Yate, M. (2015) *Ultimate CV: Over 100 Winning CVs to Help You Get the Interview and the Job*, London: Kogan Page.

Zuboff, S. (2019) *The Age of Surveillance Capitalism*, New York: Public Affairs.

Index